Crime Scene:
Britain and Ireland

To Mum and Dad

Crime Scene:
Britain and Ireland
A Reader's Guide

John Martin

Five Leaves Publications

Crime Scene:
Britain and Ireland:
A Reader's Guide
by John Martin

Published in 2014
by Five Leaves Publications,
14a Long Row,
Nottingham NG1 2DH

www.fiveleaves.co.uk
www.fiveleavesbookshop.co.uk

ISBN: 9781910170052

Cover design: JT Lindroos
Designed and typeset
by Four Sheets Design and Print
Printed by Imprint Digital in Exeter

Contents

There are worse crimes
than burning books.
One of them is not reading them.

JOSEPH BRODSKY, on the acceptance of the
post of U.S. Poet Laureate, 19th May 1991

***

For me, as for many others, the reading
of detective stories is an addiction,
like tobacco or alcohol.

W.H. AUDEN, *Harpers Magazine*, May 1948

Introduction

Regional noir began ... with writers such as Ian Rankin (Edinburgh), John Harvey (Nottingham) and my own Manchester-based Kate Brannigan. But it has lost nothing of its early vigour and reveals us to ourselves in a way that few other styles of writing can manage. Its concern with the bigger picture, its willingness to engage with society, and its descriptions of ... landscapes have as powerful a grip as ever.
VAL MCDERMID, from an article in *The Guardian*, July 21 2013

The aim of this book is to encourage reading, by whetting the appetite for British and Irish crime fiction and encouraging readers to discover new crime writers, both contemporary and historic.

For crime fiction, perhaps more than most genres, the setting of the book is crucial. A crime is often the product of the society around it, and that in itself is heavily influenced by the environment. In addition the setting evokes emotion and knowledge in the reader, which helps to give the narrative a context. *The Hound of the Baskervilles* is a Victorian murder mystery set on Dartmoor, and the descriptions of the moor, the mists, the Tor, and the Grimpen Mire serve to give the whole story an air of gothic mystery, of mystique, which would not be felt in the same way if the story was set in nineteenth century Surrey.

People love to read about the places they know, recognising a town, a street, the local moorland. This helps to draw them into the action, so that they can feel part of the story. Authors usually do this in one of two ways: either by using real places, streets and landmarks in a real place (examples include Graham Hurley — Portsmouth, John Harvey — Nottingham), or by creating a fictional setting within a real place (such as Stephen Booth — Derbyshire). This book examines British and Irish crime fiction, showing how authors have used specific British and Irish settings.

The number of crime fiction novels currently available via libraries, bookshops and the digital world is staggering, so many readers may need a little guidance to find new authors that will interest them.

Then there are those readers who know what they want, and love the thrill of the chase, the pleasure of finding that long sought-after book or author in a library, a second-hand bookshop or car-boot sale. Where do they go though, to get their next read? Who will they be looking for tomorrow?

Hopefully, this book will help. Dividing Britain and Ireland into thirteen regions, it shows which authors have set books within each area, so if your interest is Scottish crime or Cornish crime, police procedurals or historical mysteries, this book will provide lots of ideas.

Not everything will be easy to find. The works of many authors are out of print, and will be languishing in second-hand bookshops, on eBay or in car-boot sales, waiting for someone to show interest. However, the advent of ebooks has seen many titles become available again, and overall interest in crime fiction is at an unprecedented level, so there has never been a greater opportunity for the crime fiction fan to look beyond the obvious, and try something different.

How to use this book

This book covers only crime fiction which is set in Britain or Ireland. Although I have concentrated on books published in the last fifty years, I have included many important earlier authors and titles as well.

The book is divided into thirteen regions:
— England
    — The West Country
    — The South and South East
    — London
    — East Anglia
    — The Midlands
    — The North West
    — The North East
— Wales
— Scotland
    — Glasgow and the West of Scotland
    — Edinburgh and the Borders
    — The Highlands and Islands and the North of Scotland
— Ireland
    — Northern Ireland
    — The Republic of Ireland

I have tried to include all major British and Irish crime series of the last fifty years which have been set in a specific real place e.g. Colin Dexter's Morse series (Oxford), and have also included many individual novels set in one particular area or place such as Robert Goddard's *Play to the End* (Brighton). I have also included a selection of series and novels from earlier times, especially from the Golden Age of detective fiction, which is generally accepted to run from 1920–1940.

Where an author's fictional setting is widely accepted to be based on a real place, I have included the author under that region, for example, Kate Ellis's Wesley

Peterson novels are set in Tradmouth, which is, as the author freely acknowledges, based on Dartmouth. She is therefore listed under Devon for this series, and under Yorkshire for her novels set in the fictional Yorkshire city of Eborby.

I have generally not included authors who are disingenuous or vague about their locations These include Susan Hill, whose wonderful books about the city of Lafferton could be based on Exeter, Salisbury or Gloucester. I have made an exception for Miss Marple's St Mary Mead, which Agatha Christie described as "about 25 miles from London", which puts it within the South and South East region.

For the sake of space I have not always been able to feature all books that an author has set in an area. Only on rare occasions have I been able to feature more than two or three books from an author. For example all of the Morse books by Colin Dexter are set in and around Oxford, but I have only focused on a few of them in his entry in the Midlands section.

In addition, no author is listed in more than three regions, even though some use multiple locations. I have tried to include these authors under their three most interesting settings.

I have not generally included short stories — the main exception being the Sherlock Holmes short stories of Sir Arthur Conan Doyle.

Each entry is listed with an accompanying website which can be used for further information — where possible this is the author's own website, but where none exists I have given a link to a reliable source — often the wonderful *Fantastic Fiction*: **www.fantasticfiction.co.uk**. They are valid as at August 2014.

I have given ten personal recommendations at the end of each chapter, including a variety of styles and types of novel.

Any errors or omissions are, of course, mine.
John Martin, Leicester, 2014

For more information on crime fiction, you can find me on Facebook (John Martin – Crime Fiction Connoisseur) or visit my website (**www.crimefictionguide.info**).

Crime Fiction Awards

There are a number of high-profile awards made for crime fiction in Britain and America. The principle ones are listed below.

Britain and Ireland

The Daggers

The Crime Writers' Association's Dagger Awards have a long and illustrious history. The Crime Writers' Association (CWA) was founded by John Creasey in 1953, and the first award for crime novel of the year was made to Winston Graham for his book *The Little Walls* in 1955. At this point the award was called The Crossed Red Herring, but it became The Gold Dagger in 1960 and has remained so ever since. A Silver Dagger has been awarded on occasions.

A number of other Dagger awards have been added over the years. The Awards are usually made at the annual Theakston Old Peculier Crime Writing Festival in Harrogate, and the current listing is as follows:

— The CWA Diamond Dagger — sustained excellence in Crime Fiction

— The CWA Gold Dagger — the best crime novel of the year

— The CWA Ian Fleming Steel Dagger — the best thriller of the year

— The CWA John Creasey Dagger — the best new crime writer of the year

— The CWA International Dagger — the best crime novel translated into English

— The CWA Dagger in the Library — the author whose work is currently giving greatest enjoyment to library readers

— The CWA Short Story Dagger — the writer of the best crime short story

— The CWA Debut Dagger — the best new writer who has not had a novel published commercially

— The CWA Ellis Peters Historical Dagger — the best historical crime novel of the year

— The CWA Non-fiction Dagger — the best non-fiction work on a real-life crime theme

— The CWA Last Laugh Dagger was awarded between 1988 and 1996 for the year's best humorous crime novel. It is now known as the Goldsboro Last Laugh Award and is awarded at the annual Bristol CrimeFest.

The eDunnit Award

This is for the best crime fiction ebook and is awarded at the Bristol CrimeFest.

The Theakstons Old Peculier Crime Novel of the Year Award

This is run in partnership with WH Smith, and celebrates the very best in British crime writing. It is open to British and Irish authors whose work has been published in paperback during the preceding twelve months, and is usually presented at the annual Theakston Old Peculier Crime Writing Festival in Harrogate.

The Deanston Scottish Crime Novel of the Year

This is awarded at the annual Bloody Scotland Crime Festival.

The Ireland AM Crime Fiction Book of the Year

This award is open to all Irish authors and was inaugurated in 2009.

America

— **The Agatha Award** is awarded annually in memory of Agatha Christie at the Malice Domestic fan convention in Washington.

— **The Anthony Awards** were created in 1986 and are awarded by attendees at the annual Bouchercon Crime Convention.

— **The Barry Awards** are awarded at the annual Bouchercon Crime Convention by the editorial staff of *Deadly Pleasures Mystery Magazine.*

— **The Edgar Awards** are named after Edgar Allen Poe and are awarded by the Mystery Writers of America.

— **The Grand Master of the Mystery Writers of America** is an honour conferred by The Mystery Writers of America themselves.

— **The Macavity Awards** are decided by the readers of *Mystery Readers International* and awarded at the annual Bouchercon Crime Convention.

— **The Shamus Award** is given annually by the Private Eye Writers of America for the best detective novel of the year.

Abbreviations

The following abbreviations are used throughout this book:
CWA – Crime Writers' Association
DC – Detective Constable
DCI – Detective Chief Inspector
DCSupt – Detective Chief Superintendent
DI – Detective Inspector
DSgt – Detective Sergeant
DSupt – Detective Superintendent

Acknowledgments

No book of this kind can written without the help of many people. In particular I must thank Ross Bradshaw, radical bookseller and publisher at Five Leaves Bookshop/Five Leaves Publications, for taking a punt on an unknown (if enthusiastic) writer, and Five Leaves' copy-editor Pippa Hennessy, who turned base metal into gold.

I am grateful also to various friends and colleagues of the publisher for their input: Mat Coward, Jonathan Davidson, Allan Guthrie, Dr Deirdre O'Byrne, John Payne, Cathi Unsworth, and Andrew Whitehead. In addition I have used a wide variety of resources, from books to blogs.

Books

Ashley, Mike (compiler), *The Mammoth Encyclopaedia of Modern Crime Fiction*, Robinson, 2002

Earwaker, Julian & Becker, Katherine, *Scene of the Crime*, Aurum, 2002

Evans, Jeff, *Penguin TV Companion*, Penguin, 2006

Forshaw, Barry, *The Rough Guide to Crime Fiction*, Rough Guides, 2007

Forshaw, Barry (ed), *British Crime Writing: An Encyclopaedia*, Greenwood, 2009

Haining, Peter, *The Classic Era of Crime Fiction,* Prion Books, 2002

Jakubowski, Maxim (ed*), Following the Detectives: Real Locations in Crime Fiction*, New Holland, 2010

James, Russell, *Great British Fictional Detectives — A-Z*, Remember When, 2008

Ousby, Ian, *The Crime and Mystery Book: A Reader's Companion*, Thames and Hudson, 1997

Rae, Simon (ed), *The Faber Book of Murder*, Faber and Faber, 1994

Symons, Julian, *Bloody Murder,* Macmillan,1992

Wagstaff, Vanessa & Poole, Stephen, *Agatha Christie: A Reader's Companion*, Aurum, 2004

Internet sources

Much information has come from the internet, and I have used authors' own websites, association websites, and the considerable number of e-zines and blogs available — my thanks are due to authors, editors and contributors alike.

Associations

The Crime Writers' Association: **www.thecwa.co.uk**

The Crime Readers' Association: **www.thecra.co.uk**

Websites

Fantastic Fiction: **www.fantasticfiction.co.uk**

Eurocrime: **www.eurocrime.co.uk**

Shotsmag: **www.shotsmag.co.uk**

Bloody Scotland: **www.bloodyscotland.com**

Tangled Web: **twbooks.co.uk**

Reviewing the Evidence: **www.reviewingtheevidence.com**

Crimetime: **www.crimetime.co.uk**

Crime Fiction Lover: **www.crimefictionlover.com**

The Bookbag: **www.thebookbag.co.uk**

Stop, You're Killing Me!: **www.stopyourekillingme.com**

Blogs

Avid Mystery Reader:
www.avidmysteryreader.com

Grumpy Old Bookman:
www.grumpyoldbookman.blogspot.co.uk

Crime Always Pays:
www.crimealwayspays.blogspot.co.uk

Do You Write Under Your Own Name?:
www.doyouwriteunderyourownname.blogspot.co.uk

The Guardian Books blog:
www.theguardian.com/books/crime

The Rap Sheet:
www.therapsheet.blogspot.co.uk

Mean Streets:
www.writersworkshop.co.uk/crimefiction

Finally...

I must thank my family and my partner Veronica for their help and encouragement. This quote from the great American musician Frank Zappa seems very apt: "So many books, so little time."

REGION ONE
England — The West Country

The lowest and vilest alleys in London do not present a more dreadful record of sin than does the smiling and beautiful countryside... look at these lonely houses... think of the deeds of hellish cruelty, the hidden wickedness which may go on, year in, year out, in such places.
SHERLOCK HOLMES, in "The Adventure of The Copper Beeches" by Arthur Conan Doyle, *Strand Magazine*, 1892

The West Country is an area of outstanding natural beauty, full of classic market towns, fishing villages, and gorgeous, quintessential English countryside from Cornwall to the Cotswolds. It includes the ruggedness of Dartmoor and Exmoor, the historic ports of Bristol and Plymouth, and cathedral cities such as Salisbury, Exeter and Truro. There is a long coastline, and the Jurassic cliffs of Dorset near Lyme Regis are a World Heritage Site, as is Stonehenge in Wiltshire.

Connections to major names in crime fiction are rife. Agatha Christie was born in Torquay, and it was her work in a local dispensary during World War I which gave her the knowledge of poisons that she used so extensively during her long career. Arthur Conan Doyle was a GP in Plymouth early in his career, and *The Hound of The Baskervilles* is surely the greatest book ever set on Dartmoor. The indomitable P.D. James has set novels in Cornwall and Dorset, while Robert Goddard has used various West Country locations, including Truro, Saltash, and the Teign Valley. The beautiful city of Bath has been used by several writers, with Peter Lovesey even setting a book in the Theatre Royal, and the glorious Cotswolds are the backdrop to novels by the likes of M.C. Beaton and Rebecca Tope.

Jane A. Adams

Leicestershire-born author Jane Adams has used Dorset for the setting of her Rina Martin series (written as Jane A. Adams). Rina is an actress, who has retired to Frantham, a fictional coastal town near Lyme Regis. With her friend, DI Sebastian McGregor, she finds herself involved in various escapades, some more violent than others.

In the first book, *A Reason to Kill* (2007), Rina is newly retired, "Mac" McGregor is calming his shattered nerves after a police operation failed spectacularly, and a young boy called George Parker is trying to escape from a violent past. Suddenly their peace is ended abruptly by the murder of an elderly woman, and nothing will ever be quite the same again.

In *The Power of One* (2009) two men are found shot dead on a luxury yacht. It appears that they worked for a computer games company, and Rina suspects that they were trying to protect company secrets. When she investigates on her own, her friend DI McGregor is more than a little worried.

Jane Adams has also written a series of books about blind ex-policewoman Naomi Blake. *Blood Ties* (2010) is set in Somerset where Naomi and partner Alec have taken a short holiday. They meet Eddy, an eccentric local historian, and are shocked when he is found dead. When they become reluctantly involved in the investigation, they discover that there was more to Eddy than met the eye.

See also: East Anglia (Jane Adams), the Midlands (Jane Adams)

janeadams.wix.com/writer

Tom Bale

Originally from Sussex, Tom Bale (a pseudonym for David Harrison) has written four excellent fast-moving crime novels full of suspense and violence. Two of them feature Joe Clayton, an ex-CID officer whose police career ended with a disastrous undercover operation.

Though the first two are set in southern England, the third, *Blood Falls* (2011), begins in Bristol, when Clayton suddenly hears the voice of the man who has vowed to kill him because Clayton had sent his father to prison. To escape, Clayton goes to Cornwall, and hides out in the small town of Trelennen, which the author states is loosely based on a combination of Port Isaac and Looe. Unfortunately the town is ruled by gangster Leon Race, its idyllic nature is only skin deep, and Clayton is not safe after all.

See also: the South and South East

www.tombale.net

Belinda Bauer

Belinda Bauer is a novelist and scriptwriter who grew up in both England and South Africa.

Exmoor is the setting for her first three novels, which are compelling psychological novels of considerable suspense. All three books evoke the spirit of the Exmoor countryside, which adds considerably to their atmospheric nature. The author won the Dagger in the Library Award from the CWA in 2013.

In *Blacklands* (2009), which won the CWA Gold Dagger in 2010, a twelve-year old boy writes to the serial killer he thinks is responsible for the death of his uncle, and sets in motion a terrifying psychological tennis match between the horribly convincing child-molester villain and the unpopular, bullied schoolboy who digs holes on the moor in the frantic hope of finding his uncle's body.

Darkside (2011) is set in the same fictional Exmoor village (Shipcott), five years later. Jonas Holly is the village policeman, and he is shocked by the murder of an elderly woman. When he attempts to solve the crime, the investigation is taken away from him by an abrasive detective from Taunton. When there is another death, Jonas is convinced that he will have to solve the murders himself. However anonymous letters are sent and soon it is obvious that Jonas is being observed and judged by someone with intimate knowledge of everything he does. Then an event takes place which horrifies Jonas, his police colleagues and the villagers alike.

In *Finders Keepers* (2012), an Exmoor summer is disturbed by the frightening abduction of several children. Jonas Holly is faced with an impossible case — no ransom demands, no news, and just one clue — a note left at the site of each abduction.

www.belindabauer.co.uk

M.C. Beaton

The wonderful Agatha Raisin series of successful, light-hearted crime novels is set in the northern Cotswolds and written by the prolific Marion Chesney, under one of her various pseudonyms. She was already an experienced writer when she began the series in 1991 with *Agatha Raisin and the Quiche of Death*. Agatha is a larger than life character, whose main loves are food, booze and cats, possibly in that order. Though detection is her forte, it is not always at the forefront of her mind. The twenty-third book of her adventures (*Hiss and Hers*) was published in 2012.

In the second novel, *Agatha Raisin and the Vicious Vet* (1993), Agatha falls for the local vet, who she thinks has fallen for her. When he dies in an accident, she sets her eyes on the vet's neighbour — a distinguished military man. She hopes that by helping him to investigate the vet's death, a romance liaison may be forthcoming. However, danger may get in the way.

In *Agatha Raisin and The Deadly Dance* (2004) Agatha investigates when the daughter of a wealthy local woman receives a death threat, and is then attacked. As she investigates, Agatha is helped by her old friend, Sir Charles Fraith, a man of supreme charm. Agatha is bowled over — the longer the case goes on, the happier she is.

In *Agatha Raisin and the Busy Body* (2010) the death of an unpopular Health and Safety Inspector leaves Agatha with so many suspects she barely knows where to start.

See also: Scotland: Highlands and Islands
www.agatharaisin.com

Simon Beckett

Sheffield-born author Simon Beckett has been shortlisted for various awards (including the CWA Gold Dagger) since the publication of his first David Hunter crime novel, *The Chemistry of Death*, in 2006. Hunter is a forensic anthropologist and all the novels have relatively remote rural settings.

The Calling of the Grave (2010) is a brilliantly atmospheric novel, set on Dartmoor. Hunter is drawn back to the area where he had once been instrumental in apprehending a vicious serial killer, Jerome Monk. Monk has now escaped from Dartmoor Prison, and is hell-bent on retribution against all involved. The old mine workings on the moors become central to the plot, and to Hunter's very survival, as he sets out to track Monk down. When he follows Monk into them, it soon becomes clear that the killer knows the layout far better than Hunter.

See also: *East Anglia, Scotland: Highlands and Islands*
www.simonbeckett.com

Veronica Black

This is one of the five pseudonyms used by the prolific Welsh author Maureen Peters, who wrote over 100 novels between 1968 and her death in 2008. Altogether she wrote eleven detective novels about a Cornish nun, Sister Joan, starting with *Vow of Silence* (1990). In this book, Joan is persuaded to take a teaching post at a remote Cornish convent not far from Bodmin, where one nun has died in strange circumstances, and another nun is missing.

In *A Vow of Poverty* (1996), the wonderful characters of The Daughters of Compassion are in fine form. Sister Joan finds an old photo in an attic with a mysterious phrase written on it. Two people have died and Joan's imagination is running riot — she thinks she has seen a ghost!

www.fantasticfiction.co.uk/b/veronica-black

Nicholas Blake

This was the pseudonym of Cambridge lecturer and Poet Laureate C. Day-Lewis, which he used for a series of crime novels featuring amateur sleuth Nigel Strangeways, the nephew of a Scotland Yard Commissioner. Cecil Day-Lewis had connections with Dorset, having been educated at Sherborne School, and the third in the series, *There's Trouble Brewing* (1937), was set in the fictional Dorset town of Maiden Astbury and features the discovery of a body boiled to its bones in a brewery vat.

Several of the other early novels also have a West Country setting, including *The Beast Must Die* (1938), in which the son of a crime writer is run down by a car near Cheltenham. The author sets out to find and kill the driver, but is thwarted by the intervention of Strangeways. The story comes to a moving end in Lyme Bay.

www.cday-lewis.co.uk

Janie Bolitho

Janie Bolitho was born in Falmouth. After a varied career her first book, *Kindness Can Kill*, was published by Constable in 1994. In the next eight years she wrote two series – one continuing from this featuring DCI Ian Roper, and one set specifically in Cornwall featuring photographer/painter and amateur sleuth Rose Trevelyan. Both series were popular but were cut short when the author died of cancer in 2002.

In *Framed in Cornwall* (1998), Rose is shocked by the death of her elderly friend Dorothy Pengelly, and finds that there's more to it than meets the eye, while in *Killed in Cornwall* (2002) she discovers that being the confidant of many friends and neighbours can be problematic, especially when the police start investigating a series of local burglaries and assaults.

www.janiebolitho.info

Hilary Bonner

Originally from Bideford, Hilary Bonner is a former Fleet Street journalist and a former Chair of the CWA. As well as several showbiz biographies, she has written a number of high-quality psychological crime novels, often based on real events, and usually set in West Country, where she still lives.

A Deep Deceit (2000) is set in St Ives, Cornwall, where Suzanne and Carl Peters are living an idyllic life. There is a dreadful secret in their lives, and the arrival of a series of poison pen letters causes consternation. Before long their careful, enclosed world crashes around them, and a chilling story of sexual collusion and all-consuming love unfolds.

No Reason to Die (2004) is set on Dartmoor. Several men and women have died suddenly at the remote Hangridge Army Camp, and journalist John Kelly thinks that the Army's plausible explanations do not ring true. When he takes his ideas to the police it becomes clear that there are people at a high level who would prefer that the truth remained hidden. The book was based on tragic deaths at Deepcut Barracks and elsewhere in the British Army between 1995 and 2002. The author interviewed several of the families concerned to produce a novel of immense power, and a conspiracy theory that could be close to the truth.

www.hilarybonner.co.uk

Damien Boyd

A solicitor by profession, Damien Boyd is the author of a series of fast-moving crime novels set in Somerset. The central character is DI Nick Dixon, a former Metropolitan Police Officer who has returned to his home area.

In *As the Crow Flies* (2013), he investigates when his former climbing partner, Jake Fayter, is killed in an apparent accident. When it transpires to be murder, Nick is drawn to the seaside town of Burnham-on-Sea, and uncovers a conspiracy that will shatter the town.

The second novel, *Head in the Sand* (2014), features Burnham again, when a severed head is found on a local golf course, while the third (*Kickback*, 2014) begins when a jockey is found kicked to death at a racing stables near Bridgwater.

www.damienboyd.com

John Bude

John Bude was the pseudonym of Ernest Elmore, who wrote around thirty crime novels between 1935 and 1957. He was a founder member of the CWA, but had a fairly undistinguished career.

The Cornish Coast Murder (1935) was republished by the British Library in 2014. It is a classic, genteel murder mystery from the Golden Age, reminiscent of, but not as good as Allingham or Christie. It is set in the village of Boscawen, where a much-disliked magistrate is found shot dead. The local policeman is confused, but the vicar, Reverend Dodd, and his friend, the local doctor, team up

to help solve the baffling mystery.
See also: the North West
www.fantasticfiction.co.uk/b/john-bude

W.J. Burley

William John Burley, a Cornishman who originally trained as an engineer, was a schoolteacher in Newquay for many years. Born in 1914, he came to writing late, and his first novel was not published until he was fifty-two. He invented the character of Superintendent Charles Wycliffe for the novel *The Three-Toed Pussy*, which was published in 1968, and another twenty-one Wycliffe novels followed before his death in 2002. The books were televised in the 1990s with Jack Shepherd in the title role and the scenery of Devon and Cornwall as a dramatic backdrop — as in the original books.

Wycliffe's eighth case, *Wycliffe and the Scapegoat* (1978), sees Wycliffe investigating the shocking present-day re-enactment of an old pagan legend in which a man is strapped to a blazing wheel which is rolled into the sea. A local man, Jonathan Riddle, has vanished and slowly the awful truth emerges.

In *Wycliffe and the Last Rites* (1992), a bizarre murder disturbs the quiet Cornish village of Moresk. A woman is found dead on the steps of the church. Wycliffe's inquiries do not go well, but when a second murder takes place he is sure he knows the perpetrator. However, knowing is one thing — proving it is quite another.
www.fantasticfiction.co.uk/b/w-j-burley

Agatha Christie

Agatha Christie is the best-known crime writer in the world, and between 1920 and 1976 she wrote over eighty crime novels. Over a billion copies of her books have been sold in the English language, and another billion copies in other languages. She was born in Torquay, Devon, in 1890, lived in the county for much of her life and used Devon as the setting for a number of her best stories.

In *And Then There Were None* (1939, originally entitled *Ten Little Niggers*), ten strangers are lured to an island hotel (a fictional version of Burgh Island off the Devon Coast) and are then subjected to an extraordinary accusation by an unseen voice — that they are guilty of murder in their past and think they have got away with it. One by one the ten strangers are killed in mysterious circumstances until only one is left... at which point Christie unleashes one of her great surprises.

Evil Under the Sun (1941) is set in a hotel on Smuggler's Island, another fictional version of Burgh Island. Hercule Poirot is on holiday here when an attractive woman, who has been flirting with another woman's husband, is found strangled. Everyone seems to have an alibi, but Poirot does not believe all he hears.

In *Peril at End House* (1932), Poirot is on holiday in Cornwall when someone takes a pot-shot at Nick, a young woman living nearby. Also, *The Sittaford Mystery* (1931) takes place on Dartmoor during a fierce snowstorm, and *Dead Man's Folly* (1956) is set at a writer's country house, which seems to be modelled on Christie's own holiday home, Greenway, near Dartmouth.

See also: the South and South East, London
www.agathachristie.com

Michael Clynes

Under this pen-name, the prolific Paul Doherty wrote a series of historical mysteries set in Tudor England.

In *The Grail Murders* (1993), Sir Roger Shallot (who is a bit of a rogue) is forced to watch the execution of the Duke of Buckingham on Tower Hill in London. It appears that Buckingham has been unsuccessful in some royal quest. Then Sir Roger is ordered by Henry VIII's henchmen to visit Templecombe Manor in Somerset, in an effort to find the ancient relics that Buckingham had been searching for — The Holy Grail and King Arthur's sword, Excalibur. Failure will be punished in the usual medieval way — death.

See also: London (Michael Clynes, Paul Doherty), the South and South East (Paul Doherty, C.L. Grace)
www.paulcdoherty.com

Judith Cutler

Judith Cutler has written several separate crime series set in different parts of the country — the Midlands, Kent and Devon.

In *The Food Detective* (2005), Josie Welford is settling into her new life, running a pub in an idyllic Devon village. However a simple change of food suppliers causes local friction. Then the local vet disappears, and the village's dark side becomes horribly apparent.

See also: the South and South East, the Midlands
www.judithcutler.com

Freda Davies

There are only three novels in Freda Davies's short series of books featuring Gloucestershire-based D.I. Keith Tyrell, but they are intriguing, atmospheric police procedurals. In her debut novel *A Fine and Private Place* (2001), Tyrell discovers that the village of Tolland is home to some nasty secrets when the skeleton of an American soldier who disappeared during World War II is dug up in a field. The discovery of a second, more recent body only complicates matters.

Flawed Scales (2005) also has an American aspect, as Tyrell is sidelined from murder investigations to confirm the identity of a terrorist suspect living in the area. A dead body, arson and death threats to his wife convince Tyrell that the case is serious.

www.fantasticfiction.co.uk/d/freda-davies

Sir Arthur Conan Doyle

Sir Arthur Conan Doyle is perhaps second only to Agatha Christie in popularity. An Edinburgh-born doctor, in Sherlock Holmes he created perhaps the most famous detective of them all. The great Sherlock Holmes

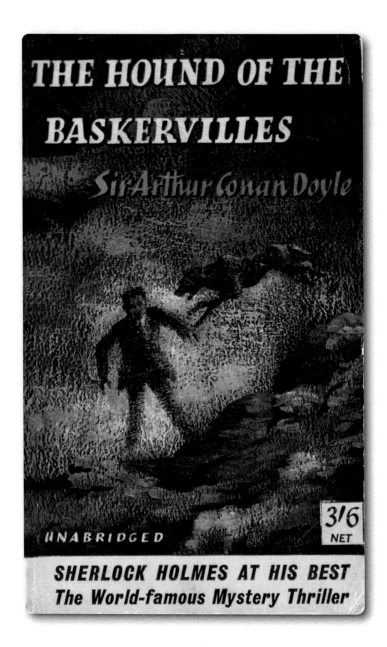

THE HOUND OF THE BASKERVILLES

Sir Arthur Conan Doyle

3/6 NET

UNABRIDGED

SHERLOCK HOLMES AT HIS BEST
The World-famous Mystery Thriller

first appeared in print in 1887, and by 1893 his popularity was assured through regular stories in *The Strand Magazine*. Conan Doyle wanted to be taken seriously for other work and claimed that Holmes was a distraction he could do without, so he decided that Holmes should die at the Reichenbach Falls at the end of *The Final Problem* (1893). Many readers were hugely disappointed, and cancelled their subscriptions to the magazine in protest.

By 1900 there was considerable pressure on Conan Doyle to resurrect Holmes, and eventually he did so in one of the great crime novels, *The Hound of the Baskervilles* (1902). This is a magnificent novel set on lonely Dartmoor. Holmes travels to Devon to help Sir Charles Baskerville, whose life is threatened by a family curse. He and Watson expose the curse and the spectral hound as fakes, and Sir Henry's enemy is consigned for all time to the fictional Grimpen Mire — a huge bog based on one of Dartmoor's great wastelands.

This was not Holmes's only visit to Dartmoor, as it is also the setting for one of the most famous short stories, *Silver Blaze* (from *The Memoirs of Sherlock Holmes*, 1892), in which Holmes investigates the disappearance of a valuable racehorse and the murder of its trainer.

Only on one occasion did he venture to Cornwall, for *The Devil's Foot,* from *His Last Bow* (1917), and Holmes referred to it as the strangest case he had ever handled.
See also: the South and South East, London
www.sherlockholmesonline.org

Margaret Duffy

Margaret Duffy was born in Essex, and has worked for both the Inland Revenue and The Ministry of Defence. Bath is a regular setting for her novels featuring private detective Joanna Makepiece and her ex-lover DCI James Carrick.

In *Prospect of Death* (1995), Makepiece investigates after Carrick is found unconscious in his crashed car after Burns Night celebrations, and meets Patrick Gillard from the author's long-running Langley and Gillard series.

This latter series often features Bath as well, as Gillard and his wife — novelist Ingrid Langley — live nearby. For example, in *Rat Poison* (2011), gang warfare has broken out in the city, as a London gangster is trying to take over. Carrick is aided by Langley and Gillard (both ex-British Intelligence operatives) but the ganglord always seems to be ahead of the game.

www.margaretduffy.co.uk

Carola Dunn

Though best known for her cosy Daisy Dalrymple series, this English-born but American-based author has written a trilogy set in Cornwall in the 1960s. The main character is Eleanor Trewyn, an elderly widow who retired to the village of Port Mabyn and founded a small charity shop. Her niece is a Detective Sergeant with the local police and, despite her age, she finds herself mixed up with robbery and murder in this most peaceful of settings.

In *Manna from Hades* (2009), Eleanor and the vicar's wife discover a corpse in the stockroom of the shop — and jewels from a London robbery turn up in the shop's donations. To understand what happened Eleanor must endure lies, treachery and danger.

See also: London

www.caroladunn.weebly.com

Kate Ellis

Kate Ellis is a Liverpudlian by birth, but her superbly plotted crime novels are set in the south Devon coastal town of Tradmouth. As anagram lovers would expect, this is based on Dartmouth. The fictional town is, however, much larger than its real equivalent, having a hospital and a large police headquarters.

The ingenious, atmospheric novels feature one of the few black policemen in British crime fiction in DSgt Wesley Peterson, a former Sergeant in the Metropolitan Police who leaves London for the quiet backwaters of Devon. Life does not work out like that. Wesley is a quiet, dedicated policeman with a degree in archaeology — which certainly makes him unusual, but helps with the historical aspects of the stories. His boss is DCI Gerry Heffernan, a no-nonsense Liverpudlian.

History features heavily in the books, and historical events and themes are regularly part of Wesley's investigations. For example, in *The Jackal Man* (2010), Wesley finds similarities between contemporary attacks on local women and the mysterious history of the nearby Varley Castle.

In *The Funeral Boat* (2000), DCI Heffernan thinks the disappearance of a Danish tourist is linked to a series of vicious robberies. Wesley is thinking of something far older, and that there may be a link to an ancient mystery.
See also: the North East
www.kateellis.co.uk

Debby Fowler

An experienced writer of books and stories for magazines, Debby Fowler began the Cornwall-set Felicity Paradise series in 2006 with *Letting Go*. Felicity is a mature woman, independent and determined, who investigates the death of her husband in a hit-and-run.

Later books involve a missing boy, a serial arsonist and money problems, all alongside the latest travails in Felicity's life, and her relationship with Inspector Keith Penrose. The author's Cornish background is reflected in the settings used for the books, and even the publisher (Truran) is Cornish.

The second in the series is *Intensive Care* (2007), which is set in St Ives and Zennor. Felicity has come across a small boy who she thinks she has met before. When she realises

where, she has to act fast to uncover the facts — with a little help from Inspector Penrose of the Cornish Police.
www.felicityparadise.com

Dick Francis

One of the great names of British crime fiction, Francis was a former champion jockey who knew the racing game backwards. He turned to writing thrillers set around the world of horse racing after he retired, and his first novel, *Dead Cert*, was published in 1962. He received a CBE in 2000 and died in 2010 at the age of ninety. Since then his son Felix has continued to write under the Dick Francis banner.

As one of the premier racecourses in the country, Cheltenham regularly features in his books.

In *Comeback* (1991), civil servant Peter Darwin returns to his childhood home and finds himself caught up in the mysterious deaths of a string of valuable racehorses.

In *Under Orders* (2006), private investigator and ex-jockey Sid Halley is on the trail of murder and mayhem at the Cheltenham Gold Cup.

The 1993 novel *Decider* features the fictional Wiltshire racecourse Stratton Park, which is facing financial ruin when a massive explosion takes place at the course.

See also: the South and South East, East Anglia
www.dickfrancis.com

Anthea Fraser

For ten years (1986–96) Anthea Fraser was the Secretary of the CWA. Her sixteen books featuring DCI David Webb were published over fifteen years (1984–1999). They are set in the fictional county of Broadshire, which seems to be largely based on Wiltshire.

Her novels were relatively gentle procedurals, exploring families, feelings, relationships and bitterness, and how the whole can lead to explosive outbursts of violence. *Six Proud Walkers* (1988) is a fine example, as Webb finds many unsavoury secrets in the background to a family feud in the quiet village of Honeyford.

In *I'll Sing You Two-O* (1991) Webb investigates the murder of twins known as "The Lily-White Boys" and the sudden proliferation of violent events in the fictional town of Shillingham.

www.fantasticfiction.co.uk/f/anthea-fraser

Elizabeth George

Though American, Elizabeth George has set virtually all of her bestselling novels in England.

She is best known for her series featuring Scotland Yard detectives Inspector Thomas Lynley and Sergeant Barbara Havers. The series has won many awards and has been televised in the UK by the BBC.

As the eighth Earl of Asherton, Lynley's family home is Howenstow, a country estate in Cornwall, and in *A Suitable Vengeance* (1990) he takes his fiancée home to meet his family, only to find himself involved in a murder mystery which will tear the local community apart and expose a dreadful family secret.

In *Careless in Red* (2008), after a personal tragedy he goes home to Cornwall, to hike the county's bleak and forbidding coastline in an effort to forget the past. However, when he stumbles upon the body of a man who has apparently fallen to his death from a cliff, he becomes both a witness and a suspect in a murder investigation.

See also: London, the North West

www.elizabethgeorgeonline.com

Robert Goddard

Robert Goddard has written more than twenty bestselling mystery novels, many set wholly or partly in the West Country. They are wonderfully complex, with plots often arching over long periods of time, and ordinary, honest protagonists thrust into situations not of their making.

Goddard lived and worked in Devon before becoming a full-time writer, and his wonderful first novel *Past Caring*

(1986) is set mainly in the Devon hinterlands north of Teignmouth. Martyn Radford is a distracted, bored ex-teacher who takes up an offer to investigate a political mystery from Edwardian times. Edwin Strafford was MP for the Teign Valley, and a member of Lloyd George's Cabinet, when he suddenly and mysteriously disappeared. Delving into the mystery with the help of an attractive professional historian, Radford finds himself enmeshed in a web of deceit where the danger is only too real. Goddard's original ideas were based on the real-life disappearance of Labour politician Victor Grayson in 1920.

Beyond Recall (1997) is an atmospheric story set mainly in and around Truro, Cornwall, moving between a wedding party in 1981 and a murder mystery in 1947. Chris Napier undertakes a long journey into family reminiscences to get to the bottom of the post-war tragedy that broke up a childhood friendship.

The fine 2012 novel *Fault Line* concerns the mysterious history of a Cornish china clay company from St Austell, the intrigues surrounding the family which runs it, and the employee whose investigations into a company secret uncover a network of lies.

Dying to Tell (2001) centres on mysterious events at a farm near Glastonbury in 1963 that led to the disappearance of Lance Bradley's old school-friend Rupert Adler, nearly thirty years later. Bradley sets out to uncover the truth, but has no idea what lies ahead.

See also: the South and South East
www.robertgoddardbooks.co.uk

Lesley Grant-Adamson

Londoner Lesley Grant-Adamson was a writer for *The Guardian* newspaper before moving into crime fiction. She wrote fifteen stylish crime novels between 1985 and 1999. The first and last of them are set in Somerset.

The first novel, *Patterns in the Dust* (1985), features the fictional village of Nether Hampton, where a notorious Fleet Street columnist has come to relax from the hurly-burly of London. Is it just coincidence that sudden death arrives as well?

Undertow (1999) is centred around another fictional part of the Somerset coast, Stark's Point. A woman has moved to the town to patch up her relationship with her boyfriend, but becomes involved in a forty-year-old murder mystery which still taints the community.

www.crimefiction.co.uk

J.M. Gregson

A teacher and lecturer for many years, J.M. Gregson eventually decided to concentrate on writing full-time, and his forty-second crime novel was published in 2012. Though somewhat formulaic, the books have a gentle sense of humour which aids their readability.

The Lambert and Hook police procedural series started with *Murder at the Nineteenth* (1989), and the golfing theme has never been too far away since, as the Gloucestershire CID detectives are portrayed as enthusiasts of the game.

An Academic Death (2001) opens with a university lecturer being reported missing, though as his wife says, he is not exactly missed. When he turns up not far away with a bullet in his head, Lambert and Hook have to go to university — but not to study books.

In *Murder at the Eleventh Hole* (2002), Superintendent Lambert and his sergeant Bert Hook are enjoying a game on a local course in Gloucestershire when they find a body. When it is identified as a woman known for prostitution and drug dealing, it brings them into contact with some very unpleasant people indeed.

See also: the North West

www.fantasticfiction.co.uk/g/j-m-gregson

Martha Grimes

American author and long-time anglophile Martha Grimes has written more than twenty crime novels set in various parts of Britain. In 2012 she was made a Grand

Master of the Mystery Writers of America.

Her Richard Jury series has been running for nearly thirty years. Jury is a Scotland Yard detective who rises through the ranks to become a Superintendent. He is often assisted by Melrose Plant, an aristocrat who no longer uses his title. On several occasions they are helped by the dedicated Brian Macalvie of the Devon and Cornwall Police.

In *Help the Poor Struggler* (1985) Richard Jury joins forces with Macalvie, then merely a constable, to investigate the deaths of three children on Dartmoor, while in *I Am the Only Running Footman* (1986), they examine the links between two murders, one in Mayfair and one in Devon.

The Lamorna Wink (1999) is set in Cornwall. Jury is called in to help investigate the murder of a woman and to ascertain whether it can be linked to the disappearance of two children several years before.

See also: the Midlands
www.marthagrimes.com

Gregory Hall

Despite the interruption by cancer of his writing career in 2004, Gregory Hall has written several West Country-based mysteries in the style of Robert Goddard. His first novel, *The Dark Backward*, was shortlisted for the CWA John Creasey Award in 1995.

In *A Sleep and a Forgetting* (2003), an unexpected suicide note forces academic Catriona to go to the Cotswolds to discover what had forced her sister to take such a drastic course of action. Soon she realises that to understand her sister's actions, she will have to return to their shared childhood, and expose the various truths that they both tried to forget.

www.gregoryhallwriter.larkhallmarketing.co.uk

Simon Hall

Simon Hall is the BBC Crime Correspondent in south-west England. He used his inside knowledge to create Plymouth-based crime reporter Dan Groves, whose friendship with DCI Adam Breen enables him to be closely involved in high-profile crimes.

In *The Death Pictures* (2008), an artist is found dead with his wrists slashed. His death makes no sense, as he has created a series of paintings as a riddle for the public to solve, with a valuable prize at the end — but he died before the solution was revealed. Dan Groves investigates. Are there links to a series of rapes that took place in the area?

The TV Detective (2010) shows how the TV reporter and policeman first met, on a violent case about the murder of an unpopular local businessman. Breen invites the newly-appointed crime reporter to shadow him on the case, and it is Groves who comes up with the answer to a crucial question — cracking the case wide open.

www.thetvdetective.com

Ray Harrison

Between 1983 and 1998 Ray Harrison wrote fifteen novels about the careers of Victorian policemen Sergeant Bragg and Constable Merton. They were mainly set in London, but *A Harvest of Death* (1988) finds Bragg caught up in a murder mystery while staying in a village near Dorchester, and in *Akin to Murder* (1992) Bragg is drawn into the mysterious death of a well-off Dorset surveyor.

See also: London

www.fantasticfiction.co.uk/h/ray-harrison

Patricia Harwin

American author Patricia Harwin wrote two gentle crime novels set in East Gloucestershire, introducing elderly ex-librarian Catherine Penney as a sort of up-to-date

Miss Marple who has relocated from America to Gloucestershire to be with her married daughter.

In *Arson and Old Lace* (2004) Catherine has just moved in to her new Cotswold home. She tries to get to know her neighbour, Arthur Crocker, but he is killed in a house fire. It is considered an accident, but having listened to the old man's recent ramblings, Catherine is not so sure.

www.fantasticfiction.co.uk/h/patricia-harwin

Mo Hayder

Though she left school at fifteen, Mo Hayder has a degree in film from an American university and a degree in Creative Writing from Bath University, where she now lectures. Her books have won many awards including the CWA Dagger in the Library in 2011. Her novels are gruesome, chilling and macabre, and remain with the reader long after they are finished.

The first two books were set in London, but in 2008 her protagonist DI Jack Caffrey is transferred to the Major Crimes Unit in Bristol. Subsequent novels featuring Caffrey have been set in the Avon and Somerset area. He is young, virtually unshockable and hard-working, but with enough demons in his make-up to make him realistic.

The trilogy of *Ritual* (2008), *Skin* (2009) and *Gone* (2010) have become known as The Walking Man series. In *Ritual* (2008), a police diver finds a human hand with no body attached. It is identified as that of a young boy who has vanished, and Caffrey discovers a frightening underworld in Bristol, where ancient superstitions and modern science clash.

Gone (2010) begins with a simple car-jacking, but it turns out that a young girl was in the back of the car when it was taken. That is bad enough, but when the kidnapper communicates and hints that this is just the first, Caffrey is under enormous pressure to find him before more children are taken.

Hanging Hill (2011) is not part of the Caffrey series, and is set in Bath. It concerns the lives of two estranged sisters (one a police inspector), and the effects on them of the murder of a teenage girl.

See also: London

www.mohayder.net

Peter Helton

An artist and writer, Peter Helton has so far written two fine series of murder mysteries, one set in Bristol and the other in Bath.

In his Bath series, Chris Honeysett is a painter, gourmet cook and amateur sleuth, who investigates stolen paintings in his home town (*Headcase*, 2005) and missing women (*Slim Chance*, 2006).

Following the success of the Chris Honeysett series, Helton created Bristol-based detective DI Liam McClusky, who as the series opens (*Falling More Slowly*, 2010) is just getting used to his new job, having been transferred from Southampton, where he was injured in the line of duty. He is plunged into a horrific case where explosive devices designed as everyday objects are being left all over Bristol, with terrible consequences.

In *Four Below* (2011), drug use and violence cause chaos in the city during a particularly harsh winter.

www.peterhelton.com

Stan Hey

Stan Hey was best known as a television scriptwriter for many years (*Auf Wiedersehen Pet, The Manageress* and others), but he also tried his hand at crime fiction. He wrote two novels featuring private investigator Frank Brennan, set around Bradford-on-Avon.

In *Sudden Unprovided Death* (1996), Brennan is a struggling journalist who is given information about a quarrying company which could be planning considerable environmental damage to the Mendips.

www.bbc.co.uk/wiltshire/s_o_p/writers_story.shtml

Joanna Hines

Joanna Hines lived for many years on the Lizard peninsula in Cornwall. She wrote a number of clever, well-crafted thrillers about strong-willed women, of which *The Murder Bird (*2006), was the last. Set in Cornwall and London, it concerns poet Kirsten Waller, who was working on a poem of this title just before her mysterious suicide. Her daughter is convinced that her mother would not commit suicide, and sets out to prove it was murder.

www.joannahines.co.uk

David Hodges

David Hodges is a former police superintendent who has written three books set in and around the Somerset Levels.

In *Slice* (2011), a razor-wielding killer is on the loose around a fictional area based on Bridgewater. DSupt Jack Fulton is horrified when a gory murder enquiry leads him to believe that a fellow officer may be involved, and the investigation becomes shockingly personal.

Firetrap (2011) sees a police surveillance operation on the Somerset Levels firebombed, and DC Kate Hamblin only narrowly escapes with her life — but two colleagues died. Kate is blamed and suspended from duty. Desperate to clear her name and prove what really happened, she risks everything by trying to get close to the killer.

www.fantasticfiction.co.uk/h/david-hodges

Graham Hurley

After finishing the acclaimed Faraday and Winter series with *Happy Days* in 2012, Graham Hurley began a new, equally authentic series set in and around Exmouth, featuring the newly-promoted Jimmy Suttle, one of the great characters from the earlier series.

As a naive DC in Portsmouth's Major Crimes Team, Jimmy learned a lot from colleagues such as Joe Faraday and Paul Winter. Now he has taken the post of Detective Sergeant with the Devon and Cornwall force.

In *Western Approaches* (2012), Suttle investigates the suspicious death of a much-disliked member of the local rowing club, while trying to settle in to a new area with his wife and young son. The past in Portsmouth is never completely out of his mind, and his world is complicated by his disintegrating home life. His colleagues don't support his view of Kinsey's death, and Jimmy has to sink or swim by his own actions.

Touching Distance (2013) examines the detrimental effects of wartime service on ex-military personnel. Three murders take place near Exeter, all extremely professional and apparently motiveless. While Suttle and his colleagues investigate, his estranged wife Lizzie, a journalist, is interested in a services rehabilitation unit in Plymouth. When the various strands come together Suttle finds himself in mortal danger.

See also: the South and South East
www.grahamhurley.co.uk

Francis Iles

Anthony Berkeley was a journalist who was, with others such as Agatha Christie, a founder member of The Detection Club — formed by a group of British crime writers in 1930 for professional and social purposes. He wrote under several pseudonyms, including Francis Iles. He was a vital element of the development of crime fiction in the 1930s.

Still seen as one of the masterpieces from the Golden Age, Francis Iles's *Malice Aforethought* (1931) is set in the fictional Devon village of Wyvern's Cross, where Doctor Edmund Bickleigh hosts a garden party for the great and the good, while planning to murder his wife. Although not a murder mystery, as the killer is revealed at the very beginning, the book is a crime novel with a wonderful mixture of thrills and suspense.

www.fantasticfiction.co.uk/i/francis-iles

P.D. James

Phyllis Dorothy James is one of the true greats of twentieth-century literature. That she has never even been long-listed for The Man Booker Prize is, in my view, a blot on the history of the award. She has won numerous other awards, including the Cartier Dagger of the CWA for Lifetime Achievement and the Grand Master Award from the Mystery Writers of America. She is best known for her Adam Dalgleish novels. He is a London policeman, who rises through the series to the rank of Commander, but murder often comes to him, even when he is on holiday or visiting friends, so the books are set in various parts of the country.

Several of her books are set in the West Country, specifically in Dorset and Cornwall. *The Black Tower* (1975) was the fifth Dalgleish novel. Unhappy in his job, Dalgleish is considering retirement, and accepts an invitation to visit an old friend who is a chaplain at Toynton Grange, a home for the disabled in Dorset. When he gets there he finds his friend is dead of natural causes, and a resident has been murdered. The killer needs to be found before there are any more deaths, but there are plenty of suspects. The chilling ending is one of the author's best.

Thirty-three years later the author returned Dalgleish (with his small team of detectives) to the county, this time to look into the death of an investigative journalist at a Dorset convalescent home, in *The Private Patient* (2008). Once again there are suspects galore, and the image of Agatha Christie is intact. Dalgleish even summons them to the library for the denouement.

The Lighthouse (2005) is set even further west, on the imaginary Combe Island off the Cornish coast. Privately owned, it is a retreat for the stressed and wealthy. When one of the residents is murdered, Dalgleish and his team are called in, but they are stretched to the limit and a second murder soon follows.

Then Dalgleish is struck down by something less human but just as lethal as murder.

See also: London, East Anglia

www.randomhouse.com/features/pdjames

Michael Jecks

Michael Jecks is the author of more than thirty medieval West Country mysteries set in the early 14th century. He lives on Dartmoor, and his love of the county of Devon is apparent, as is the depth of his research. He is a former chairman of the CWA, and a founder member of The Medieval Murderers, a group of historical crime writers who write and perform collaboratively.

His stories include such wonderful Devon settings such as Crediton (*The Crediton Killings*,1997), Tavistock (*The Abbot's Gibbet*, 1998) and Exeter (*City of Friends*, 2012). The mysteries are unravelled by the sleuthing duo of Simon Baldwin, Bailiff of Lydford, and former Knight Templar Sir Baldwin Furnshill.

In *The Crediton Killings*, the town is beset by a group of vicious mercenaries just as the Bishop of Exeter is due to visit, and when a young girl is murdered Simon and Sir Baldwin must unmask the killer before the visit becomes a disaster.

In *The Abbot's Gibbet*, it is the time of the Tavistock Fair and visitors — good and bad — are everywhere. Simon and Sir Baldwin are in town as guests of the Abbot when a headless body is discovered. — The Abbot asks them to investigate, but the web of intrigue surrounding the town is complex.

www.michaeljecks.co.uk

Morag Joss

As well as several high-class stand-alone novels, Scottish author Morag Joss has written three books featuring cellist and amateur detective Sara Selkirk.

All are set in Bath.

The first, *Funeral Music* (1998), centres on a murder in the famous Roman Baths. The Museum director has been found dead, and Sara, taking a break after a stress-related error-strewn performance in Paris, finds that she knows several people close to the investigation. Her curiosity leads her into danger.

In *Fearful Symmetry* (1999), Sara is having an affair with a music-loving detective, which gives her inside knowledge about a local murder. A second death takes place, and she knows the victim. She is sure that she has identified a connection, but a little knowledge can be a dangerous thing.

www.moragjoss.com

Brian Kavanagh

Australian Brian Kavanagh has many years of experience in the Australian film industry.

His first Belinda Lawrence crime novel, *Capable of Murder*, was published in the UK in 2005, and sees the heroine inherit a cottage in a small village outside Bath. However, nothing is quite as it seems, and soon she finds herself in danger after her next-door neighbour is killed.
See also: the South and South East

www.belindalawrenceamateursleuth.com

Erin Kelly & Chris Chibnall

Broadchurch was the big TV hit in early 2013, showing how the murder of a young boy affects a small Dorset seaside town. Erin Kelly, writer of three powerful psychological novels, then joined forces with original writer Chris Chibnall to produce a novelisation based on the original screenplay.

The body of eleven-year-old Danny Latimer is found on the beach, to the horror of the whole town of Broadchurch. DSgt Ellie Miller knew the Latimer family and is desperate to help. She is annoyed when a new detective, DI Alec Hardy, is brought in to head up the case. As the media frenzy is stepped up, pressure and tension lead to a further death and as secrets tumble into the light Ellie begins to realise that for the whole town nothing will ever be the same again.

With increased insight into the characters and the location, the book will appeal to crime readers everywhere.

See also: London (Erin Kelly)

www.erinkelly.co.uk

Bernard Knight

As the Home Office Pathologist, Professor Bernard Knight was a central figure in many major murder investigations of the late twentieth century, including the Fred and Rosemary West case in 1994. He wrote the script for the BBC TV series *The Expert*, and contributed scripts to *Bergerac* in the 1980s.

He has written a series of colourful medieval crime novels set in twelfth century Devon, all featuring Sir John De Wolf (known as Crowner John). After fighting in the Crusades with Richard the Lionheart, he returns to England and is appointed Coroner for Exeter in *The Sanctuary Seeker* (1998), and later becomes the first Coroner for the whole of Devon.

The Tinner's Corpse (2001) sees him on the moors, examining the body of a murdered tin miner. The subsequent investigation proves incredibly difficult for Crowner John, as problems pile up. Then his indispensible right hand man, Gwyn, is arrested for murder. The Tinners have their own laws, and their own methods of enforcing them.

In *The Grim Reaper* (2002), Crowner John is called in to investigate a spate of murders in which a biblical text has been left next to the victims. He is sure a priest is guilty, but which one? There are twenty-five parish churches in Exeter alone.

See also: Wales

www.fantasticfiction.co.uk/k/bernard-knight

Deryn Lake

Historical novelist Dinah Lampitt writes the John Rawlings Georgian mysteries under the pen-name Deryn Lake. Though mainly set in London, the series includes books set in Devon and Cornwall.

In *Death and the Cornish Fiddler* (2006), apothecary John Rawlings visits Cornwall in May 1765 and is drawn into the mysterious disappearance of a child from the Hellstone (*sic*) Floral Dance.

Death at the Wedding Feast (2012) is set in Devon. Rawlings is visiting Sidmouth to be with his pregnant mistress. When he is told about the impending marriage of Lady Sidmouth's young daughter to a much older man he is worried, and soon his sense of foreboding is proved all too accurate.

See also: the South and South East, London
www.derynlake.com

Janet Laurence

Janet Laurence wrote ten mostly West Country-set foodie mysteries between 1989 and 2000.

Amateur sleuth Darina Lisle is a high class cook and caterer who, like the author, lives in Somerset.

In *Recipe for Death* (1992), she investigates a sudden death at a Somerset farm, owned by cookery competition winner Verity Fry.

In *Death and the Epicure* (1993), Darina is invited to write a cookery book by Finer Foods, a West Country firm importing exotic foods. However, the company is in financial trouble, and its problems are exacerbated when a death occurs in the demonstration kitchen. A second death is only just avoided, and when the police seem to be moving in the wrong direction, Darina decides to seek the truth herself.

See also: London
www.fantasticfiction.co.uk/l/janet-laurence

Christopher Lee

Best known for his 1995 BBC series about Britain, *This Sceptred Isle*, Christopher Lee also wrote three Bath-set crime novels about the eccentric DI James Boswell Hodge Leonard.

In *The Bath Detective* (1995) Inspector Leonard is given the task of solving the gruesome murder of a beggar. When his investigations take him into city society, he finds a network of lies among the elite.

www.fantasticfiction.co.uk/l/christopher-lee

Michael Z. Lewin

An American who has lived in Somerset for many years, Michael Z. Lewin has been writing crime novels since the early 1970s. He has written two series set in his home city of Indianapolis, and has been nominated for an Edgar Award three times.

He also wrote three novels about the Lunghi family of private detectives, an extraordinary group which includes three generations of one Bath family. Clever and witty, they are light enough on the surface but the dark notes are there, if you look for them.

In *Family Way* (2011), all the generations are enjoying Nation Day, a huge celebration bringing big crowds to the city. Then a body is found, with drastic consequences.

www.michaelzlewin.com

Peter Lovesey

After being a teacher, Peter Lovesey became a full-time crime writer in 1975. Originally known for his Sergeant Cribb novels set in Victorian London, he won the CWA Gold Dagger for *The False Inspector Dew* in 1982, and has been nominated for many other awards both in the UK and in America.

He has written a stylish series of crime novels set in the beautiful city of Bath, featuring DSupt Peter Diamond. A no-nonsense, determined character with a great deal of charm, he has appeared in thirteen novels since 1991.

In *The Vault* (1999), bones are discovered below the city's Georgian tea-rooms. They prove not to be historic, and bear signs of violence. Meanwhile, the wife of an English professor has disappeared. Diamond has plenty on his plate when suddenly there is another murder, and it implicates the professor.

Peter Lovesey also wrote the brilliant *Rough Cider* (1986), a classic psychological novel about American GIs and the discovery of a body in a Somerset cider barrel during World War II.

The stand-alone mystery, *The Reaper* (2000), was set in the fictional Wiltshire village of Foxford, where local vicar Otis Joy has a secret other life — as a murderer. This novel won the CWA/Cartier Diamond Dagger in 2000.

See also: London
www.peterlovesey.com

Fergus McNeill

A veteran of the computer games industry since the early 1980s, Fergus McNeill's first foray into crime fiction is *Eye Contact* (2012). The book opens with a body found at Severn Beach, which leads Inspector Harland to the discovery of a frightening serial killer, who chooses his victims completely at random.

A follow-up novel (*Knife-Edge*) was published in 2013. This time, Harland is sent to investigate the vicious murder of a woman in her Bristol home. It appears at first to be a random attack, but soon Harland begins to have doubts.

www.fergusmcneill.blogspot.co.uk

Edward Marston

The murder of an unpopular monk in the bell-tower of Gloucester Abbey is the centrepiece of Edward Marston's *The Owls of Gloucester* (2000). This is book ten of the eleventh-century Doomsday series, which is set all over England. Edward Marston is one of the pseudonyms used by the very prolific Keith Miles.

See also: the South and South East, London, Wales, the North West

www.edwardmarston.com

David Ralph Martin

Dave Martin was a television scriptwriter whose best-remembered work was for Doctor Who — he created the robot dog, K9, and wrote several highly-rated series with fellow Bristolian Bob Baker. He published four hard-hitting crime novels set in the West Country, featuring DS Vic Hallam, a cop who doesn't necessarily play by the rules.

In *Dead Man's Bay* (2005) Hallam is sent to the South Coast when a disembowelled body is found off Portland Bill. With his partner, DC John Cromer, Hallam is forced to go undercover to penetrate the lucrative local drugs trade.

www.dorsetbooks.com/david.martin

The Medieval Murderers

This is the pseudonym used by a group of well-known writers for a fine series of medieval crime novels. The authors take it in turns to write chapters, or short stories, which are woven around a central theme. They use a variety of locations around Britain and Ireland, but some of the best stories are set in the south west, as that is where several of the authors (Michael Jacks, Bernard Knight, Philip Gooden) are based.

In *King Arthur's Bones* (2009), an ancient relic is uncovered during excavations at Glastonbury Abbey, and an inscription suggests that the nearby bones are those of the great king and his wife Guinevere. The bones are stolen, and in future generations their secrets are maintained despite blackmail, treachery and murder.

Hill of Bones (2011) is set on and around Solsbury Hill in

Somerset, where a mysterious dagger has been buried as a tribute to a dead soldier from King Arthur's army. From this point on the hill is the scene of murder and duplicity.
www.michaeljecks.co.uk/medievalmurder

Barbara Michaels

A past president of the American League of Crime Writers, Barbara Michaels had a forty-year writing career and wrote around thirty crime novels. She used many settings for her work, but gave her mystery novel *Wait for What Will Come* (2007) a classic Cornish setting, as Carla Tregellas finds that her inherited Cornish mansion on the cliff brings with it more problems than just an old family curse.
www.mpmbooks.com

Fiona Mountain

Snowshill in Gloucestershire is the setting for Cotswold author Fiona Mountain's two crime novels featuring Ancestor Detective Natasha Blake.

In *Bloodline* (2004) she delves into the 1940s to solve the murder of an old man, who has been shot dead at an isolated farm. The family secrets she uncovers link No Man's Land on Christmas Day 1914 to the present day.
www.fionamountain.com

Caro Peacock

Caro Peacock is a pseudonym of former journalist Gillian Linscott, who is the creator of headstrong young Victorian detective Liberty Lane.

Though based in London, Liberty is persuaded, in *The Path of the Wicked* (2013), to go to Cheltenham to try to save the life of accused murderer Jack Picton, a known political troublemaker. In doing so, she discovers that beneath the town's haughty façade lies a web of secrets and lies, as the underclass seek to avoid the workhouse.
See also: London (Caro Peacock, Gillian Linscott).
www.caropeacock.com

Robert Richardson

As a journalist Robert Richardson wrote for a number of papers including *The Times, The Telegraph and The Observer*. He was at one time Chair of the CWA.

The fourth novel to feature playwright and part-time detective Augustus Maltravers, *The Dying of the Light* (1990), centres on the fictional Cornish fishing village of Porthennis, where Maltravers's girlfriend is performing in a summer theatre (similar to the real Minack Theatre). At the behest of a local psychic he looks into the supposedly accidental death of a local sculptress, who was found crushed to death by one of her own works.

See also: the South and South East

www.fantasticfiction.co.uk/r/robert-richardson

Michael Robotham

Australian Michael Robotham has been a journalist in America and the UK as well as his home country. He has written nine novels, and biographies of celebrities and pop stars under a pseudonym.

His protagonist is Joe O'Loughlin, a clinical psychologist, and Metropolitan policeman Vincent Ruiz often appears in lesser roles. Several books of the series are set in the Bristol/Bath area. *Shatter* (2008) opens in shocking fashion, as a naked woman jumps to her death from the Clifton Suspension Bridge, having been talked into jumping by a terrifying adversary — a man with the persuasive power to break minds.

The next book in the series (*Bleed for Me*, 2010) is set in Bath, where O'Loughlin is called to examine a fourteen-year-old who appears to have bludgeoned her father (a former detective) to death in her bedroom.

See also: London

www.michaelrobotham.com

Rosemary Rowe

Rosemary Rowe is the pseudonym (actually her maiden name) of Cornwall-born Rosemary Aitken. She is the author of more than a dozen Roman murder mysteries mainly set in and around Glevum (Roman Gloucester). They are set during the period 183–190AD, at the time of the Emperor Commodus. The series began with *The Germanicus Mosaic* (1999).

In these well-researched stories the sleuth is Libertus, a former slave now working as a pavement-maker, who uses his knowledge of puzzles and patterns to solve a number of interesting mysteries.

In *Requiem for a Slave* (2010), Libertus has to clear the name of his own slave when a man is found dead in his workshop, and in *The Vestal Vanishes* (2011) the disappearance of a soon-to-be-married vestal virgin looks suspicious to Libertus, especially when a second woman disappears. It looks as if the Druids may be involved, and Libertus faces a dangerous task to ensure the safety of the missing women.

www.raitken.wyenet.co.uk

Betty Rowlands

The Cotswolds are the setting for two series of relatively gentle murder mysteries from a very fine writer. In some ways Melissa Craig is the author's alter-ego, living in a Cotswold village writing crime fiction. However she is also an amateur sleuth, who appears in twelve books between 1990 and 2004.

In *Finishing Touch* (1991), she investigates a murder at the local technical college where she teaches, while in *No Laughing Matter* (2011), she delves into a case of poisoning in the residential home where her mother is staying.

The second series features Scenes of Crime Officer "Sukey" Reynolds, whose intuition often succeeds where her superiors have failed.

In *Smokescreen* (2008), a best-selling author is found dead in her bath in her country pile outside Bristol, just days after a break-in by a disturbed fan. Finding the suspect is just the start of an extraordinary case.

www.bettyrowlands.com

Andrew Saville

The *Bergerac* BBC TV series set on the Channel Island of Jersey was hugely popular during the 1980s. Crime writer Andrew Taylor (writing under the pseudonym of Andrew Saville) wrote six novels based on the TV character, with fresh, original storylines.

In *Bergerac and the Traitor's Child* (1988) Bergerac's boss DCI Barney Crozier is on the receiving end of a blackmail threat, while in *Bergerac and the Fatal Weakness* (1988) it is Bergerac and Jersey that are under threat from an IRA assassination team and a major outbreak of scarlet fever.

See also: London (Andrew Taylor), Wales (Andrew Taylor)
www.andrew-taylor.co.uk

Kate Sedley

Bristol-born Kate Sedley has set her twenty-two historical crime novels all over the south-west. They take place in the fifteenth century, and recount the adventures of Roger the Chapman, a former monk who has given up the monastic life to become a peddler in the West Country.

Her second novel, *The Plymouth Cloak* (1992), sees Roger fighting to clear his reputation when a King's Messenger is murdered on board a ship in Plymouth Harbour.

In *The St John's Fern* (1999), it is 1477 and Roger is back in Plymouth. He investigates the murder of a wealthy old man in the city. The old man's nephew has vanished, and is thought to be guilty, having eaten St John's Fern — a herb which supposedly renders the eater invisible. Roger does not believe this theory.

The Midsummer Rose (2004) sees Roger attacked in a Bristol house which was the scene of a murder thirty years before. At first no-one accepts his version of events, but after a body is found in the river, Roger's story is verified. It seems that there is more to the old house than meets the eye.

www.fantasticfiction.co.uk/s/kate-sedley

Mark Sennen

Though he grew up in Surrey and Shropshire, Mark Sennen now lives in Devon, and has set his dark, visceral thrillers in Plymouth and other parts of the West Country. DI Charlotte Savage is the central character, along with a number of other characters from Plymouth CID.

The first novel, *Touch* (2012), is told from three points of view — the police, the killer and the victims. A series of assaults on students is stretching CID resources, and when a body is found on a beach it proves to be just the first of many, as Charlotte and her team race to find a vicious serial killer.

In the follow-up, *Bad Blood* (2013), a child's body is found under a patio, and a local paedophile is found murdered. Then a member of Charlotte's team is abducted, and more murders follow. Charlotte is up against a violent murderer who is selecting his victims for a reason. Could she be next? All the time her colleague lies in a makeshift prison, waiting for the final bullet.

www.marksennen.com

Neville Steed

Neville Steed's six Peter Marklin mysteries were published between 1986 and 1991.

Marklin was an unusual amateur sleuth, a quiet, dependable man who owned an antique toy shop in the shadow of Corfe Castle.

In *Tin-plate* (1986), he finds himself out of his depth after the theft of valuable antique toys, and in *Boxed-in* (1992), he becomes involved in murder when he opens a car boot at an auction and finds a dead boy.

www.fantasticfiction.co.uk/s/neville-steed

Charles Todd

Charles Todd is the pen name of an American mother and son writing team, but their novels are quintessentially

English. They all feature Inspector Ian Rutledge, an unusual character who has been invalided back from the trenches of France during World War I suffering from shell-shock. He hears voices in his head, principally that of Hamish, a young soldier whose execution Rutledge had ordered during the horrors of battle.

Though he works for Scotland Yard, Rutledge is regularly sent to deal with cases around the country. *Wings of Fire* (1998) finds Rutledge in Cornwall investigating the sudden death of a well-known war poet, whose work had helped to keep Rutledge sane on the front line.

In *Search the Dark* (1999) Rutledge tries to help a fellow World War I veteran who is accused of murdering his wife in Dorset, although the man claims that she was killed in a London bombing raid. Their children have also vanished...

See also: East Anglia, Scotland: Highlands and Islands
www.charlestodd.com

Rebecca Tope

Brought up on a Devon farm, Rebecca Tope had her first book published in 1999, since when she has written more than twenty more.

Though best known for her Cotswold mysteries, her Den Cooper and Drew Slocombe series are both set in Devon. Cooper is a CID officer, while Slocombe is a trainee undertaker.

In *A Dirty Death* (1999), Cooper investigates the death of a much-hated local farmer, while in *Dark Undertakings* (1999), Slocombe has his doubts about the death of fitness fanatic Jim Lapsford.

In *The Sting of Death* (2002), they team up when they come to live in the same village and have to deal with the dark side of country life, including the aftermath of a foot and mouth outbreak, as well as abduction and murder.

In 2004 *A Cotswold Killing* introduced Thea Osborne, a forty-two-year old widow and amateur detective. Since then Rebecca Tope has written twelve more charming novels about Thea, whose career as a house-sitter leads her into various dangerous situations with lots of dubious people, while her relationship with DSupt Phil Hollis ebbs and flows.

Many of these stories are set in real Cotswold villages. *Death in the Cotswolds* (2006) is set in Cold Aston, where village secrets are brought into the open after a body is found on Notgrove Barrow.

A Cotswold Ordeal (2005) is set in Frampton Mansell. Someone has done the unthinkable and committed suicide in the barn of the house where Thea is acting as house-sitter. Then her sister arrives, with a tale of her own woe. Soon the police are involved, but Thea is not sure who she can trust.

See also: the North West

www.rebeccatope.com

Nicola Upson

Cambridge-educated Nicola Upson was the crime reviewer for *The New Statesman* for five years, and has also worked in the theatre.

She has written a short series of crime novels set in the 1930s with the real-life crime novelist Josephine Tey as an amateur detective. They are full of period atmosphere and are reminiscent of the novels of the Golden Age.

She has used various settings, including Cornwall. In *Angel With Two Faces* (2009), Josephine is on holiday with Inspector Archie Penrose in Porthleven. When the Minack Theatre is the site of both tragedy and murder, Josephine finds that red herrings abound and past crimes resonate through the apparently unspoiled rural community.

See also: Wales

www.nicolaupson.com

Minette Walters

Previously a writer for romantic magazines, over the last twenty years Minette Walters has become one of the best exponents of the psychological crime novel. She loves Dorset and this is reflected in her choice of settings. She won the CWA John Creasey Award with her first book *The Ice House* (1992), and has twice won the CWA Gold Dagger.

The Ice House is a compelling, complex murder mystery with many subplots. A body is found in the grounds of Streech Grange, a large country house based on the real Creech Grange. The police investigate, and connect the death with a missing man who vanished ten years earlier. But as so often happens, the simple explanation may not be the right one.

In *Fox Evil* (2002), which won the Gold Dagger in 2003, the author again focuses on the psychological aspects of the characters in an extraordinary story involving an elderly, wealthy landowner, a small remote Dorset village, a drug-addict daughter, a mysterious death and a large group of travellers, led by a man known as Fox Evil.

www.minettewalters.co.uk

Gordon M. Williams

Sam Peckinpah's controversial film *Straw Dogs* (1971) was partly based on the 1969 novel *The Siege of Trencher's Farm* by Gordon M. Williams, in which a mild-mannered American professor and his family rent a remote Cornish farmhouse so that he can finish a book in peace. Unfortunately the peace is shattered when he accidentally runs down a man, thus upsetting some very unpleasant locals. Their revenge is brutal.

www.fantasticfiction.co.uk/w/gordon-m-williams

M.P. Wright

Though born and bred in Leicestershire, former private investigator M.P. Wright has set his exciting debut novel *Heartman* (2014) in 1960s Bristol. Disgraced ex-detective J.T. Ellington has not been in the city very long — he has only recently arrived from Barbados and is unsure and uncertain in a strange place. He is hired to find a missing

girl — a young, deaf-and-dumb black girl who the police have given up on far too easily. Faced with animosity, bitterness and bigotry at every turn, Ellington is soon embroiled in a seedy, dangerous world full of backstreet pubs, prostitutes, and nightclubs.
www.mppwrightauthor.blogspot.co.uk

Ten Recommended Reads

1: *Darkside* by Belinda Bauer (2011)

2: *Wycliffe and the Last Rites* by W.J. Burley (1992)

3: *The Hound of the Baskervilles* by Sir Arthur Conan Doyle (1902)

4: *A Painted Doom* by Kate Ellis (2002)

5: *Past Caring* by Robert Goddard (1986)

6. *The TV Detective* by Simon Hall (2010)

7. *Ritual* by Mo Hayder (2008)

8: *The Crediton Killings* by Michael Jecks (1997)

9: *Rough Cider* by Peter Lovesey (1986)

10. *The Ice House* by Minette Walters (1992)

REGION TWO
England — The South and South East

Faraday was watching a tiny fishing smack butting against the tide... Centuries ago, a heavy iron chain was laid across to the Gosport shore, resting on the seabed. In times of war, the chain could be raised, barring the entrance to the harbour, and the remains of this primitive barrier were still visible, brown and rusting, at low tide. These days of course, there were other ways of keeping the enemy at bay, but the longer Faraday spent in the city, and deeper he plumbed its depths, the more certain he became about what made the place tick. Portsmouth owed its very existence to aggression.

GRAHAM HURLEY, *Angels Passing*, Orion, 2003

This region includes the South Coast from Southampton to the Thames estuary, Hampshire, Sussex, Kent and all the Home Counties surrounding London. It takes in the wonderful natural beauty of the New Forest and the South Downs, the historic Weald of Kent and the ecclesiastical centre of Canterbury. Its coastline includes perhaps the most famous naval port in the country (Portsmouth), and holiday destinations such as Whitstable, Margate and Brighton, while The White Cliffs of Dover are for many a symbol of Britain.

Great names in crime fiction with local connections include Peter James, who went to Charterhouse School, lives in Sussex and sets his novels in Brighton, Arthur Conan Doyle, who lived in Surrey and Sussex, Agatha Christie (when she famously disappeared in 1926 her car was found abandoned near Guildford), and Ruth Rendell, who sets her Wexford novels in the fictional Sussex town of Kingsmarkham. Brighton is also the setting for works by Graham Greene and Robert Goddard, while Graham Hurley and Pauline Rowson focus on the historic naval city of Portsmouth.

Gilbert Adair

Film critic, novelist and journalist Gilbert Adair wrote three wonderful Agatha Christie pastiches featuring murder mystery writer and amateur detective Evadne Mount.

In *A Mysterious Affair of Style* (2007), Evadne investigates when an actress is murdered on a crowded film set at Elstree Studios in Hertfordshire.

www.fantasticfiction.co.uk/a/gilbert-adair

Catherine Aird

A long-time resident of Kent, Catherine Aird (a pseudonym of Kinn Hamilton Mcintosh) has said that any similarity between her fictional Calleshire, where all of her Inspector Sloan novels are set, and Kent itself is a coincidence. However, I believe there are enough coincidences throughout her well-plotted novels to justify her inclusion in this section.

Inspector CD ("Seedy") Sloan's many cases include a body in a suit of armour (*The Complete Steel*, 1969) and an Egyptian mummy being replaced with a dead body (*Little Knell*, 2000). Cleverly straddling the line between cosy crime and police procedural, the stories are imaginative and thoughtful.

In *Hole in One* (2005), when two lady golfers discover a body in the much feared Hell's Bells bunker at a local golf course, Sloan is called in and finds that the club committee is divided by more than just their golf handicap.

www.catherineaird.com

Rennie Airth

When South African journalist Rennie Airth found a scrapbook detailing the life of an uncle who had been killed in World War I, it gave him the idea for the beautifully written, expertly researched John Madden trilogy.

The first book, *River of Darkness*, was published in 1999, and was nominated for Anthony, Macavity and Edgar Awards in the USA. Madden is a sympathetic character, a war veteran who has lost his family. He is the detective in charge of the investigation into the horrific murder of five people in a small, peaceful Surrey village shortly after the end of the Great War. While others are prepared to believe it was robbery gone wrong, Madden insists that there is more to it.

The final novel, *The Dead of Winter* (2009), takes place in 1944 by which time Madden has retired to a Surrey farm. When a young Polish refugee girl is viciously murdered, the hard-pressed police are prepared to see it as a random killing until Madden, for whom the girl had been working, decides to use his Scotland Yard contacts to take the case forward, and soon there are links to stolen diamonds and another murder.

www.rennieairth.net

Tom Bale

Tom Bale is the pseudonym of David Harrison, and his first novel *Skin and Bones* (2010) is set in rural Sussex, where a Hungerford-style massacre takes place in a quiet, sleepy village. Julia Trent is a survivor, and her account does not tally with the official view — that it was a lone gunman. Working with the son of one of the victims, she sets out to uncover the truth. However, by not letting it rest, she has put herself in even more danger.

In the follow-up, *Terror's Reach* (2011), an exclusive island enclave off the south coast is attacked by a group of merciless killers. Joe Clayton, an ex-policeman now working as a bodyguard, finds himself caught in the crossfire of a violent vendetta.

See also: the West Country
www.tombale.net

Christianna Brand

This is one of a number of pseudonyms used by Malayan-born Mary Christianna Lewis, whose writing career lasted from 1941 to 1982. With interesting plots and a fine sense of humour, her crime novels can be compared to classics from the Golden Age of detective fiction.

She created the character of Inspector Cockrill of the Kent County Police for *Heads You Lose* (1941), who also appeared in *Green for Danger* (1944), which is often cited as one of the classic mysteries of the period. The story is set in a military hospital at the height of the Blitz, where a patient has died during an operation and the nurse in charge has been murdered. The Inspector finds himself with a number of suspects, but no apparent motive.

www.fantasticfiction.co.uk/b/christianna-brand

Simon Brett

A writer and producer for the BBC for many years, Simon Brett is perhaps best known for his crime novels featuring jobbing actor Charles Paris, but his series of Fethering novels have brought him many new readers. Fethering is a fictitious retirement community on the Sussex coast, and his amateur sleuths are retired civil servant Carole Seddon and her friend and accomplice Jude Nichols. The relationship between these two very different characters is central to these charming, cosy crime novels.In their first investigation, *The Body on the Beach* (2001), Carole finds a body, which she reports, only for it to disappear before the police arrive. They disbelieve her, but her friend Jude persuades her to turn detective and the two women decide to investigate for themselves.

In *Blood at the Bookies* (2008), they investigate when the body of a Polish immigrant is found dead in the local betting shop. There are plenty of suspects, including a university lecturer and a mysterious woman. Then Jude is attacked, and they realise they must apprehend the killer before he or she strikes again.

See also: London, Scotland: Edinburgh and the Borders
www.simonbrett.com

John Dickson Carr

One of the all-time great crime novelists, John Dickson Carr was the grand master of the locked-room mystery. An American by birth, he lived for many years in England, and often used English settings. His novels were full of unlikely scenarios, and he specialised in impossible murders.

In *The Crooked Hinge* (1938) his protagonist Dr Gideon Fell is staying in a small Kent village when a man is murdered in front of three people, all of whom claim to have seen nothing.

See also: London
www.jdcarr.com

Glenn Chandler

Best known as the creator of TV series *Taggart*, Glenn Chandler is a playwright of note and the author of two powerful crime novels set in Brighton, featuring DI Steve Madden, a sad and cynical detective recovering from a broken marriage.

In *Savage Tide* (2003), Madden is called to a murder scene, only to find that the victim is his own son, who had just announced that he was gay. To find the truth about his death Madden has to enter Brighton's gay underworld.

In the follow-up, *Dead Sight* (2004), Madden investigates a frightening murderer who kills without compunction.

www.fantasticfiction.co.uk/c/glenn-chandler

Agatha Christie

Born in Devon in 1890, Agatha Christie was an extremely productive crime writer, with more than eighty novels and a vast number of short stories to her credit, as well as a number of plays including *The Mousetrap* — the longest running play of all time.

The character of Miss Jane Marple, spinster, was originally introduced in *The Murder at The Vicarage* (1930). She lived in St Mary Mead, a classic English village. Its exact location is never made clear, but it is described as being about twenty-five miles from London, which puts it in the Home Counties.

Miss Marple is elderly, and though she has rarely left her home village, she has become a student of human nature, and considers herself a good amateur sleuth. Surprisingly, she only appeared in one novel in the first twenty years of Agatha Christie's writing career.

Miss Marple's second full-length appearance is in *The Body in the Library* (1942), in which a body is found in the country house belonging to her friends, the Bantrys. The body is thought to be that of a dancer from nearby Danemouth, and there are quite a number of suspects. The police are baffled, and then a second young girl is killed. It takes Miss Marple's ingenuity to uncover a cruel and vicious murderer.

In *The Mirror Cracked From Side to Side* (1962), a murder takes place at the home of film star Marina Gregg, which was formerly owned by the Bantrys. It transpires that the film star may have been the intended victim, and Miss Marple becomes interested because Mrs Bantry had been at the party where the murder took place. Further deaths occur before she is able to ascertain the truth.

Overall Agatha Christie wrote twelve Miss Marple novels, as well as many short stories. Miss Marple has been played by several different actresses on TV and radio, with varying results. The BBC adaptations featuring actress Joan Hickson are my personal favourites, and are the most faithful to the original stories.

See also: the West Country, London

www.agathachristie.com

Alys Clare

A former student of archaeology, Alys Clare has written a superb series of historical crime novels centred around the magnificent Hawkenlye Abbey in Kent. The Abbey is a mixed community of monks and nuns, all in the charge of the formidable Abbess Helewise. Set in the late 1100s at the time of Richard the Lionheart, they feature a highly unusual detective partnership — a nun (Abbess Helewise) and a knight (Sir Josse D'Acquin), who meet in the first of the series (*Fortune Like the Moon*, 1999) when King Richard employs his old colleague D'Acquin to find the killer of a young nun.

In *The Faithful Dead* (2001), an elderly pilgrim has died at the Abbey, and a decomposing body is found. Soon Josse and Helewise find themselves embroiled in a mystery whose roots go back into the depths of recent history, well beyond the Second Crusade.

By the time of *The Rose of the World* (2011) life has moved on. Helewise has left the Abbey and moved to Hawkenlye Manor with Sir Josse, and as King John has been excommunicated, his men have arrived to take over the Abbey. When Helewise's granddaughter vanishes, Sir Josse and Helewise face a danger that could ruin their lives.

www.severnhouse.com/author/Alys+Clare/9378

N.J. Cooper

Natasha Cooper is a former Chair of the CWA, and writes for many newspapers and magazines. After two mystery series set in London she has set her most recent series on the Isle of Wight. The main character is forensic psychologist Karen Taylor.

In the first book, *No Escape* (2009), Karen is conducting interviews for a paper on Severe Personality Disorder. She is trying to probe the mind of imprisoned psychopath Spike Falconer, but she starts to doubt his guilt — which is not a universally popular point of view on the island.

The fourth in the series, *Vengeance in Mind* (2012), sees Karen working to unlock the memories of a devastated woman who was a witness to a gruesome murder. A wealthy businessman has been found dead, horribly mutilated in what looks like a revenge attack. The only witness was his personal assistant, who is suffering from traumatic amnesia. As the story starts to come out it is Karen herself who is most at risk. This novel was shortlisted for the CWA Gold Dagger in 2012.

See also: London

www.natashacooper.co.uk

Freeman Wills Crofts

A Dubliner by birth, Freeman Wills Crofts was part of the Golden Age in the 1920s and 1930s. He was a contemporary of Christie and Sayers, and was an early member of the Detection Club, the group of authors who drew up a series of "fair-play rules" for crime writers.

His main character, Inspector French, was for a time seen as a major rival to Hercule Poirot, and had been promoted to Chief Inspector by the time of *Mystery on Southampton Water* (1934), in which French investigates an explosion on a launch in the Solent.

Crofts lived in Guildford for many years and set a number of his books in the area, including *The Hog's Back Mystery* (1933), where Inspector French is puzzled by the mysterious disappearance of several local people, and *Crime at Guildford* (1935), in which French investigates the connection between a jewel robbery in London and the death of a Guildford businessman.

www.fantasticfiction.co.uk/c/freeman-wills-crofts

Judith Cutler

Born and bred in the West Midlands, Judith Cutler moved to Kent a few years ago and started to write a series of novels set there, featuring DCSupt Frances Harman, a realistic and sensitive character who tries to find the balance between her police work as an experienced senior detective and the demands of her family.

The first book in the series (*Life Sentence*, 2005) deals with a terrible case — a woman who was attacked, raped and left in a coma. If she dies, it will be a murder enquiry, which will be just another addition to Fran's huge caseload. Fran is not far from retirement, and has a number of personal issues, but the job will not let her go.

In the fourth book, *Burying the Past,* 2012, she is anticipating her wedding to Assistant Chief Constable Mark Turner when preparations are thrown into chaos by the discovery of a skeleton in the garden of their prospective new home.

See also: the West Country, the Midlands
www.judithcutler.com

Lindsey Davis

Birmingham born and bred, Lindsey Davis originally worked as a civil servant before turning to writing full time. She is best known for the Falco series, featuring Marcus Didius Falco, former legionnaire and informer, later Imperial Agent (a sort of private eye) in Ancient Rome. She is a highly respected author and has won both the CWA Ellis Peters Historical Dagger and the Dagger in the Library. Her research is impeccable, and in the character of Falco, her sense of humour shines through. The series began with *The Silver Pigs* (1989) and is generally set around AD 70.

The thirteenth in the series, *A Body in the Bathhouse* (2001), sees Falco sent to the construction site of Fishbourne Palace in Sussex to investigate corruption and murder. He has to survive on his wits when he uncovers unexpected menace.

www.lindseydavis.co.uk

Paul Doherty

A prolific author under his full name and several pseudonyms, Dr. Paul Doherty has written several series of historical crime novels.

In his *Canterbury Tales of Mystery and Murder,* published between 1994 and 2012, a group of pilgrims embark on the long journey from London to Canterbury. Stopping at various points *en route,* each one recounts a grisly tale of murder and mayhem.

In *Ghostly Murders* (1997) the pilgrims take shelter in a ruined church and the priest tells his tale. — Two brothers are appointed priests in the small Kent village of Scawsby. They set about building a new church and graveyard for the village, but when graves are moved to the new site, some are empty and others contain bodies of men clearly buried alive. The subsequent investigations lead the brothers into barely imaginable horror.

After a ten-year gap, the seventh tale — *The Midnight Man* — was published in 2012. This is the physician's tale. Brother Anselm and his novice are summoned to perform an exorcism at St Michael's Church, Candlewick. Before long they are overtaken by a series of shocking events — murder, satanism, triumph and tragedy.

See also: the West Country (Michael Clynes), London (Michael Clynes, Paul Doherty), the South and South East (C.L. Grace)

www.paulcdoherty.com

R.S. Downie

Since winning a writing competition in 2004 Ruth Downie has written five well-researched novels about Gaius Petreius Ruso, a doctor in the Roman Army based in Britain. The author's sense of humour and knowledge of the period come to the fore in a very readable series.

Ruso and the River of Darkness (2010) is set in Roman Verulamium, now St Albans, where Ruso has settled following an escapade in France. Persuaded to try to find a missing tax man and some missing money, which may or may not be connected, Ruso finds that the people of Verulamium may not be as supportive of the Romans as they are thought to be. Soon he finds himself in a conspiracy involving theft, forgery, treasure and the legacy of Queen Boudicca herself.

See also: the North West

www.rsdownie.co.uk

Sir Arthur Conan Doyle

Sir Arthur Conan Doyle was born and educated in Edinburgh but lived much of his life in southern England, including many years in Surrey and Sussex. He created Sherlock Holmes in 1887, and wrote about him for almost forty years.

He set short stories all around southern England, including in Surrey, Sussex and Hampshire.

"The Adventure of The Reigate Squire" was originally included in *The Memoirs of Sherlock Holmes* (1893). While recuperating at a country house near Reigate, Holmes hears of a burglary and a murder nearby. There is only one clue — a piece of torn paper with a few apparently meaningless words on it. Holmes uses his knowledge of handwriting to help solve the mystery.

"The Five Orange Pips" was originally written for the *Strand Magazine* in 1891, and was later collected for *The Adventures of Sherlock Holmes* (1892). Holmes is called on to investigate a series of odd events at an estate in Horsham, West Sussex, including two deaths and the receipt of a strange letter from India, containing five orange pips.

The Adventure of The Crooked Man appeared in *The Memoirs of Sherlock Holmes* (1893). Holmes investigates the death of a military colonel at the army barracks in Aldershot. The colonel's wife is the prime suspect, but

Holmes is not convinced. The colonel's military service in India proves to be vital.

See also: the West Country, London
www.sherlockholmesonline.org

Liz Evans

Grace Smith is a hard-up private investigator in the down-at-heel coastal community of Seatown who is called in to help out in various strange investigations such as the death of a beach donkey called Marilyn Monroe (*Who Killed Marilyn Monroe?*, 1997) and clearing the name of a woman who freely admits to murder (*Sick as a Parrot*, 2004).

See also: London (Patricia Grey)
www.lizevans.net

Dick Francis

As a jockey, Dick Francis is best remembered for failing to win the 1956 Grand National on the Queen's horse Devon Loch, but as a writer he was the author of many award-winning crime novels, and he was awarded the CWA Cartier Dagger for lifetime achievement in 1989.

Even Money (2010) was the third collaboration between Dick Francis and his son Felix.

It starts on the first day of a major event at Ascot Racecourse, Berkshire, when bookmaker Ned Talbot, who has always understood himself to have been orphaned by a car crash when he was very young, is amazed to meet a man claiming to be his father. An hour later the man is dead, and Ned is drawn into a conspiracy that could cost him his life.

Sandown Park in Esher, Surrey is a high-class, historic racecourse which has hosted horseracing since 1875, and features in several Dick Francis novels, including *Reflex* (1980) and *High Stakes* (1975).

See also: the West Country, East Anglia
www.dickfrancis.com

Robert Goddard

Hampshire-born Robert Goddard read History at Cambridge, and has been a bestselling writer for more than twenty years.

His second novel, *In Pale Battalions* (1988), featured the beautiful Meon Valley in Hampshire as the backdrop to a classic Goddard mystery, set at the time of World War I. Elderly widow Leonora Galloway visits a war memorial in France to pay tribute to her father, who was killed at the Somme. The date given for her father's death is eleven months before she was born. What appears at first to be a simple case of wartime illegitimacy turns out to have violent repercussions that Leonora could not possibly have expected.

See also: the West Country

www.robertgoddardbooks.co.uk

Dolores Gordon-Smith

Jack Haldane is the hero of Dolores Gordon-Smith's excellent series of novels, set in the years immediately after World War I. He was a pilot for the Royal Flying Corps, and is living in 1920s Sussex, trying to make his way as a crime writer.

In *A Fate Worse Than Death* (2007), the amiable Jack is drawn into the mystery of a death at a local fête. The body turns out to be that of Jeremy Boscombe, like Jack a former RAF pilot. After a second death Jack teams up with the local police. Soon they realise that the deaths are connected to the Great War, and specifically events surrounding the Battle of the Somme.

In *A Hundred Thousand Dragons* (2010), a murder in Sussex and a note left in a book at the London Hotel are instrumental in Haldane facing up to a long-evaded truth about his part in The War.

www.doloresgordon-smith.co.uk

C.L. Grace

This is another pseudonym of the extraordinary Paul Doherty (he uses at least six). Kathryn Swinbrooke is a medical practitioner in fifteenth-century Canterbury. In *The Merchant of Death* (1995), it is Christmas 1471, and Kathryn is horrified at the news that young painter Richard Blunt has confessed to murdering his wife and two alleged lovers. In addition a crime has taken place at The Wicker Man Inn, where a tax collector has been killed and the King's money stolen. Kathryn is determined to find out the truth.

In *Saintly Murders* (2001), Kathryn is called in to deal with a plague of rats, but finds that the odd events surrounding the corpse of a beatified friar are more interesting. When she discovers that the friar was murdered, she becomes involved in a desperate search for a killer.

See also: the West Country (Michael Clynes), London (Michael Clynes, Paul Doherty), the South and South East (Paul Doherty)

www.paulcdoherty.com

Clio Gray

Clio Gray was born in Yorkshire and has now settled in the Scottish Highlands, where she works in her local library.

She has written an atmospheric series of historical crime novels featuring the gentle, middle-aged Missing Persons Finder Whilbert Stroop.

The Brotherhood of Five (2009) is set on the Isle of Thanet in 1808, as Stroop tries to find the answers behind a series of mysterious deaths. He uncovers a devastating plot that began years before on the battlefields of Europe — but is it too late to stop it?

See also: the North East, Scotland: Highlands and Islands

www.cliogray.com

Graham Greene

One of the really great writers of the twentieth century, Graham Greene was a sub-editor for *The Times* before becoming a full-time writer. His writing career lasted more than fifty years, and included both crime thrillers and more serious novels, though they often covered similar subjects.

Brighton Rock was published in 1938, and it proves that a crime story can be a serious novel too. It centres on the two faces of Brighton in the years before World War II —on the one hand a glitzy, tourist-friendly place full of fun and humour, on the other a dark, violent underworld of mobsters and terror. Throw into this the character of Pinkie, a psychotic teenager desperate to cover up his involvement in a gangland killing, and you have an explosive mix, brilliantly described. It is without doubt a classic.

www.greeneland.tripod.com

Peter Guttridge

From 1998 to 2002 Peter Guttridge was the director of the Brighton Literature Festival, and he has been a crime writer since 1997.

In 2010 he published the first in a series set in Brighton, *City of Dreadful Night*. This is a classy thriller in which a present-day journalist tries to discover the truth behind the Brighton Trunk Murder of 1934, by linking up with disgraced ex-cop Bob Watts. The second in the series is *The Last King of Brighton* (2011) in which gangster John Hathaway is under siege from criminals even more vicious than himself. Brighton is awash with violence, and people are forced to make unpalatable decisions. The clever linking of Brighton's past with its present is a central feature in all the books.

www.peterguttridge.com

Elizabeth Haynes

Elizabeth Haynes is a police intelligence analyst, and *Revenge of the Tide* (2012) is the author's second novel. This is a stylish murder mystery about a young woman, Genevieve, who leaves her stressful job in London to fulfil her dream and live on a houseboat in Kent. Unfortunately the night of her boat-warming party is ruined when a body is washed up alongside, and Genevieve realises that she knows the victim.

www.elizabeth-haynes.com

Graham Hurley

In 1990 Graham Hurley published a thriller, *Rules of Engagement*, which was turned into a TV series, and more thrillers followed. In the late 1990s he turned his hand to crime fiction, and has not looked back since.

The first book in his twelve-novel series, *Turnstone,* was published to critical acclaim in 2000. It introduced the central characters — the introspective, slightly lonely bird-watcher DI Joe Faraday, the silver-tongued, amoral, but effective DC Paul Winter, and the historic naval city of Portsmouth.

The long-running battle to control or convict Bazza Mackenzie, a drug baron with a wide-ranging criminal empire, is a thread which runs throughout the latter half of the series, and in *Cut To Black (*2004), Portsmouth CID attempt to trap Mackenzie with a financial sting operation. The original DI in charge of the plan is run down by a gang of Liverpudlian dealers trying to muscle in on Bazza's patch, and Faraday is called in to replace him. However, Faraday's personal life is desperately complicated, and in the end personal and professional events conspire to leave him compromised and the plans in tatters.

All the while Winter ploughs his own course inside and outside the force, bending the law as it suits him and using both colleagues and criminals for his own ends. In *The Price of Darkness* (2008), Winter goes undercover and joins Mackenzie's drug empire. Then a property developer is murdered, a drugs raid by another force threatens to unravel Winter's life of deception and a government minister is assassinated on a visit to the city. As his bosses search for answers, Faraday comes under immense pressure to find the truth, whatever it takes.

The series eventually comes to a shattering close with *Happy Days* (2012) in which Portsmouth CID are determined to end Mackenzie's criminal career at all costs, as he is arrogantly attempting to stand for Parliament. By now Winter has decided once and for all whose side he is on, and the scene is set for a decisive climax.

See also: the West Country

www.grahamhurley.co.uk

Peter James

Peter James was educated at Charterhouse School, and started writing in the 1980s. In the 1990s he was described as Britain's answer to Stephen King. A series of brilliant horror novels brought him a considerable readership, but in 2005 he changed tack and turned his hand to crime fiction. His first novel, featuring Brighton detective Roy Grace, *Dead Simple* (2005) — which incidentally features one of the best car chases ever written — was a huge success. He served two terms as Chair of the CWA and has won awards in a number of countries including France, Germany and the UK.

All his books are meticulously researched, and his experience as a horror writer and Hollywood producer (he was the executive producer for *The Merchant of Venice*, starring Al Pacino) ensure that his books are not for the faint-hearted. He has an excellent relationship with the police, and has even been able to accompany them in order to accurately represent their work.

The Roy Grace series is now one of the highlights of contemporary crime fiction worldwide, and the series has been nominated for many awards across the globe. A new Roy Grace novel is a major highlight of the crime fiction calendar. All the novels feature Brighton settings, often with international links.

Dead Simple (2005) begins with a stag night prank which ends in disaster. Michael Harrison is reported missing by his fiancée, but Grace soon realises that there is something odd about the whole situation. As he investigates, his discomfort is increased by thoughts about the disappearance of his own wife many years before.

In *Looking Good Dead* (2007), Grace finds himself investigating the impossible, as his chief suspect in the murder of Brighton socialite Katie Bishop appears to have been in two places at once. In *Not Dead Yet* (2012), an obsessed stalker is hunting a rock superstar who is in Brighton for the filming of a movie about George IV and Maria Fitzherbert.

www.peterjames.com

Alison Joseph

In 2013 Alison Joseph (best known for her London-based mysteries featuring Sister Agnes Boudillon) used the Kent coast as the setting for an unusual one-off novel featuring DI Berenice Killick (*Dying to Know*). The deaths of three physicists working on a top secret project suggest a possible vendetta, but Berenice has to trust her instincts to discover the full truth. However, making her voice heard in the misogynistic world of the local police is easier said than done.

See also: London

www.alisonjoseph.com

Brian Kavanagh

Brian Kavanagh has worked in the Australian film industry for many years, and his films have won awards in Australia and elsewhere..

Bloody Ham (2007), the third in the author's series about lively ex-pat Australian Belinda Lawrence, sees

Belinda suspected of murder after a double death on a film set in Ham House in Surrey.

A Canterbury Crime (2010) finds Belinda querying the death of a retired academic, who was about to publish a book which would rewrite the story of Thomas Becket. Is there more to his death than meets the eye?

See also: the West Country

www.belindalawrenceamateursleuth.com

Deryn Lake

In 2010 Deryn Lake moved away from her John Rawlings series of historical novels and began a series of contemporary mysteries set in the somewhat eccentric Sussex village of Lakehurst. It features a trendy vicar-cum-sleuth (Nick Lawrence) and a hard-pressed inspector from Sussex police (Dominic Tennant).

In *The Mills of God* (2010), a killer is on the loose, leaving a note by his victims, calling himself "The Acting Light of the World". In the follow-up *(Dead on Cue, 2012)* a body is found after a party thrown by a brash American actor and his wife, who are new to the area and have no idea what is in store for them.

See also: the West Country, London

www.derynlake.com

Edward Marston

One of this author's many series features Inspector Robert Colbeck, a railway policeman based at Ashford, Kent in the 1850s.

His cases take him to many different parts of the country. In *The Excursion Train* (2005), the investigation of a death on a Great Western train leads Colbeck back to a miscarriage of justice in his home county. In *Murder on the Brighton Express* (2008), Colbeck investigates when the Brighton Express is derailed with terrible consequences.

See also: the West Country, London, Wales, the North West

www.edwardmarston.com

Andrew Martin

A qualified barrister, Andrew Martin won the *Spectator* Young Writer of the Year Award in 1988, and has since written for various broadsheet newspapers, as well as writing and presenting documentaries for the BBC. The ninth book in his Jim Stringer series of railway-based detective novels was published in 2013. Settings vary from York and London to India and wartime France.

Stringer is a lowly railway porter working at Waterloo Station in Edwardian London when he first appears in *The Necropolis Railway* (2002). In this evocative and ingenious novel, his duties are restricted to working with the coffin trains that serve the huge, rather strange Brookwood Cemetery in Surrey, and when his predecessor vanishes, he finds himself involved in an extraordinary mystery.

The Jim Stringer series was nominated for the CWA Dagger in the Library award in 2008.

See also: the North West, the North East

www.jimstringernovels.com

Jennie Melville

The pseudonym of prolific writer Gwendoline Butler who died in 2013, Jennie Melville wrote more than twenty novels featuring CID Inspector Charmian Daniels, who rises in rank throughout the series and eventually becomes a chief superintendent. Most of the series is set in and around Windsor, and it was one of the first police procedural series to concentrate on the career of a senior policewoman.

In *Windsor Red* (1988), Charmian is on sabbatical but cannot stand idly by while limbs and bodies are found all over the town. In *Dead Again* (2000), a child-murderess returns to Windsor after serving a prison sentence, only for dead bodies to turn up, suggesting that she has returned to her evil ways.

See also: London (Gwendoline Butler)

www.fantasticfiction.co.uk/m/jennie-melville

Gladys Mitchell

One of the major names from the Golden Age of Crime Fiction, Gladys Mitchell, had a fifty-year writing career and set her books in various different parts of the country.

Death and the Maiden (1947) is set in and around Winchester in Hampshire, as the renowned Mrs Bradley is drawn into a mystery surrounding the deaths of two young boys.

www.gladysmitchell.com

Amy Myers

Formerly a director of a London publishing firm, Amy Myers has written four different series of crime novels. Three of them feature Kent as a background to some, if not all the stories. August Didier is a master chef and amateur detective in Victorian London who, in *Murder Makes an Entree* (1992), has to clear his name when a guest drops dead of poisoning during a literary dinner in Broadstairs — in front of the Prince of Wales.

Jack Colby, Car Detective, is an amateur detective and lover of classic cars. In *Classic in the Barn* (2011) he is captivated by a 1938 Lagonda V12 which is languishing uncared-for in a Kent barn. When its owner is murdered he has to find out why.

The third series features wheelchair-bound ex-policeman Peter Marsh and his daughter Georgia. In *Murder in Hell's Corner* (2006), a group of Battle of Britain veterans meet up in a country hotel in Kent, where many years ago a well-known war hero met an untimely death. In attempting to solve this mystery, Peter and Georgia Marsh stir up old memories, and then a second murder takes place.

www.amymyers.net

Malcolm Noble

Former policeman Malcolm Noble now runs a second-hand bookshop in Leicestershire, but his books are set in his old stamping ground of Portsmouth, and feature a highly unusual sleuth — a local prostitute, known as Timberdick.

Her real name is Billie Elizabeth Woodcock, and she has now appeared in nine novels since 2004. They cover a period from the 1920s to the 1960s, and feature a host of interesting, unusual characters as well as a well-defined sense of time and place.

The Case of the Dirty Verger (2007) is set just after World War II, when Timberdick is new to the streets. Life is tough for everyone, and when a body is found under the arches of a railway bridge, the police look to Timberdick for help.

In *The Poisons of Goodladies Road* (2012), the residents of Goodladies Road are concerned that the discovery of a body has thrown doubt on an old murder conviction. They ask their local policeman to investigate, but despite his best efforts his enquiries are going nowhere until Timberdick becomes involved.

The author has also started a second series of quirky village mysteries set in the south of England, featuring PC Pinch and his wife Peggy. In *The Body in the Bicycle Shed* (2014) it is 1926, and PC Pinch is shocked to discover the victim of a savage murder — in his own bicycle shed...

www.malcolmnoble.com

Mark Peterson

Flesh and Blood (2012) is a debut novel, set in Brighton, by Londoner Mark Peterson. A major anti-drugs operation goes wrong, resulting in the death of an undercover police officer, and a huge drugs shipment hits the streets. The unfortunate DS Minter seems to have joined the team at Kemptown police station at just the wrong time.

In the second novel, *A Place of Blood and Bone* (2013), Minter is faced with a dismembered body on a station platform, and a killer who loves inflicting pain.

www.fantasticfiction.co.uk/p/mark-peterson

James Raven

James Raven is a former Managing Director of ITV Granada Sport, and has recently written two crime novels set in the New Forest.

In *Rollover* (2012), a journalist ends up on the run from both police and a murderer who has kidnapped his family after a close friend wins the lottery. In *Urban Myth* (2012), a family holiday in a New Forest cottage becomes a nightmare of epic proportions.

www.james-raven.com

Ruth Rendell

The list of awards won by Ruth Rendell in a career of almost fifty years is enormous. She has won three Edgars in America, and four Gold Daggers in Britain, as well as the title Grand Master from the Mystery Writers of America. She was made a life peer (Baroness Rendell of Babergh) in 1997.

Since 1964 she has written more than twenty novels featuring Chief Inspector George Wexford, mainly set in and around the fictional Sussex commuter town of Kingsmarkham. Memorably played on television by George Baker, Wexford is a superb character. He is sympathetic, yet he has a temper. He's obstinate and opinionated, but he retains a sense of humour.

Wexford's family feature regularly, and in *Road Rage* (1997), his wife is held hostage by environmental activists.

Rendell often tackles difficult subjects, as can be seen by *Simisola* (1994), which deals with racism in a small town, and *Harm Done* (1998), in which a paedophile, having done his time, is released back into the community with terrifying consequences.

By *The Vault* (2012) Wexford has retired, but the series continues. In *No Man's Nightingale* (2013), his old colleague Mike Burden asks for his advice when Wexford's cleaning lady discovers a body. Wexford is intrigued, but makes an error which affects the murder investigation.

Psychologically powerful, the novels are intricately plotted and expertly written. That she has never even been long-listed for the Man Booker Prize is nothing short of a travesty.

See also: London, East Anglia (Barbara Vine)
www.authors.simonandschuster.com/Ruth-Rendell/62237729

Robert Richardson

A former chair of the CWA, Robert Richardson wrote a number of highly regarded crime novels set in different parts of the country.

The Hand of Strange Children (1993) was shortlisted for the CWA Gold Dagger. It concerns an appalling crime which has lain uncovered within a Hertfordshire family for many years, but which comes to light with terrible consequences for all concerned. When two bodies are discovered in the house of a merchant banker, details given to the press are scanty. But through the voices of those involved the reader is drawn into a compelling mystery.

See also: the West Country
www.fantasticfiction.co.uk/r/robert-richardson

Imogen Robertson

Born and bred in the north east, Imogen Robertson read Russian and German at Cambridge before becoming a TV director. Her first novel was published in 2009, and there has been a new one every year since.

Sussex in the 1780s is the setting for *Instruments of Darkness* (2009), which introduced Georgian sleuths Harriet Westerman and Gabriel Crowther — an unusual pairing of the inquisitive, headstrong wife of a serving naval Commodore, and a strange, reclusive anatomist. This is an excellent historical mystery from a very fine writer. It centres on Thornleigh Hall, the home of the crippled Earl of Sussex. Harriet finds a dead body nearby, and a man is

ruth
rendell

ROAD RAGE

A CHIEF
INSPECTOR
WEXFORD
MYSTERY

killed in a London music shop. These two events lead Harriet towards a family secret which has torn one family apart and may damage many others,

See also: the North West

www.imogenrobertson.com

Pauline Rowson

Pauline Rowson was a respected marketing and training guru before she turned to writing crime fiction. DI Andy Horton has featured in her excellent police procedurals since early 2006. He is a tough uncompromising detective often found either riding a Harley Davidson around Portsmouth, or battling with the elements at sea.

In *Footsteps on the Shore* (2012) Andy finds that not only has his beloved Harley been vandalised, but two bodies have been found and a convicted murderer is on the loose in the city. His bosses want results, but the pressure on Andy has only just begun.

Undercurrent (2013) opens with a body found in Portsmouth's historic dockyard. It is quickly identified and thought to be a suicide. Then another body is found, and DI Horton is certain that both were murdered. His superiors are unconvinced, and Horton has to take matters into his own hands. Blocked at every stage, he starts to suspect a cover-up at the highest level.

www.rowmark.co.uk

Leigh Russell

Leigh Russell was an English teacher for many years prior to her writing career. She is the author of a series of gripping psychological novels featuring DI Geraldine Steel, a determined resourceful detective with a pleasing touch of humanity.

In her debut, *Cut Short* (2009), DI Steel is a newly promoted member of the Kent Murder Squad, and finds herself balancing home problems with the need to find a serial killer who is preying on lone women in local parkland.

Geraldine's home problems persist in the second story. In *Road Closed* (2010), she investigates the death of a man in a gas explosion and another in a hit-and-run. After the third book in the series, Geraldine joins the Metropolitan Police in London, but the author returns to Kent with *Cold Sacrifice* (2013), which features DS Ian Petersen, who was a part of the Murder Squad in the first three DI Steel books.

See also: London

www.leighrussell.co.uk

C.J. Sansom

The brilliantly researched Matthew Shardlake mysteries are set against the backdrop of Henry VIII's England, and are full of so much period detail that you can virtually smell it.

The first of the series, *Dissolution* (2003), is set in the freezing winter of 1537. Thomas Cromwell is chief minister to Henry VIII, and when one of his commissioners is murdered in the monastery of Scarnsea in Sussex, he sends his top lawyer, the hunchbacked Matthew Shardlake, to discover what happened.

In *Heartstone* (2010) it is 1545, England is preparing for battle with France, and the English fleet has gathered at Portsmouth. Shardlake is presented with a difficult case by an elderly servant of the new Queen (Catherine Parr) which leads him to the town, and eventually to a denouement in Portsmouth Harbour, aboard the King's flagship, *The Mary Rose*.

C.J. Sansom has been shortlisted for many awards including The Dagger in the Library, and *Dark Fire (2004)* won the CWA Ellis Peters Award in 2005.

www.cjsansombooks.com

Dorothy L. Sayers

One of the greatest names of crime fiction, Dorothy L. Sayers wrote fourteen full-length novels between 1920 and 1939, and the thirteenth, *Busman's Honeymoon*

(1937), was set in Hertfordshire. Aristocratic sleuth Lord Peter Wimsey has bought an old farmhouse in which to spend his honeymoon, but when he and his bride Harriet Vane discover the previous owner dead in the cellar with severe head injuries, Lord Peter not only has to clear their names but discover the real truth.

www.sayers.org.uk

Sara Sheridan

Sara Sheridan has been writing for adults and children for around fifteen years. With *Brighton Belle* (2012) she introduced Mirabelle Bevan, a former Secret Service operative living in post-Second World War Brighton and working for a debt collection agency. With her friend, Vesta Churchill, she sets out to help a pregnant Hungarian refugee, only to find that her old abilities are still needed after all, as they follow a trail of gold coins and bodies.

Vesta and Mirabelle reappear in a second novel — *London Calling* (2012). A childhood friend of Vesta's is suspected of involvement in the disappearance of a seventeen-year-old girl in London's Soho. With Mirabelle, Vesta sets out to prove her friend's innocence.

www.sarasheridan.com

John Sherwood

John Sherwood wrote eleven light-hearted murder mysteries featuring Celia Grant, a Sussex-based horti-culturalist. Many of the stories were set locally, though she occasionally ventured elsewhere. A Miss Marple-like figure, Celia uses her horticultural knowledge to unravel various mysteries including kidnapping (*Creeping Jenny*, 1993) and the neglected gardens of a country house (*Flowers of Evil*, 1987).

In *A Bouquet of Thorns* (1994), Celia's head gardener is arrested and charged with the murder of a violent alco-holic. Celia does not believe he is guilty, and uses her knowledge of local secrets to unravel the mystery.

www.fantasticfiction.co.uk/s/john-sherwood

Dorothy Simpson

Dorothy Simpson was a French teacher and counsellor before becoming a full-time writer. She wrote fifteen highly-rated stories featuring Inspector Luke Thanet and Sergeant Lineham, set in and around the fictional town of Sturrenden in Kent. They are part police procedural and part psychological drama, and always worth reading.

In *Last Seen Alive* (1985), their investigation into the death of a young woman murdered just hours after returning to the village of her youth won the CWA Silver Dagger.

A Day for Dying (1995) finds Thanet investigating the death of crime writer Max Jeopard. He soon finds that the writer had many enemies, and that below the surface Jeopard led a less than perfect life.

www.dorothysimpson.co.uk

Edwin Thomas

The streets of Dover feature heavily in *The Blighted Cliffs* (2003), a historical mystery by Edwin Thomas, a former chair of the CWA. It is the first of three historical mysteries to follow the career of Lieutenant Martin Jerrold, a man who survived Trafalgar "without an ounce of credit". When he discovers a body and is suspected of murder, he has to search the town from top to bottom to clear his name.

In the follow-up, *The Chains of Albion* (2004), Jarrold moves from Chatham to Dartmoor and Brighton in an effort to recapture a lost French prisoner of war.

www.edwin-thomas.com

L.C. Tyler

L.C. Tyler is originally from Essex, and after a career in the civil service was the Chief Executive of the Royal College of Paediatrics and Child Health for eleven years. His books are wonderfully funny, and he won the CWA

Last Laugh award for *The Herring in the Library* in 2010. He has also been shortlisted for the Dagger in the Library, and is currently the Vice-Chair of the CWA.

His series features eccentric crime writer Ethelred Tresidder and his literary agent Elsie Thirkettle. Their adventures are a wonderful spoof of the Golden Age with such great titles as *Ten Little Herrings* (2009) and *The Herring on the Nile* (2011).

In *The Herring Seller's Apprentice* (2007), Ethelred's ex-wife has vanished near his Sussex home, and she is thought to be the victim of a serial killer. Elsie, who sees herself as Miss Marple in a short skirt, disagrees, and sets out to prove it.

In *The Herring in the Library* (2010), Elsie and Ethelred are invited to dine at Muntham Court in West Sussex. During the evening, their host is found dead — in a locked room. The police conclude that Sir Robert has committed suicide, but Lady Muntham is unsure and persuades Ethelred (with Elsie's help, or possibly hindrance) to find out the truth.

www.lctyler.com

Jill Paton Walsh

A Fellow of the Royal Society of Literature, Jill Paton Walsh has a long career writing for adults and children. In 1998 she was acclaimed for completing *Thrones, Denominations*, a Lord Peter Wimsey novel left unfinished by Dorothy L. Sayers at the time of her death.

This was followed by a completely new Lord Peter story, *A Presumption of Death* (2002), in which Lord Peter's wife Harriet has to act alone to help find the murderer of a young woman killed during an air raid practice in a nearby Hertfordshire village.

www.greenbay.co.uk/jpw.html

Jacqueline Winspear

Born and raised in Kent but now living in America, Jacqueline Winspear has written a series of crime novels featuring the redoubtable Maisie Dobbs, psychologist and private investigator between the wars. In her adopted country Winspear has won two Agatha awards and been nominated for an Edgar. Her stories are full of rich period detail, and the county of Kent is a regular setting.

An Incomplete Revenge (2008) sees Maisie delve into a series of crimes, including arson, in an idyllic Kent village during the hop-picking season. The apparently straight-forward investigation turns out be far more complex than expected.

See also: London
www.jacquelinewinspear.com

Ten Recommended Reads

1: *The Dead of Winter* by Rennie Airth (2009)

2: *Vengeance in Mind* by N.J. Cooper (2012)

3: *The Hog's Back Mystery* by Freeman Wills Crofts (1933)

4: *City of Dreadful Night* by Peter Guttridge (2010)

5: *Cut to Black* by Graham Hurley (2004)

6: *Dead Simple* by Peter James (2005)

7: *Murder in Hell's Corner* by Amy Myers (2006)

8: *Harm Done* by Ruth Rendell (1999)

9: *Heartstone* by C.J. Sansom (2010)

10: *The Blighted Cliffs* by Edwin Thomas (2003)

REGION THREE
England — London

Why, Sir, you find no man, at all intellectual, who is willing to leave London. No, Sir, when a man is tired of London, he is tired of life; for there is in London all that life can afford.
SAMUEL JOHNSON, 1777

London is one of the world's great cities. With over eight million residents, it is vast and sprawling with, at its heart, one of the biggest financial centres in the world. It is a city containing suburban Metroland and grim tower blocks, leafy Richmond and darker areas like Wapping or Limehouse. It is said that in London you can buy and sell anything — at a price.

London is the home of two of the greatest names in all fiction, Sherlock Holmes, who lived at 221B Baker Street, and Hercule Poirot of Whitehaven Mansions. Other fictional detectives roving the streets include Tom Thorne (Mark Billingham), Gideon of the Yard (J.J. Marric), Adam Dalgleish (P.D. James) and Slim Callaghan (Peter Cheyney). High quality villains can be found too, especially in the East End novels of Martina Cole, G.F. Newman and Lynda la Plante.

The cosmopolitan nature of the city is reflected in the works of Barbara Nadel and Mike Phillips, and different periods of its history are laid bare by the likes of Susanna Gregory, Peter Ackroyd, Anne Perry, Arthur Conan Doyle and Laura Wilson, to name just a few.

Ben Aaronovitch

A former bookseller for Waterstones, Ben Aaronovitch cut his writing teeth as a screenwriter for *Doctor Who* and *Casualty*.

He gives a very different take on the London crime novel with his *Rivers of London* series, which mixes crime fiction with Harry Potter-style fantasy. The books follow the adventures of Peter Grant, police constable and apprentice wizard. The author's love of London is reflected in the eccentrically-detailed descriptions.

In the third book of the series (*Whispers Underground*, 2011), Grant is concerned with a dead body found at Baker Street tube station, while his boss DCI Thomas Nightingale (the last registered wizard in England) is hunting a rogue magician called The Faceless Man.

In *Broken Homes* (2013) Grant has to contend with murder and theft, and the reappearance of his old arch-enemy, The Faceless Man.

www.the-folly.com

Peter Ackroyd

A prodigiously talented man, Peter Ackroyd is a literary biographer (of Dickens, Shakespeare, and Blake), historian, critic and novelist who makes no secret of his love for London, the city which is at the heart of many of his written works. He would not claim to be a crime novelist, yet with *Hawksmoor* (1985) he has written one of the most extraordinary crime novels of the last fifty years. The book won both the *Guardian* Fiction Prize and the Whitbread Novel Award.

Hawksmoor is not a standard crime story, by any means. It follows two narratives, one in the present and one in the past.

In 1985, London policeman Nicholas Hawksmoor is investigating a bizarre series of murders in London churches — all of which were designed by the eighteenth-century architect Nicholas Dyer (who is based on the real architect of that time, Nicholas Hawksmoor). In the early eighteenth century Dyer is engaged in a programme of church building — — all the while secretly indulging in Satanic practices. Back in the twentieth century, Hawksmoor finds that not only has the murderer left no traces, but the power of the churches and their history affects his investigation. Eclectic and mysterious, *Hawksmoor* remains one of the classic novels of twentieth century fiction.

www.fantasticfiction.co.uk/a/peter-ackroyd

Margery Allingham

A Londoner by birth, Margery Allingham studied drama at Regent Street Polytechnic. She is recognised as one of the great crime writers from the Golden Age and is best known for her novels featuring Albert Campion, an amateur sleuth with a gentle manner and an aristocratic background.

The best of these is *The Tiger in the Smoke* (1952), in which Campion joins forces with the police as they brave terrible winter smog to search across London for heart-less killer Jack Havoc, who is out of jail and rampaging across the city.

See also: East Anglia

www.margeryallingham.org.uk

Jake Arnott

Prior to his writing career, Jake Arnott was a player with a radical theatre company and a part-time social worker. His London trilogy covers the last forty years of the twentieth century and his eye for detail brings the period lovingly to life.

Arnott's first novel, *The Long Firm* (1999), features gay East End gangster Harry Starks, and is set in the

Swinging Sixties. In common with most of Arnott's works, the book includes scenes with, or references to, real characters — in this case the Kray twins, politician Tom Driberg and actress Judy Garland. It is unusual in that it has multiple narrators.

The follow-up *He Kills Coppers* covers the period from England winning the World Cup in 1966 to Thatcher's Britain of the 1980s, telling the stories of Billy Porter, a criminal on the run after shooting three London policemen in cold blood, and the detective and journalist who are trying to find him. It is loosely based on the true story of gangster Harry Roberts.

The final part of the trilogy, *Truecrime* (2003), takes up the thread from where *He Kills Coppers* left off, with discovery of a body in Harry Starks' Spanish Villa.

www.jakearnott.com

R. Austin Freeman

Richard Austin Freeman has a good claim to have invented the first true scientific detective in Dr John Thorndyke, who features in his series of novels and short stories. Freeman was a physician, surgeon and a knowledgeable amateur scientist, and Thorndyke always explains the tests he uses to solve seemingly impossible mysteries.

Thorndyke is a lecturer at London's St Margaret's hospital and in his debut, *The Red Thumb Mark* (1907), he is faced with missing diamonds, a safe untouched but for two thumb-prints, and a young man suspected of theft. By breaking down the evidence scientifically, Thorndyke sets out to prove him innocent.

In *A Silent Witness* (1914) a dead body is found in Millfield Lane, London. When the man who reports it returns to the spot with the police, it has vanished. Thorndyke is called in to investigate.

www.fantasticfiction.co.uk/f/r-austin-freeman

Marian Babson

American author Marian Babson may have been born in Massachusetts, but she has lived in London for a long time, and many of her crime novels are set there. The author's gentle humour and love of cats is reflected in her many books.

Douglas Perkins and Gerry Tate are partners in a London public relations firm and appear in four novels published between 1971 and 1990. In *Murder at the Cat Show* (1972) Perkins and Tate are engaged to provide the PR for a major cat show, but robbery and murder changes their perspective.

Trixie and Evangeline are ageing London-based thespians who get mixed up in murder. In *No Co-operation from the Cat* (2012), the seventh novel in which they appear, murder strikes at a cooking demonstration, while in *Past Regrets* (1990) an American woman flies to London to find her missing daughter, a London student.

www.fantasticfiction.co.uk/b/marian-babson

Mark Billingham

As well as a career as a stand-up comedian (he still appears occasionally at London's Comedy Store) Birmingham-born Mark Billingham has written a series of high-quality police procedurals featuring DI Tom Thorne. They are well-written, witty and descriptive, often exposing the seediness of twenty-first-century London. The series has been televised with David Morrissey as Tom Thorne.

So far Thorne has dealt with a number of serious concerns. The clever, disturbing *Lifeless* (2005) sees him go undercover into London's homeless community when it is targeted by a vicious murderer.

The serial killer novel has possibly been overdone over the years but *Scaredy Cat* (2002) is one of the very best. Thorne spots a connection between various murders, but is confused by certain aspects. When he realises the truth, he knows that he is on the trail of someone who

Serial killers *normally* work alone . . .

MARK BILLINGHAM

SCAREDY CAT

'The best book I've read in years'
MARTINA COLE

loves to inspire terror. The book was nominated for the CWA Gold Dagger.

Death Message (2007) involves Thorne in a frightening case, when he starts to receive pictures of dead bodies on his mobile phone, and finds himself up against a horribly difficult adversary — a man with nothing left to lose.

Billingham has also written two excellent stand-alone crime novels, including *In the Dark* (2008), which centres on London's teenage gangs. Full of dead bodies and shocking secrets, it provides a satisfying read and has a great final twist.

www.markbillingham.com

Helen Black

The daughter of a Yorkshire miner, Helen Black has a law degree and worked with teenagers in London. It is this work which has given her the background for her crime novels, which raise some very serious issues about society in the twenty-first century.

In a stand-alone novel, *Twenty Twelve* (2012) she raises the spectre of a bomb at the London Olympics, with an administrative assistant from the Department of Culture, Media and Sport thrust into the limelight as a heroine.

Her main protagonist is Lily Valentine, a feisty northern lawyer with a passion to do the right thing and the strength of will to see it through. She specialises in working with those from difficult backgrounds, and has various problems of her own.

London often features in these books. In *A Place of Safety* (2008) a boy watches as two fellow pupils rape an immigrant girl, and is so shocked that he runs away to try to survive on the streets of London.

www.hblack.co.uk

S.J. Bolton

Lancastrian Sharon Bolton worked in the City of London (in public relations and marketing) before starting her writing career. Following three very successful stand-alone novels, she introduced the resourceful DC Lacey Flint and her colleague DI Mark Joesbury in *Now You See Me* (2010)

Bolton is not afraid to use an element of horror in her books, and in *Now You See Me* Lacey finds herself up against a sadistic killer using similarities to Jack the Ripper to terrify the capital. In a compelling and spine-tingling novel Lacey is forced to revisit aspects of her past that she would prefer to forget as she races against time to apprehend London's most vicious murderer yet.

In *Like This, For Ever* (2013), the discovery of a body on a Thames Beach is just the beginning of another desperate race to catch a terrifying murderer. As the number of bodies increases, so the media frenzy grows and so Lacey and Mark are driven to follow any lead, no matter how strange. When Lacey becomes emotionally entangled again, the tension is racked up to breaking point.

See also: East Anglia, Scotland: Highlands and Islands
www.sjbolton.com

Gyles Brandreth

The multi-talented Gyles Brandreth has been a Tory MP, a regular radio broadcaster, a celebrated after-dinner speaker and master of ceremonies. In addition to all this he has a written a fascinating series of Victorian murder mysteries featuring Oscar Wilde, Arthur Conan Doyle, Bram Stoker and their circle.

In *Oscar Wilde and the Candlelight Murder* (2007), Wilde and Conan Doyle set out to solve the murder of sixteen-year-old Billy Wood in London in 1889, and in *Oscar Wilde and the Nest of Vipers* (2010), Oscar and Arthur are asked by Prince Edward to investigate a death at the heart of Victorian society.

www.gylesbrandreth.net

Simon Brett

A writer of crime novels, radio programmes and TV series (*After Henry, No Commitments* and others), Simon Brett is an accomplished author. He has written four different crime series, all laced with his innate sense of humour and wit. He is perhaps best-known for the Charles Paris series, which centres on a charming middle-aged actor with a penchant for drink and women, who becomes embroiled in various murder mysteries in the world of the theatre — often (though not always) in London's Theatreland.

In *The Dead Side of the Mike* (1980), Paris gives a talk at the BBC and, after a studio manager is murdered, ends up uncovering fraudulent practices and complicated scandals in Broadcasting House, while in *Murder Unprompted* (1982) he takes a part as an understudy in a West End play, only to be drawn into murder and mayhem when the lead actor is shot dead on stage on the opening night.

See also: the South and South East, Scotland: Edinburgh and the Borders

www.simonbrett.com

Ken Bruen

A finalist for crime awards in both the UK and America, Ken Bruen has written a bleak series of novels about Inspector Brant and DCI Roberts of the Metropolitan Police, who are hard-nosed cops facing tough, uncompromising criminals in violent, crime-ridden London. In some ways they are little better than the criminals they chase.

In *A White Arrest* (1998), they find themselves chasing the brutal murderers of England cricketers while simultaneously hunting the vigilantes who are meting out their own rough justice to drug dealers in Brixton

In *Calibre* (2006), Brant faces up to "The Manners Killer", who takes his own revenge on those he considers to be rude or out of line. The retribution may be fine by Brant, but it is too messy to be allowed on his patch.

See also: the Republic of Ireland

www.fantasticfiction.co.uk/b/ken-bruen

Sian Busby

Londoner Sian Busby, who died of cancer in 2012, had written three intelligent non-fiction books before her first high-class historical novel, *McNaughten,* was published in 2009. Prior to her death she had embarked on a second, a crime thriller set in London just after World War II, and the final partly-finished chapters were transcribed by her husband, the financial journalist Robert Peston. The book was eventually published in 2013.

A Commonplace Killing (2013) is a powerful, evocative story. Two boys find a woman's body in an abandoned churchyard in July 1946. She is identified as Lillian Parry, who had lived nearby. DI Jim Cooper, a hard-working copper ground down by his lot, investigates. As the mystery unfolds, a harsh post-war London is exposed, full of dingy cafés, shattered bomb sites, thin-faced spivs and disillusioned ex-servicemen. Melancholy and moving, it is a fine post-script for an author lost too soon.

www.fantasticfiction.co.uk/b/sian-busby

D.S. Butler

With a background in hospital pathology and scientific research, Danica Butler is well-qualified to give her contemporary crime novels a different twist. They feature DS Jack McKinnon from the City of London Police Murder Investigation team.

The background to the series is set in *Deadly Obsession* (2012), as Jack searches for a missing Polish student and is drawn into the world of easy fame and reality television.

In *Deadly Justice* (2013), a spate of suicides are linked by similar suicide notes. It appears that someone does not think the police are doing their job properly, and is taking matters into their own hands.

www.dsbutlerauthor.wordpress.com

Gwendoline Butler

Gwendoline Butler, who died in 2013, was a crime novelist for more than fifty years. A graduate of Oxford University, she also lectured there, but her crime novels were mainly set in London. She was a contemporary of P.D. James and Ruth Rendell.

The first novel to feature London policeman John Coffin was *The Murdering Kind* (1958), set in Blackheath, and twenty-nine more followed, the last in 2002. During the series Coffin rises from a mere Inspector to Chief Commissioner of the Metropolitan Police.

He is described as both intelligent and intense, and the books carry a feeling of unease, never more so than in *Coffin's Game* (1997), when an unrecognisable body found after a terrorist attack is suspected to be that of his wife, Stella.

One of his last cases was also one of his most macabre, as Coffin is forced to investigate not only the murder of a midwife and her daughters, but also the bizarre find of a pile of infant skulls (*A Cold Coffin*, 2000).

See also: the South and South East (Jennie Melville)
www.fantasticfiction.co.uk/b/gwendoline-butler

John Dickson Carr

Now recognised as one of the all-time greats for his locked-room mysteries, American-born John Dickson Carr lived in London for many years. He used the city as the backdrop for some of his finest stories, including his acknowledged masterpiece, *The Hollow Man* (1935).

In this superb novel, his long-term protagonist, Dr Gideon Fell, investigates how a man can commit a murder inside a locked-room, vanish, reappear in a street outside, commit another murder in full view of witnesses, and yet not be seen in either case.

In *The Judas Window* (1938), written under his pseudonym Carter Dickson, his other major character, Sir Henry Merrivale, defends a man found next to a dead body in a locked study. Sometimes preposterous, but always enthralling, Carr's novels are worth seeking out as examples of crime writing from another era so very different to the more violent, psychological novels of today.

See also: the South and South East

www.jdcarr.com

Will Carver

DI January David is faced with a ritualistic London serial killer and a crazed vigilante in *The Two* (2012), the second heart-stopping thriller from Will Carver, a former IT worker who took the chance to write when he was made redundant.

His first book *Girl 4* (2011) also finds DI David in trouble — this time when he attends a crime scene only to find that he knows the victim.

www.willcarver.net

Jane Casey

Though she was born and brought up in Dublin, Jane Casey studied English at Oxford University. Her first novel was published in 2010.

DC Maeve Kerrigan is usually the youngest member of the murder team, but she is still the central character in Jane Casey's accomplished series, which began with *The Burning* (2010). Kerrigan is a strong personality, determined and ambitious, who is intent on succeeding as a detective in the misogynistic world of the Metropolitan Police.

All the books are set in contemporary London, and are full of psychological tension.

In *The Reckoning* (2011), Kerrigan is forced to think about her own views when her team investigates the savage murders of convicted paedophiles in South London.

The Stranger You Know (2013) forces Maeve to consider the unthinkable — that one of her colleagues could be the man who has strangled three women in their own homes.

www.maevekerrigan.co.uk

Kimberley Chambers

Originally from an East End family, Kimberley Chambers has used her first-hand knowledge of that part of London and Essex (she once worked at the Roman Road market) as a background for all of her novels.

The Mitchells and the O'Haras are two warring families trying to control the East End, and *The Feud* (2010), *The Traitor* (2010) and *The Victim* (2011) describe how even the most innocent members of the families can become involved in this deadly world.

Beside this trilogy, Chambers has written several stand-alone novels based in the East End. *The Betrayer* (2009) is set on a tough council estate in Stepney and covers the period from 1975 to 2005. The Hutton family centres around mum Maureen and eldest son Tommy. Though she does her best, Maureen's hopes for Tommy are dashed when he is sentenced to ten years for murder.

www.kimberleychambers.com

Paul Charles

Mostly set around Camden Town and Primrose Hill, the Inspector Christy Kennedy novels by Paul Charles are not as well known as they should be. The author's background in the music business gives him an authentic voice, and his love for London is clear. Kennedy is a much milder creation than many — his strongest tipple is tea — but his contentment with life is part of his strength as a policeman.

In his first novel, *I Love the Sound of Breaking Glass* (1997), the disappearance of a record company executive leads Inspector Kennedy into the world of music publishing and chart rigging.

The Ballad of Sean and Wilko (2000) also has a music business backdrop. Sean and Wilko are two old-style rock musicians who never made it first time round. They get back together for a comeback tour but on the first night Wilko is found murdered in his locked dressing room. When another body is found in another locked room, the unfortunate Inspector is faced with plenty of suspects but no clues.
See also: Northern Ireland
www.paulcharlesbooks.com

Peter Cheyney

Reginald Evelyn Peter Southouse Cheyney was born in the East End of London in 1896. His Slim Callaghan novels were published between 1938 and 1953 and were written in the hard-boiled American style that he also used for his more successful Lemmy Caution series — Caution was an FBI agent and the books were set all over the world. Callaghan was a tough, hard-edged London private eye, and the books had an American feel to them, despite the English setting.

In *They Never Say When* (1944), Callaghan is hired by a woman who says she is being blackmailed. She has employed a man to steal a valuable jewel from her husband's safe, but now the man is holding on to it and blackmailing her instead. When Callaghan investigates, he discovers that everyone is lying to him, and someone is happy to use violence to stop him getting at the truth.

It Couldn't Matter Less (1941) sees Callaghan engaged to find the missing boyfriend of an attractive London singer. Easy — he thinks. However the missing man is poet Lionel Wilbery, whose penchant for drugs and unsavoury friends means that Slim's search will be tricky. Then the singer is found stabbed to death, and Slim has even more trouble on his hands.
www.petercheyney.co.uk

Agatha Christie

Without doubt the most popular crime novelist of all, Agatha Christie has sold more than two billion copies of her novels in English and, remarkably, another one billion in other languages. London features heavily throughout her books, as Hercule Poirot lives there for much of his time in England (in Whitehaven Mansions, sometimes shown as Whitehouse Mansions or White-friars Mansions) and Tommy and Tuppence meet at Dover Street tube station.

Hercule Poirot is, like Sherlock Holmes, one of the most recognisable characters in literature. With his egg-shaped head, little moustache and patent leather shoes, and his accent, he is unmistakeable.

In *Cards on the Table* (1936) Mr Shaitana invites four investigators (Poirot, Colonel Race, Ariadne Oliver and Superintendent Battle) and four suspected murderers to a bridge party in his London flat. During the game he is stabbed to death, but no one had seen anything amiss. Poirot and his colleagues investigate a classic locked-room style mystery.

The hotel in *At Bertram's Hotel* (1965) is said to be based on Brown's Hotel, just off Piccadilly, and Chelsea is the setting for *One, Two, Buckle My Shoe* (1940), when Poirot's dentist is found dead in his Harley Street practice.

Third Girl (1966) finds Poirot in Swinging Sixties London. His breakfast is disturbed by a dishevelled girl who blurts out that she may have committed a murder. What follows is a complex case full of the usual red herrings, doubtful characters and family secrets.

See also: the West Country, the South and South East
www.agathachristie.com

Rory Clements

Formerly a national newspaper journalist, Rory Clem-ents is the author of a fascinating, closely-researched series of historical thrillers set in Elizabethan England. He pulls no punches over the brutality of the times, and violence is meted out to both Protestant and Catholic alike. Many real characters are used (Elizabeth I, Earl of Essex, Earl of Leicester), but the protagonist is the fictional John Shakespeare, William Shakespeare's older brother. The novels take in many different locations, but London is central to each of them, especially Westminster, Greenwich, Southwark and Deptford. The descriptions leave little doubt as to unsanitary conditions of the city at the time.

Martyr (2009) is set in 1587, the year before the Spanish Armada. There is a plot to assassinate Sir Francis Drake, and a cousin of the Queen has been found murdered and defiled. John Shakespeare, chief intelligencer in the spy network run by Sir Francis Walsingham, is given the task of solving both cases.

Prince (2011) moves on to 1593, when a series of horrific bombings in the capital lead Shakespeare into the theatrical underworld where he is pitted against the frightening, ruthless priest-hunter, Richard Topcliffe.

www.roryclements.com

Michael Clynes

A pseudonym of the prolific Paul Doherty, Clynes's hero is Sir Roger Shallot, rogue, charlatan and secret emissary of Henry VIII.

In *The Gallows Murders* (1995), Shallot is embroiled in the mystery of the Princes in the Tower. Cardinal Wolsey is receiving threatening letters, supposedly sent by one of the Princes. The terrifying threats have upset the King as well, and he is also worried by a series of grisly murders among the hangmen of London. The King orders his cousin, Benjamin Daubney, and Sir Roger, to discover the truth.

See also: the West Country, London (Paul Doherty), the South and South East (Paul Doherty, C.L. Grace)

www.paulcdoherty.com

Liza Cody

Back in 1982 Liza Cody won the CWA John Creasey Memorial Dagger for her novel *Dupe* (1980) featuring Anna Lee — an ex-policewoman now running a small detective agency on Kensington High Street — whose first case leads her into the darkest reaches of the film industry.

Five more witty adventures for Anna followed, finishing with *Backhand* (1991), and Anna also appears in the author's short series about female wrestler Eva Wylie.

In *Head Case* (1985), Anna is asked to find a missing teenager but the police get to her first. The girl, a student, is found in a catatonic state, and is accused of murder. Anna is suspicious and investigates further. Through interviews with the girl's lecturers Anna soon realises that she has been leading a double life.

www.lizacody.com

Martina Cole

A hugely successful novelist, Martina Cole was born and brought up in Essex, and her hard-hitting novels are set in and around the East End of London. From the first novel, *Dangerous Lady* (1992), in which a seventeen-year-old girl takes on the hardest men in London's gangland, she has pulled no punches. Tough and often violent, the books deal with the struggles of people living in difficult circumstances, and what they may have to do to survive. They tend to deal with women's issues, and the line between good and bad is smudged.

The Ladykiller (1994) and its sequel *Broken* (2000) feature a hardened criminal (Patrick Kelly) whose daughter is murdered by a vicious sexual sadist, forcing him to consider anything that might lead to the capture of his daughter's killer, up to and including working with the officer in charge of the case, DI Kate Burrows. Their relationship blossoms, but that leads to problems of its own.

Martina Cole's books have sold more than ten million copies worldwide, and have been made into TV programmes and stage plays. *The Take* won the BCA Crime Thriller Award in 2006.

www.martinacole.co.uk

J.J. Connolly

In 2004 Daniel Craig (of James Bond fame) appeared in the film of J.J. Connolly's contemporary London gangland thriller, *Layer Cake* (2004), as a successful drug dealer who is looking for a way out of the business when he is asked to find the missing daughter of another major criminal.

In the 2012 follow-up, *Viva La Madness*, the still unnamed drug dealer is brought back to London from his Caribbean retirement for another fast and furious take on the London underworld.

www.fantasticfiction.co.uk/c/j-j-connolly

N.J. (Natasha) Cooper

As a lifelong Londoner, Natasha Cooper puts the city of London at the heart of many of her novels. She is a former Chair of the CWA and a book reviewer for *The Times*.

In the light-hearted Willow King books, a part-time civil servant and romantic novelist becomes mixed up in various murder mysteries in London, such as in *Festering Lilies* (1990), in which the minister for King's department is battered to death.

After six Willow King mysteries, the author moved on to the grittier Trish Maguire series. Maguire is an ambitious lawyer with a heightened sense of right and wrong, which leads her to move outside her professional world into more threatening areas.

A good example is *A Place of Safety* (2003), where Maguire finds the art world is full of truth and lies as she investigates the origins of the Gregory Art collection and discovers it may not only be paintings that are fakes.

In *A Greater Evil* (2007), Trish's life has become very complicated, and her caseload is just the same. She is torn apart by a difficult case involving the murder of a pregnant woman and an awkward insurance claim.

See also: the South and South East

www.natashacooper.co.uk

Mat Coward

Mat Coward is probably the only crime writer to work as a researcher for the BBC TV show *QI*, and he has written a variety of books on subjects as diverse as cats and radio comedy. He also reviews crime fiction for the left-wing daily, the *Morning Star*.

His clever, quirky crime novels feature North London coppers DI Don Packham and DC Frank Mitchell — and the stories are funny but with more than a grain of seriousness. Packham is an interesting character who suffers with a manic depression syndrome, which means he moves from being upbeat one day to total despair on the next.

Over and Under (2004) features death at the annual cricket match between the Writers and the Comedians. One team member has been murdered — with a baseball bat — at a cricket match that is sacrilege in itself!

In *Open and Closed* (2005), Packham and Mitchell are called in when library campaigner Bert Rosen is found murdered in a North London librarian's office during a protest against library closures.

www.matcoward.com

James Craig

A Scot by birth but a long-time London resident, James Craig has set out to use the familiar landmarks around Covent Garden, Trafalgar Square and the West End in his series of novels featuring Inspector John Carlyle of the Metropolitan Police.

London Calling (2011) sees Carlyle facing a killer who is focusing on members of London's elite, and is threatening that the next victim will be Edgar Carlton, the country's Prime Minister-in-waiting.

In *Buckingham Palace Blues* (2012), Carlyle's investigations into child-trafficking lead him on a trail from Russia to a part of London he was not expecting to visit.
www.james-craig.co.uk

John Creasey

Overall, during an astonishing career, John Creasey used twenty-eight pseudonyms and wrote nearly six hundred novels — almost all of them crime fiction. He created a huge range of characters, including two London policemen ("Gideon of the Yard" and "Handsome West"), and the amateurs, "The Toff" and "The Baron". The CWA has an award named after him (the John Creasey New Blood Dagger). Creasey is the most prolific crime writer of them all.

Inspector Roger West was created by Creasey in 1942, and these books were written under his own name. West was a suave, confident and practical detective, who featured in forty-three novels between 1942 and 1978.

In *Inspector West Kicks Off* (1949), he investigates the death of a London businessman which leads back to one of the capital's top football clubs, while in *Inspector West at Home* (1944), West's career comes under scrutiny as he is accused of bribery and corruption.
See also: London (J.J. Marric)
www.johncreasey.co.uk

Adam Creed

Adam Creed is an Oxford graduate who abandoned a career in the City to start writing. He is now Head of Writing at John Moores University in Liverpool, though all his books are set in London, and feature the same central character. DI Will Wagstaffe is a hard-pressed policeman in contemporary London, dealing with the causes and consequences of horrific crimes, as well as his own feelings and failings.

In *Suffer the Children* (2009) Wagstaffe has to deal with the gruesome murder of a convicted paedophile, and he starts to ask himself just how far a man will go to protect his children.

In the following book, *Willing Flesh* (2010), his investigations into the murders of two prostitutes lead him into a conflict with the British establishment that threatens not just himself but those he cares for most.

www.fantasticfiction.co.uk/c/adam-creed

Deborah Crombie

Texan by birth, but anglophile by nature, Deborah Crombie's excellent books are mainly set in London. Her main characters, Duncan Kincaid and Gemma James, are Scotland Yard detectives, so even though their adventures sometimes take them elsewhere, London is their home patch.

Mourn Not Your Dead (1996) sees Kincaid and Jones investigating the murder of a commander in the Metropolitan Police, who turns out to have been not quite the paragon of virtue that was expected, especially where his career was concerned.

In *Where Memories Lie* (2008), their efforts to help an elderly neighbour recover a piece of stolen jewellery lead them into a case that has links to Nazi Germany, with shadows that reach the present day.

To Dwell in Darkness (2014) sees Kincaid transferred to the London Borough of Camden and investigating a deadly bomb explosion at St Pancras Station. All is not what it seems, though, and soon Kincaid realises that even the events in his professional life could be part of a greater, and very dangerous, conspiracy.

See also: the North West
www.deborahcrombie.com

Neil Cross

A high-class novelist since 1998 (his book *Always the Sun* was nominated for the Man Booker Prize in 2004) Neil

Cross created the character of DCI John Luther of the Metropolitan Police for BBC TV in 2010, and wrote a prequel novel for the character in 2011 — *The Calling*. This was the serial killer case that pushed Luther to the limit, and sometimes beyond.

In it, Luther has to deal with the most gut-wrenching of cases — a double murder which includes a pregnant woman and almost certainly her child, who was ripped from the body of the butchered woman. The case breaks Luther, at home and at work, but his intuition helps him to pin down the murderer. But can Luther control himself when it comes to the climax?

www.neil-cross.com

Denise Danks

Denise Danks was formerly a writer in the IT business. In Georgina Powers, she created a streetwise, savvy heroine for the nineties, which was when the books were originally published.

In *Better Off Dead* (1991), Georgina is horrified when her friend Carla Blue, an aspiring music star, and rock legend Johnny Waits, die in close succession, and when unreleased tapes by both appear on a stall on a London market she is certain something is badly wrong.

Phreak (1998) sees Georgina caught up in a gangland turf-war and a phone-hacking scandal.

www.fantasticfiction.co.uk/d/denise-danks

David Stuart Davies

David Stuart Davies is an acknowledged Sherlock Holmes expert, playwright and writer, and was a friend and biographer to the late Jeremy Brett, who portrayed Holmes so memorably on television. He has written two fine series of crime novels, one consisting of new adventures for Sherlock Holmes, and the other following the career of private investigator Johnny Hawke, known as Johnny One-Eye because he has lost an eye in a military accident.

The Veiled Detective (2004) is set in 1880, when Holmes and Watson first met. It fills in many of the gaps in the original stories, and fleshes out characters such as Watson and Lestrade. It is a clever pastiche and provides the perfect lead-up to Doyle's classic *A Study in Scarlet*.

In *Comes the Dark* (2006), it is 1941 and London is being hammered by the Blitz. Johnny has infiltrated the Britannia Club, a suspicious underground organisation with fascist overtones. Meanwhile, several prostitutes are found murdered on the London streets. Johnny searches for a connection, but what he finds is worse than he could possibly have imagined.

www.fantasticfiction.co.uk/d/david-stuart-davies

Stephen Davison

Stephen Davison is a full-time chiropractor, and his medical background and love of London are used to good effect in his first two fast moving novels.

Kill & Cure (2009) follows the predicament of London chiropractor David Stichell who witnesses the murder of his fiancée. He reports it to the police, but when they go to his flat all signs of the murder have vanished. Then a lab technician is found dead, the police suspect Stichell and suddenly there is nowhere to hide.

Dead Innocent (2011) asks the question "what's your blood worth?" After a simple road accident, scientist Rita Sidhu is tormented and compromised. DCI Terence Varcy uncovers a shocking trail of violent death when he investigates the murder and torture of a young man.

www.stephendavison.com

Luke Delaney

A former Metropolitan Police detective, Luke Delaney's first-hand experience has given him all the knowledge he needs to make his crime novels grisly and disturbingly authentic.

His first novel was published in 2013. *Cold Killing* features that most frightening of killers, the random murderer. DI Sean Corrigan is certain that a series of brutal South London murders are linked, but with no clues, no motive and no forensic evidence, he is struggling. But his own childhood was dark and bitter, and he can empathize with damaged minds. He just might be able to get inside the mind of the perpetrator.

The Toy Taker (2014) is another chilling novel, this time focusing on child kidnap. Four-year-old George Bridgeman has been abducted by someone, and yet no one saw anything. Even Corrigan cannot see into this monster's mind — and then a second child is taken.

www.fantasticfiction.co.uk/d/luke-delaney

Ted Dexter and Clifford Makins

Former England cricket captain Ted Dexter joined forces with journalist Clifford Makins to write two crime novels with a sporting background. *Testkill* (1976) has a London setting, with a cricketer murdered during an Ashes Test at Lords. Full of action, it is an interesting read for any cricket fan. There was a second novel with a golfing theme (*Deadly Putter*, 1979).

doyouwriteunderyourownname.blogspot.co.uk/2009/05/forgotten-book-testkill.html

David Dickinson

Born in Dublin, Cambridge graduate David Dickinson is a former editor of the BBC's *Newsnight* and *Panorama*. He is the author of two separate crime series.

The central character of the first series is Lord Francis Powerscourt, an amateur sleuth with an Irish background. Meticulously researched, the series has now stretched to eleven books, and the location is usually, though not always, London.

In the first novel, *Goodnight, Sweet Prince* (2002), Powerscourt is asked to investigate when Prince Eddy, the eldest son of the Prince of Wales, dies suddenly in 1892.

Death at the Jesus Hospital (2012) is set in 1910, with Lord Powerscourt investigating three deaths connected to the very powerful Guild of Silkworkers, a livery company founded in the seventeenth century. Each man's body has been branded with a strange marking, which no one can identify, and Powerscourt is convinced that it is a vital clue.

David Dickinson has also written a well-reviewed series of novellas based around the character of Mycroft Holmes, Sherlock Holmes's elder brother. In *Mycroft Holmes and the Bankers' Conclave* (2012), Sherlock has retired and a financial crisis has left the City of London on the brink of collapse. As an attack on the City's lines of communication makes things worse, Mycroft must use all his cerebral powers to save England's financial system from total ruin.

See also: the Midlands

www.fantasticfiction.co.uk/d/david-dickinson

Paul Doherty

Historian and author Paul Doherty sets out to bring history to life with all his many series of historical crime novels. London settings feature prominently, as in *Satan in St Mary's* ("Hugh Corbett" series,1986) when Corbett, a clerk from the Court of the King's Bench, is drawn into dark, dangerous world of the medieval London of 1284.

The "Mathilde of Westminster" books are set in the court of Edward II (1307–1327). In *The Cup of Ghosts* (2005), she finds herself engaged in the efforts to understand a series of gory deaths including that of Sir John Baquelle, who has been crushed to death during the King's Coronation.

"The Sorrowful Mysteries of Brother Athelstan" were originally written under the pen-name Paul Harding, but are now published under the author's real name. They are set around 1380, and Athelstan is a monk who works with the Coroner of London, Sir John Cranston, to unravel a series of medieval murders. In *Bloodstone* (2011), they investigate the death of a wealthy merchant and the disappearance of a cursed relic. As usual there is a very strong plot, and the sense of history is palpable.

See also: the West Country (Michael Clynes), London (Michael Clynes), the South and South East (Paul Doherty, C.L. Grace)
www.paulcdoherty.com

Michael Donovan

Though he is from Lancashire and was a joint winner of the Northern Crime Writing competition in 2011, the setting for Michael Donovan's first novel *Behind Closed Doors* (2013) is a vividly-described London. Protagonist Eddie Flynn is a private detective with a flashy car, and his style tips its hat to Chandler's Philip Marlowe. A young girl reports her friend, Rebecca, missing, and Eddie is drawn into a strange case which leads from a high-class mansion to the London underworld, where the truth is a novelty and trouble lurks around every corner.
www.michaeldonovancrime.com

Sir Arthur Conan Doyle

Edgar Allan Poe may have created the first fictional detective in *The Murders in the Rue Morgue* (1841), but Sir Arthur Conan Doyle can be seen as the father of crime fiction. An Edinburgh-born doctor, Doyle's first Sherlock Holmes story (*A Study in Scarlet*) was published in magazine form in 1887.

Holmes is a remarkable character, able to deduce events from the flimsiest of clues. Holmes lived at 221B Baker Street — a fictional address on a real London street. Aided and abetted by his long-standing friend Dr Watson, Holmes appeared in four novels and fifty-six short stories. Many of these took place in and around the capital, and Doyle's descriptions of Victorian London are powerful and evocative. Though he never lived in central London, he was a regular visitor, and his descriptions of the dank streets, mud-coloured fogs and grimy buildings give the stories an added menace.

There are many great examples, such as "The Blue Carbuncle" from *The Adventures of Sherlock Holmes*

(1892), where a fabulous blue jewel ends up in the crop of a cooked goose after a theft at a London hotel; "The Adventure of the Bruce Partington Plans" from *His Last Bow* (1917), in which Holmes solves the disappearance of secret submarine plans during a severe London fog; *The Man with the Twisted Lip* — also from *The Adventures of Sherlock Holmes* (1892) — which includes a great description of an opium den in the East End. Holmes employs a group of local London street children (The Baker Street Irregulars) to help him on occasions as in *The Sign of Four* (1887).

See also: the West Country, the South and South East
www.sherlockholmesonline.org

Francis Durbridge

During a writing career that lasted from 1938–1986, Francis Durbridge was nothing if not an entertainer. His Paul Temple series appeared in book form as well as plays and radio dramas, while his stand-alone novels were hugely popular. Many were set in and around London, with the backdrops of hotel rooms, robberies, clergymen, Mayfair flats and Home Counties accents. Paul Temple was unusual, a crime novelist who was the central character in crime novels, solving crime with the help of his girlfriend/wife Ros.

In *Send for Paul Temple* (1938), he is called in by Scotland Yard after a night-watchman is killed in the latest of a string of jewel robberies, and in *Paul Temple and the Kelby Affair* (1970), Temple investigates when the possessor of a scandalous diary is murdered and the diary stolen.

Apart from three novels featuring businessman Tim Frazer, there were no running characters in his other novels. In *A Game of Murder* (1975), a young Scotland Yard officer is on holiday when his father dies in a mysterious golfing accident, which soon proves to be murder.

www.fantasticfiction.co.uk/d/francis-durbridge

Ruth Dudley Edwards

Irish-born Ruth Dudley Edwards has never held back from poking a little fun at the British establishment through her satirical crime novels. Her extraordinary sleuthing duo, Robert Amiss and Baroness Ida "Jack" Troutbeck, leave no stone unturned and few pillars of the establishment untouched in this ingenious series.

In *Ten Lords A-Leaping* (1995), ten members of the Upper House have simultaneous heart attacks, which is felt by the police to be a little suspicious, especially in the light of a fierce anti-hunting debate, while *Clubbed to Death* (1992) takes a massive swing at London's Gentlemen's clubs.

Other targets have included the Civil Service (*Corridors of Death*, 1981*)*, the Church of England (*Murder in the Cathedral*, 1996), and high literature (*Carnage on the Committee*, 2004). In the latter, the gloriously outlandish Baroness is invited to take the place of a suddenly deceased judge on the judging panel of a major literary prize. Though a murderer continues to whittle away at their number, he (or she) may not have reckoned with "Madam Chairwoman".

www.ruthdudleyedwards.co.uk

Stella Duffy

Saz Martin is a lesbian private investigator in London in a series of five novels from the excellent Stella Duffy, who was born in London and has come back from New Zealand to live there.

In *Fresh Flesh* (1999), Saz takes on two searches for real birth parents, one for her friend Chris, the other for outrageous celebrity cook Patrick Freeman. She thinks it will be easy work, but as it takes her through contemporary London society the cases become an emotional rollercoaster.

www.stelladuffy.wordpress.com/my-books

Carola Dunn

Though a graduate of Manchester University, Carola Dunn has lived in the United States for many years. She has written several series of books, including romances, historical romances and cosy crime novels such as the Daisy Dalrymple series. Daisy is a journalist in 1920s England with a heightened sense of curiosity and a penchant for finding dead bodies. She is also involved with, and later marries, a high-flying Scotland Yard detective.

The series is set all over the country, but one of the best is *The Bloody Tower* (2007) in which Daisy, now the mother of twins, agrees to write an article about the Tower of London, only to find one of the Yeoman Warders has been murdered.

See also: the West Country

www.caroladunn.weebly.com

Patrick Easter

A former officer of the Metropolitan Police Marine Support Unit, Patrick Easter clearly knows the River Thames very well. He has used his knowledge and love of history to great effect in two books following the career of Tom Pascoe, a river surveyor in the newly-formed Marine Police of 1798.

In the debut novel, *The Watermen* (2011), Pascoe comes up against an old adversary, Boylin, who is creating havoc in London through organised crime in the shipping world, as well as stirring the flames of Irish rebellion.

www.patrickeaster.co.uk

Charles Felix

The Notting Hill Mystery (1865) by Charles Felix is now viewed as perhaps the earliest crime novel ever published. Out of print for over a hundred years, it was republished to considerable acclaim by the British Library in 2012. The author was for many years a mystery, as Charles Felix was a pseudonym, but is now known to have been English journalist Charles Warren Adams.

The story concerns the death of the wife of a London baron, and the enquiry into her husband's guilt by insurance investigator Ralph Henderson. It is told through diary entries, chemical analysis, witness interviews and family letters, and the book even includes a crime scene map.

www.en.wikipedia.org/wiki/The_Notting_Hill_Mystery

Gordon Ferris

Originally from Kilmarnock in the West of Scotland, Gordon Ferris worked in the City as a management consultant but always wanted to get back to his first love, writing.

His first two novels are set in post-war London, an era of bomb-sites, rationing and poverty. They centre on Danny McRae, a demobbed SOE operative who now suffers from blackouts and gaps in his memory. He has become a private investigator, and in *Truth Dare Kill* (2007), he sets out to help a high-class client who thinks she has killed her boyfriend in an accident. McRae knew the boyfriend from his military service. All the while newspaper accounts of gruesome murders in the city's red light district stir memories deep in his mind. As the two cases coalesce, McRae realises that he will have to go back to wartime events for the answers.

The follow-up, *The Unquiet Heart* (2008), takes Danny from London to Berlin and back on the trail of black marketeers, double agents and terrorism.

See also: Glasgow and the West of Scotland
www.gordonferris.com

Christopher Fowler

A writer in several different genres, Christopher Fowler has won awards in most of them, including crime fiction. His wonderfully funny, stylish and eccentric series features the elderly detectives Arthur Bryant and John May of the Peculiar Crimes Unit of the Metropolitan Police.

May is the senior, suave and charming, while Bryant is rude and grumpy. The series takes them into many unusual parts of London including long-lost Underground stations, vanished pubs and subterranean rivers.

Bryant and May Off the Rails (2010) sends the intrepid duo into the Underground on the track of a killer they have caught before. Unfortunately he escaped, killing a policeman in the process, and is now on the run in the deepest recesses of London's transport system.

The Victoria Vanishes (2008) begins with Arthur Bryant watching a drunken, middle-aged woman leaving a back-street pub. The next day she is found dead at that exact spot, but the pub has vanished. A killer is at work in London pubs, and Bryant and May love a drink, making them the ideal investigators.

www.christopherfowler.co.uk

Nicci French

Not one crime writer but two, Nicci French is the pen-name of London-based journalists Nicci Gerrard and Sean French. Together they have written twelve best-selling psychological thrillers, and have recently started a series set in London featuring psychotherapist Freida Klein.

In *Blue Monday* (2011), a child is abducted, and one of Freida's clients has been having disturbing dreams featuring a child who is the spitting image of the vanished boy. The police take little interest until a link is found to an unsolved abduction that took place twenty years earlier. Suddenly Freida is central to the investigation, trying to get inside the mind of a psychopath. But doing so may lead to danger for all concerned.

In *Tuesday's Gone* (2012), a man is found dead in the London house of a mentally disturbed woman. Through interviews, Freida unlocks the woman's memory and the identity of the man is revealed. He is Robert Poole, a master conman, and many people have a motive for his murder. The more Freida and the police find out, the more ghosts from the past appear, and some of these relate to Freida herself.

www.fantasticfiction.co.uk/f/nicci-french

Frances Fyfield

One of the queens of the psychological crime novel, Frances Fyfield (the pen-name of Frances Hegarty) has spent much of her adult life in London, and has used the city as the setting for several of her books.

Helen West is a Crown Prosecutor who lives in Highbury, within hearing distance of the old football ground. In *Deep Sleep* (1991), which won the CWA Silver Dagger, she is drawn into a frightening story of drugs and terror in the East End.

The last Helen West novel was published in 1996, and since then the author has written a number of clever, award-winning, stand-alone novels. In *Blood From Stone* (2008), which won a CWA Dagger in 2008, doubts surround the apparent suicide of ruthless and successful Kensington barrister Marianne Shearer. Her last case resulted in an acquittal, but when her erstwhile colleague Peter Friel examines the transcripts he finds clues to a wide-ranging deception.

www.francesfyfield.co.uk

Robert Galbraith

When *The Cuckoo's Calling* was published in 2013, Robert Galbraith was a former military policeman who had been working in the civilian security industry. In reality, "he" was Harry Potter author, J.K. Rowling, masquerading under a pseudonym.

The fine novel is set in contemporary London. A model has fallen to her death from a Mayfair balcony, and it is generally thought to be suicide. Her brother hires derelict private eye and ex-soldier Cormoran Strike (a highly unusual character) to double-check. The complex, compelling investigation takes him across the city, from Soho to the East End, and danger waits on every corner.

Strike returns in 2014 in a second novel, *The Silkworm*. This time he is investigating a murder in the London publishing world. It is clear that the author knows this world well, as the spiky descriptions of authors, agents and editors attest. Again, the minutely detailed depiction of the capital gives the novel a realistic backdrop, and the plotting can be ranked with the best.

www.robert-galbraith.com

Elizabeth George

American author Elizabeth George has written nearly twenty books about mismatched Scotland Yard detectives Inspector Thomas Lynley (the eighth Earl of Asherton) and his down-to-earth colleague Barbara Havers. Though they are often involved in investigations around the country, their base is London, and several of the books are set there.

With No One As Witness (2005) and *What Came Before He Shot Her* (2006) are in many ways the central books in this series, and are solidly based in the capital. In the former, Scotland Yard is on the defensive when it fails to act on the case of a serial killer whose victims are mainly black or mixed-race boys. Against a backdrop of claims of institutional racism Lynley and his team is called in, only for a terrible tragedy to strike. The latter novel seeks to explain the events that led to that tragedy.

The series was successfully televised by the BBC between 2001 and 2007.

See also: the West Country, the North West

www.elizabethgeorgeonline.com

Michael Gilbert

A founder member of the CWA and a Grand Master of the Mystery Writers of America, Michael Gilbert's writing career lasted for fifty years and included every kind of crime thriller.

The Petrella series, featuring painstaking and dogged London policeman Patrick Petrella, included both novels and short stories, written between 1977 and 1994. *In Roller-Coaster* (1993) Petrella takes on a new job as Superintendent of the East London docklands, and is faced by a particularly unpleasant Dutch smuggling ring.

Gilbert also wrote the classic novel *Smallbone Deceased* (1950), in which a body is found in a hermetically sealed deed box at a Dickensian firm of London solicitors.

www.fantasticfiction.co.uk/g/michael-gilbert

Ann Granger

Portsmouth-born Ann Granger has written four different series of crime novels since 1991, and two of them are set in London. The author's humour and eye for detail are clear in both. The Fran Varady series is based around a young woman, first seen when out of work and almost destitute, making her way in multicultural London as a private investigator at the end of the twentieth century. Considered a problem by the local police, she is, however, able to combat crime that they miss, and so finds herself dealing with people-trafficking (*Watching Out* (2003) and kidnapping (*Keeping Bad Company,*1997).

Lizzie Martin, on the other hand, is a lady's companion in Victorian London who investigates strange events with the aid of DI Ben Ross of Scotland Yard. In *A Particular Eye for Villainy* (2012), they find more than they bargained for when investigating the background of a man found bludgeoned to death in his lodgings.

See also: the Midlands

www.anngranger.net

Susanna Gregory

Cambridge academic Liz Cruwys uses this pseudonym for her evocative Thomas Chaloner historical mysteries which are set in London around the time of the Restoration in 1660. Chaloner is a former Parliamentarian spy who, on the return of the new King, is forced to work for the Earl of Clarendon, in whatever capacity he sees fit.

In the first book of the series (*A Conspiracy of Violence*, 2006), Chaloner is sent to discover whether gold has been buried in the Tower of London. Life becomes more complicated when he discovers that his predecessor in the Earl of Clarendon's employ had been murdered.

In *A Murder on London Bridge* (2009), Clarendon is concerned by rumours of an uprising against the new King and a murder that has taken place on London Bridge. Chaloner is sent to investigate, and soon realises he is involved in a race against time to unmask the plotters and stop their plans for an explosive event on Shrove Tuesday.

Susanna Gregory writes two other series of historical mysteries, and is a member of The Medieval Murderers.
See also: East Anglia, Wales (Simon Beaufort)
www.susannagregory.com

Patricia Grey

Crime writer Liz Evans used this pseudonym for a short series of novels set in London during World War II. Featuring DCI Jack Stamford and Sergeant Sarah McNeill, they focus on small communities in the capital, and the effects that crime can have on them.

In *Junction Cut* (1994), a fifteen-year-old girl is murdered, with ripples and consequences that shake the whole community, while *Good Hope Station* (1997) involves anonymous letters sent to the staff of an auxiliary fire station during the Blitz.
See also: the South and South East (Liz Evans)
www.lizevans.net/id8.html

Patricia Hall

Former journalist Patricia Hall (pseudonym of Maureen O'Connor) has set most of her work in her native

Yorkshire, but in 2011 she began a new series set in the world of Swinging Sixties London. As a young reporter the author had arrived in London in the time of Beatlemania, and so had experienced the era first-hand.

Photographer Kate O'Donnell comes down from Liverpool to London at the same time as the Beatles, and in *Dressed to Kill* (2013) she is shocked when a former model from her studio is found battered to death in Soho. When a second girl is killed she seeks help from a policeman friend and uncovers dark secrets in the worlds of fashion and music.

In *Blood Brothers* (2014), Kate's relationship with DS Harry Barnard is under pressure. Harry is involved in two major investigations — a brutalised body found at Centre Point Tower, and a vanished witness in a gangster trial. Meanwhile Kate is working with a crime reporter from a national newspaper — and discovers that Harry has connections to the gangster's brother.

See also: the North East
www.patriciahall.co.uk

Penny Hancock

Originally from South East London, Penny Hancock was a freelance journalist and author, writing stories for English language learners, before she undertook a course on creative writing at Anglia Ruskin University. While there, she started the first draft of *Tideline* (2012), and she has not looked back.

Tideline is a dark, creepy thriller about obsession and secrets, set in Greenwich. Sonia is alone in her home by the Thames when a fifteen-year old boy calls in on an errand. For reasons best known to herself, she does not want him to leave...

Hancock's second book, *The Darkening Hour* (2013), opens with a body being pulled from the waters of the freezing River Thames in Deptford. But who is it and who is to blame? Full of menace and very atmospheric,

this is a fine follow-up to the author's excellent debut.
www.pennyhancock.com

Oliver Harris

A Londoner by birth and a graduate of University College London, Oliver Harris has been a researcher for the Imperial War Museum as well as a TV and film extra. He is also a reviewer for the *Times Literary Supplement*.

His first novel, *The Hollow Man* (2012), is set in Hampstead and surrounding areas. DC Nick Belsey is the central character, a shady cop with a drink problem and a dodgy reputation, who investigates a simple missing person report only to be dragged into a murder case involving some of the most expensive locations in the city.

In the follow-up, *Deep Shelter* (2014), Belsey is shocked when a girl he is dating disappears, virtually in front of his eyes. His investigations take him deep into the subterranean world beneath London's streets, where an implacable enemy will do whatever is necessary to protect Cold War secrets.

The locations used in the books are shown on a map on the author's website, each denoted with a policeman's helmet!

www.oliverharris.co.uk

Ray Harrison

Sergeant Bragg and Constable Morton are the somewhat mismatched pair of Victorian detectives in Ray Harrison's series of London-based crime novels, written between 1983 and 1998.

Tincture of Death (1989) focuses on the opium trade in Victorian society, while in *Draught of Death* (1998), the sixteenth and last in the series, the body of a university professor is found in a vat of beer.

See also: the West Country

www.fantasticfiction.co.uk/h/ray-harrison

Cynthia Harrod-Eagles

Though perhaps best known for her long-running historical series featuring the Morland dynasty, Cynthia
Harrod-Eagles has also written a fine series of present-
day London-based crime novels featuring Inspector Bill
Slider. The series began in 1991.

Slider is a fine creation, a decent man in a harsh world.
He is regularly involved in cases in the Shepherd's Bush
area, such as *Orchestrated Death* (1991), which is centred
around the death of a violinist, or *Blood Lines* (1996), in
which he investigates the death of a dissolute and
conceited music critic.

www.cynthiaharrodeagles.com

John Harvey

The masterful John Harvey is best known for his
Nottingham-based Resnick series, but in *Good Bait*
(2012) he addresses the capital's current problems with
gang warfare and organised crime. It is a powerful story
which begins with two apparently unconnected London
fatalities. DCI Karen Shields and her team are stretched
to the limit, investigating the death of a young Moldovan
boy, found dead on Hampstead Heath. In Cornwall, DI
Trevor Cordon is trying to trace the daughter of a local
problem family. When Cordon travels to London to
continue his investigations the two stories come together
in a violent conclusion.

See also: East Anglia, the Midlands

www.mellotone.co.uk

Annie Hauxwell

Annie Hauxwell is an East End girl by birth, though she
grew up in Australia. She became a lawyer in England,
but gave this up to work as an investigator.

In Her Blood (2012) is the first novel featuring
Catherine Berlin, a drug addict working for the Financial
Services Authority. She finds herself the subject of a

police investigation when an informant turns up dead in the Thames, and a trip to her drug-supplying GP leads to the discovery of a further body.

The heroin-addicted investigator returns in *A Bitter Taste* (2013). A friend from her less-than-salubrious past turns up on her doorstep, desperate for help in finding her missing daughter. When Catherine agrees to help, she finds herself moving in a frightening world of drug dealers, bent coppers and violent death.

www.anniehauxwell.com

Mo Hayder

Mo Hayder left school at fifteen, but now has MAs from both English and American universities. Her dark, sometimes harrowing books have been nominated for a number of prizes and her second novel, *The Treatment* (2001), won a WH Smith Thumping Good Read award in 2002. In 2011 she won the coveted Dagger in the Library Award from the CWA.

Birdman (2000) is set in Greenwich, where Inspector Jack Caffrey's first case for the Metropolitan Police Murder Squad brings him up against a sex-obsessed serial killer, while exposing his own personal demons.

The Treatment (2001) takes place in Brixton, with Caffrey's past catching up with him as he investigates the murder of a young boy. Both books bring to life the seedy clubs, pubs and mean streets of South London at the turn of the twenty-first century.

See also: the West Country
www.mohayder.net

E.W. Hornung

Ernest William Hornung was a Yorkshireman from Middlesbrough, whose family background was Hungarian. On the other hand, Raffles, his major creation, was quintessentially English, living in Victorian Piccadilly, playing cricket for England and living a gentleman's life about

London, whilst continuing a second life burgling the rich – though never the host of a party he had just left!

With his associate and storyteller Bunny (in many ways similar to Watson — Hornung was Arthur Conan Doyle's brother-in-law), Raffles appears in three books of short stories, and one novel (*Mr Justice Raffles*, 1909). Since then there have been films, plays and TV shows and the books have been reprinted many times.

www.fantasticfiction.co.uk/h/e-w-hornung

Graham Ison

Not many crime writers can say that they spent four years as Protection Officer to the Prime Minister, guarded US presidents and served with the Diplomatic Protection Group. Graham Ison can, and his exceptional knowledge of policing in London has been fundamental to his twenty-five years as a crime writer. He has written four different series, mostly set in and around London. Though never bestsellers, they have been perennially popular in UK libraries.

His first short series of four books features Chief Superintendent John Gaffney of Special Branch, whose work often takes him into espionage territory. In *A Damned Serious Business* (1990), a routine traffic offence leads to a case involving MI5, MI6, the FBI and the Pakistani Secret Service.

Next came a series of seven novels about DCSupt Tommy Fox, head of the Flying Squad. In *Tomfoolery* (1992), Fox links a West End jewel robbery to a missing businessman and a mysterious dead body.

In 2001 Ison started another new series, this time with DI Harry Brock and his partner, DSgt Dave Poole. In *All Quiet on Arrival* (2010), they are called in when the stabbed body of a woman is found after a fire at a house in Chelsea. It soon transpires that all was not what it seemed at this respectable address.

Having set all his previous series in contemporary London, Ison then began another series in 2003 based in the capital during World War I. This features DI Ernest Hardcastle of the Whitehall Division of the Metropolitan Police. Ison's attention to detail is considerable, and the stories are tremendously evocative of time and place. In *Hardcastle's Mandarin* (2009), a high ranking civil servant at the Ministry of Munitions, Sir Nigel Strong, is murdered in his office. Another murder is linked to a possible German spy at Woolwich Arsenal. Hardcastle is concerned that there may be a link, and, with the war going badly, must find it quickly.

www.grahamison.co.uk

Lee Jackson

An acknowledged expert on Victorian London, Lee Jackson has written a number of non-fiction titles about the period, as well as two short fiction series. Full of gothic drama, these feature Inspector Decimus Webb of the 1870s Metropolitan Police, and Sarah Tanner, a somewhat mysterious woman who owns a coffee house on Leather Lane in the 1850s. Both series are steeped in period detail, and lead the reader into the sordid alleys and gas-lit parlours of Victorian society.

The Welfare of the Dead (2005) is the second novel to feature Decimus Webb, and is full of suspense as Webb's suspicions about a seemingly respectable businessman uncover the web of secrets and deceit behind the Holborn General Mourning Warehouse.

In *A Most Dangerous Woman* (2007), Sarah Tanner is drawn into the city's underworld when she is the only witness to the murder of an old friend. Her investigations take her from the gaming halls of Regent Street to the slums of St Giles.

Jackson has also written two fine stand-alone novels, set in the Victorian London he knows so well. The first, his debut novel, was *London Dust* (2003), which tells the story of Natalie Meadows, who witnesses the murder of music-hall star Nellie Matthews and tries to uncover the murderer. It was nominated for the CWA Ellis Peters Award.

www.victorianlondon.org

P.D. James

P.D. James is a multi-award winning author and was created Baroness James of Holland Park in 1991. She has won three CWA Silver Daggers, plus the CWA Lifetime Achievement Dagger, and has an honorary doctorate from seven British universities.

As at 2013, the Grande Dame of British crime fiction has written fourteen novels featuring Inspector, now Commander, Adam Dalgleish of the Metropolitan Police. Not all of these are set in London — Dalgleish is often found investigating murder elsewhere — but several of her true masterpieces are set in the city: *A Taste for Death* (1986), *Original Sin* (1994), *A Certain Justice* (1997) and *The Murder Room* (2003).

Few authors evoke atmosphere as well as P.D. James. *Original Sin* (1994) is set in the devious world of publishing. When Gerard Etienne, managing director of a publishing house in Wapping, is found dead with a stuffed snake in his mouth, it appears to be the culmination of a series of vicious pranks. However, it soon becomes clear that the case is incredibly complex. With no shortage of suspects, the intelligence of Dalgleish, and his colleagues Kate Miskin and Daniel Aaron, is tested to the full. Amongst all the descriptions of waterside London is a highly impressive crime novel

In *A Certain Justice* (1997), Dalgleish investigates the murder of successful lawyer Venetia Aldridge, who has been found stabbed to death in her London Chambers. There are a number of suspects, including an ex-husband, a lover, colleagues and former clients. When a second death takes place, the case takes on a very different hue. Faced with an array of motives including naked ambition, obsession and revenge, Dalgleish and his team must probe every corner of the barrister's life to unmask the killer.

See also: the West Country, East Anglia
www.randomhouse.com/features/pdjames

Hanna Jameson

This young author from Winchester is still in her twenties, but she devised the story for her novel at seventeen. Her first book was nominated for the John Creasey New Blood Dagger.

Something You Are (2013) is the first in a projected series about a London club called The Underground. Brutal, shocking, gory, it is full of characters damaged in one way or another. The central character is Nic, a young hitman with a drug habit. He is employed to track down the killer of the daughter of an arms dealer, any way he can. But he develops an unhealthy interest in the girl's mother, who has her own dubious agenda, and soon Nic is in trouble — way over his head. Sometimes uncomfortable, this is nevertheless an addictive read.

www.fantasticfiction.co.uk/j/hanna-jameson

Alison Joseph

Contemporary nun Agnes Bourdillon is the creation of playwright and scriptwriter Alison Joseph, whose work has often been heard on BBC Radio 4. Agnes is part of an open order, living in contemporary Southwark and working in a hostel for the homeless. Despite her religious views, Agnes still loves the trappings of modern life, such as cars and clothes, and this brings a tension to the stories.

In *The Hour of Our Death* (1995), Agnes stands in as a hospital visitor at St Hughs, and becomes suspicious about the death of a staff member and faked post-mortem results. Though sidetracked by a handsome portrait painter, she finds herself embroiled in a difficult case of medical politics.

For *The Dying Light* (1999), Sister Agnes is seconded to Silworth, a women's prison in South London, and she faces bullying, violence and misplaced loyalties as she tries to help when the father of a prisoner is shot dead.

In 2013 Alison Joseph became Chair of the CWA, succeeding Peter James.

See also: the South and South East

www.alisonjoseph.com

Dan Kavanagh

Leicestershire-born Julian Barnes won the Man Booker Prize with *The Sense of an Ending* in 2011, and has been shortlisted a further three times. In addition to his literary output he also wrote four crime novels under the pseudonym Dan Kavanagh, three of which are set in London. Written in a somewhat basic, coarse style, they are all blackly comic, peopled with rich, well-defined characters such as the protagonist, Duffy, a bisexual ex-policeman.

The first in the series, *Duffy* (1980), is set in Soho, and resonates with black humour as Duffy searches amongst the pimps and porn-kings for a vicious blackmailer. The follow-up, *Fiddle City* (1981), is set at Heathrow Airport and should not be read by anyone who is intending to fly in the near future, as it deals with the frankly terrifying scams which criminals use to avoid customs and immigration control. The third in the series, *Putting the Boot In* (1985), lifts the lid on dodgy dealings at a third-division football club, dealing with two 1980s social problems: AIDS and football hooliganism.

www.dankavanagh.com

Jessie Keane

Jessie Keane is a hard-hitting novelist who sets her books in London's gangland. They always feature strong female characters, and her work is often compared to Martina Cole or Lynda La Plante.

The Annie Carter books centre round a woman, originally gangster's moll Annie Bailey, who rises to the top of a major London crime family in the late 1960s/early 1970s.

In the first novel, *Dirty Game* (2008), Annie has to use all her resources to get what she wants from crime lord

Max Carter. She is rejected, and has to fight her own battles and live her own way. In doing so she makes enemies, including two rival gangs, and survival takes all her resources.

By *Scarlet Woman* (2009), she has taken over the East End, but is horrified when a close friend is the latest victim of a killer on her own streets.

www.jessiekeane.com

H.R.F. Keating

With a writing career that spanned fifty years, H.R.F. "Harry" Keating was one of the most prolific crime writers of the late twentieth century. He was president of the Detection Club for fifteen years, and chaired the CWA.

As well as his Inspector Ghote novels, set in India, he wrote a fine series of novels featuring DCI Harriet Martens, a strong-minded, tenacious woman who realises that she has to be tough to survive in the masculine world of London's Metropolitan Police in the twenty-first century.

In *The Hard Detective (*2000), her "Stop the Rot!" campaign provokes the local criminals so much that two of her officers are murdered, and in *A Detective in Love* (2001) she has to investigate the murder of Britain's number one tennis star while trying to deal with a more personal shock — she has fallen in love with a colleague.

www.hrfkeating.com

Erin Kelly

London is the setting for Erin Kelly's debut psychological crime novel, *The Poison Tree* (2010). In 1997, Karen, a clever, slightly naive university student, meets Biba, a drama student who needs Karen to teach her German for a play she is in. During the course of these lessons in a rambling old house in Highgate she meets Biba's brother Rex, and events start to spiral out of control.

See also: the West Country (Erin Kelly & Chris Chibnall)

www.erinkelly.co.uk

Simon Kernick

Simon Kernick is the one of the current masters of the relentless, page-turning, gut-wrenching crime thriller. His books have a gritty authenticity which comes from his flawless research and wide range of contacts within the police and security services. From a specific, often shocking opening, he takes the reader on a ride through the rougher side of London. Fast-paced and frantic, the distinction between the good guys and the bad guys is often blurred.

The two main characters in his books are Tina Boyd, a Detective Sergeant with the Metropolitan Police, and Dennis Milne, former London policeman, ex-hitman and renegade detective.

Milne originally appears in *The Business of Dying* (2002), which has one of the greatest opening scenes in crime fiction. Milne is a rogue cop who thought he was punishing major villains — unfortunately the men in his gun-sights are innocent customs men. As he tries to avoid arrest he simultaneously investigates the depraved murder of a young girl. Milne is the narrator of two further thrillers.

Tina Boyd is a DS in the Metropolitan Police, and appears regularly in Kernick's books in tandem with a variety of male officers. In *The Last 10 Seconds* (2010), she finds her life in danger as she tries to recapture escaped serial killer Andrew Kent, whose conviction may not be as watertight as everyone thought.

In *Severed* (2007), ex-soldier Sean Tyler wakes up in a hotel room next to the headless corpse of a girl he has only met once before. In *Deadline* (2008), a woman answers the phone only to hear that her fourteen-year-old daughter has been kidnapped and her abductors want half a million pounds, cash, in forty-eight hours — or else...

www.simonkernick.com

Max Kinnings

Max Kinnings is currently the head of Creative Writing at Brunel University. His first major novel, *Baptism* (2012), concerns a religious fanatic who holds four hundred people hostage on a Tube train in central London. Influenced by books such as *The Taking of Pelham 123* (John Godey, 1972), the book introduced DCI Ed Mallory, a blind hostage negotiator who has to find a way to get through to a man who does not want to listen.

Mallory returns in *Sacrifice* (2013), in which a masked intruder holds a disgraced hedge-fund manager hostage in his Belgravia home.

www.maxkinnings.wordpress.com

Roberta Kray

Through her marriage to Reggie Kray (who died in 2000), and with her background in publishing, Roberta Kray is well-placed to write novels about crime in London. Her first book was published in 2006. Sprinkled with authenticity, her novels give a remarkable insight into London's underworld.

In *The Lost* (2008), private eye Harry Lind is concerned that a little girl who vanished twenty years ago may have reappeared. With the help of a journalist he sets out to prove one way or another whether or not the girl is still alive. The investigation brings him into conflict with a vicious London gangster — and that means trouble.

Nothing But Trouble (2012) opens in 1998 when a young girl disappears after breaking in to the home of a known oddball, Donald Peck. When her body is found, Peck is convicted of her murder. Still protesting his innocence, he commits suicide in prison. Years later private investigator Harry Lind takes a closer look, as some skeletons have started to rattle.

www.fantasticfiction.co.uk/k/roberta-kray

Deryn Lake

The pseudonym of former journalist and historical author Dinah Lampitt, Deryn Lake is the author of the Georgian John Rawlings mysteries. The characters of apothecary Rawlings and blind magistrate Sir John Fielding are based on two real-life figures, an eighteenth-century apothecary who invented carbonated water, and the man who founded the Bow Street Runners. Full of historical accuracy, the books are entertaining and highly readable.

The majority of the books are set in London. A good example is *Death at Apothecaries Hall* (2000), in which Rawlings is called by Fielding to investigate a case of severe food poisoning at the Grand Dinner of the Worshipful Society of Liverymen. He has to decide whether the death of a liveryman is deliberate murder or not.

In *Death at St James's Palace* (2002), a man dies in a fall at a royal ceremony in 1761. No one has seen anything, as they were all watching for the first glimpse of the new Queen, but Fielding has overheard a whispered threat, and he and Rawlings set out to search for the truth.

See also: the West Country, the South and South East
www.derynlake.com

Lynda La Plante

A prolific author, Liverpool-born novelist and scriptwriter Lynda La Plante has written six different series of crime novels since giving up her fledgling acting career. She has specialised in powerful women characters, and sets most of her work in and around London.

She is perhaps best known as the creator of DCI Jane Tennison, a tough woman taking on the men in the misogynistic Metropolitan Police, and Dolly Rawlins, the criminal mastermind who arranged for a group of women to complete a series of bank raids originally planned by their deceased husbands. Both these women were important in breaking down stereotypes in the portrayal of women in crime both in fiction and on television, and all of La Plante's work is as powerful on the page as on the screen.

DCI Tennison (memorably played by Dame Helen Mirren) was the central character in the multi-award-winning TV series *Prime Suspect,* televised between 1991 and 2006. Three of the early stories were novelised, losing none of their visceral power. In *Prime Suspect 2: A Face in the Crowd* (1992), the body of a young black girl is found in one of the city's poorest areas, cranking the racial tension up towards breaking point. As her chauvinistic and racist colleagues lose track of the murderer, Tennison's personal life is exposed by the tabloid press and the resulting chaos threatens to engulf her entirely.

The Dolly Rawlins books were based on the TV series *Widows, Widows 2,* and *She's Out,* broadcast between 1983 and 1995. Rawlins is the leader of a group of women whose armed robber husbands had been killed during a robbery which went wrong. Using their plans, she and the other women decide to pull off the raid themselves. Eventually she is sent to prison. In *She's Out* (1995), Rawlins is released, and sets out to find the diamonds that she hid following a theft years before. But her ex-gang members want a cut, and a police officer wants revenge for his sister's death in the raid.

The Anna Travis series, which began in 2004 with *Above Suspicion,* follows the career of another London policewoman. *The Red Dahlia* (2006) sees her involved in a case with frightening similarities to the famous Los Angeles *Black Dahlia* murder case, as a woman's body is found in the Thames, cut in half and unrecognisable.

www.fantasticfiction.co.uk/l/lynda-la-plante

Janet Laurence

As well as a series about foodie detective Darina Lisle, cookery writer Janet Laurence also wrote three books featuring the Italian painter Canaletto, who visits London in the 1740s.

In *Canaletto and the Case of the Privy Garden* (1998) Canaletto stumbles upon the body of a young girl in an alleyway. He summons help, but finds himself mixed up in a nightmare of terrible proportions.

See also: the West Country

www.fantasticfiction.co.uk/l/janet-laurence

David Lawrence

An acclaimed poet and TV scriptwriter, David Lawrence (real name David Harsent) has written a short series of crime novels featuring the hard-bitten DS Stella Mooney, who knows the mean streets of London better than most as she grew up there.

Like Mark Billingham, Lawrence is not afraid to show London's seedier side, and the city is virtually another character in these dark, edgy thrillers. In *Cold Kill* (2005), the police find a young woman's body, and a man confesses to the murder, but Stella is not convinced that he is telling the whole truth. Then in *Down into Darkness* (2007), Stella has to confront a vicious killer who leaves his reasons for murder scrawled on the backs of his victims.

www.fantasticfiction.co.uk/l/david-lawrence

John Lawton

John Lawton is a TV director/producer who has worked with the likes of Gore Vidal, Neil Simon and Harold Pinter. His main character, DSgt Frederick Troy, is an unusual policeman. The son of a distinguished Russian émigré, he joins the Metropolitan Police in the 1930s, and Lawton's novels follow his career through to the 1960s. Troy's involvement in the major events of the times, including the Blitz, the Cold War, and the Profumo Scandal, give these clever novels an added realism.

In *Old Flames* (1996), set in 1956, Troy has been promoted to Chief Inspector, but this only brings extra problems of responsibility when a body is found beside a Russian ship in Portsmouth Harbour just as two Soviet leaders are visiting London.

In *Blue Rondo* (2005), the time is the late 1950s. The East End is being redeveloped, corruption is everywhere and the political situation is uncertain. Troy has a lot on his plate dealing with a series of sadistic murders, especially when an old girlfriend reappears and President Eisenhower makes a farewell visit to the city.

www.authorjohnlawton.wordpress.com

Gillian Linscott

Once a BBC Radio parliamentary correspondent, Linscott has written many well-received crime novels, including an evocative series about suffragette Nell Bray. Nell is a fascinating character, who has done time in Holloway, and finds herself embroiled in various mysteries in the early years of the twentieth century.

In *Stage Fright* (1993), the staging in London of George Bernard Shaw's new play, a reworking of *Cinderella*, results in murder. His leading lady is in danger, and Shaw asks Nell to help ensure that she makes it to the first night. When a murderer strikes, it is up to Nell to investigate.

In *Absent Friends* (1999), Nell wants to stand for Parliament at the end of World War I, and is drawn into the murky world of politics, which becomes more dangerous than she expects. She is approached by the wife of a Conservative MP who has been killed in a firework accident. The woman offers to cover Nell's election expenses if she will help to examine the circumstances of the man's death.

See also: the West Country (Caro Peacock), London (Caro Peacock)

www.caropeacock.com

Joan Lock

An authority on women in the police force, former police-woman Joan Lock is the author of several authentic

Victorian crime novels featuring DS (later DI) Ernest Best. The general setting is London, and they are often based on historical facts — such as the sinking of the steamer The Princess Alice in 1878 (*Dead Born*, 2001).

In *Dead Centre* (2008), it is 1887, and London is in turmoil. A prominent socialist is found dead at the foot of Nelson's Column, and DI Best is on the case. He has caught sight of a man he knows is guilty of violent acts, but is he guilty in this case?

www.fantasticfiction.co.uk/l/joan-lock

Peter Lovesey

Peter Lovesey has had a long writing career and has won awards both in the UK and America. His first novel, *Wobble to Death*, was published in 1970. It introduced the respectable, dignified Sergeant Cribb and was set in Victorian London, when murder intervened in a marathon walking contest.

Seven more Cribb novels followed, the last being *Waxwork* in 1978, and the series gained Lovesey many admirers. It was adapted for television in 1981.

In *Abracadaver* (1972), Cribb is drawn into the clubs and music halls of central London to apprehend a violent and elusive criminal, while in *Invitation to a Dynamite Party* (1974), bomb blasts are occurring all over London, thanks to the work of plotters seeking Irish independence. Cribb must infiltrate the group to save the city.

See also: the West Country

www.peterlovesey.com

J.J. Marric

This was one of the best-known pseudonyms of the endlessly inventive John Creasey. Commander George Gideon of Scotland Yard became a household name in the 1950s when Marric's early novels were adapted for television and film.

The success of the books continued through the 1960s until Creasey's death in 1973. During this time it was said that it was not unusual for people to phone Scotland Yard to speak to Gideon, in the belief that he was a real policeman. The Gideon novels portrayed a realistic view of policemen at the time and were popular both in the UK and abroad.

The series opened with *Gideon's Day* in 1955, which pioneered the police procedural in the UK, a year before Ed McBain did the same in America with his 87th Precinct novel, *Cop Hater* (1956). In *Gideon's Day*, George Gideon is up to his eyes in problems. A child murderer is on the loose in London, a policeman is killed and his home life is in shreds.

In *Gideon's Fire* (1961), Gideon has to deal with a shocking arson attack and a homicidal maniac, while facing further problems at home. Both books show the realistic side of policing in the 1960s — hard work, no home time, and little thanks.

See also: London (John Creasey)
www.johncreasey.co.uk

Ngaio Marsh

One of the great names of the Golden Age of crime fiction along with the likes of Agatha Christie and Dorothy L. Sayers, New Zealand-born Dame Ngaio Marsh wrote a series of finely crafted detective novels featuring Scotland Yard detective (and baronet's son) Roderick Alleyn.

She was a lifelong aficionado of the theatre, and several of her books have a London theatrical background, such as *Death at the Dolphin* (1966), where murder takes place at a restored London theatre, and *Opening Night* (1951), where a struggling New Zealand actor takes a job at the Vulcan Theatre only for the first night to be overshadowed by the death of a member of the cast. *Enter a Murderer* (1935) features a murder committed during a play's London run.

www.fantasticfiction.co.uk/m/ngaio-marsh

Edward Marston

This is a pseudonym of Keith Miles, an incredibly prolific author with several series of novels to his credit. Under this name he wrote an entertaining series of historical crime novels mainly set in Elizabethan London, featuring amateur sleuth Nicholas Bracewell, a man who has sailed with Drake before finding a job at a London theatre company.

In *The Wanton Angel* (1999), new laws mean that only two theatre companies have work. Bracewell and his company face unemployment. A benefactor appears and a new theatre is to be built, but murder intervenes.

In *The Malevolent Comedy* (2005), an actor is murdered during a performance and further tragedies lead Bracewell to believe the playwright may be jinxed.

Marston is also the author of the Christopher Redmayne series, about an architect living in London after the Great Fire of 1666. In *The Parliament House* (2006), an MP is shot outside a party held in his honour. The story of Redmayne's investigation is full of skulduggery, violence and danger, with more than a dash of wit.

In 2011 Marston began another new series, the Home Front Detective series, set in London during World War I. The protagonists are Inspector Harvey Marmion and Sergeant Joe Keedy, and in *Instrument of Slaughter* (2012) they investigate the complicated case of the murder of a conscientious objector.

See also: the West Country, the South and South East, Wales, the North West

www.edwardmarston.com

D.E. Meredith

Formerly the Press Officer for the British Red Cross, Cambridge graduate D.E. Meredith is the author of two excellent, authentic Victorian mysteries, set in the dangerous, filthy, turbulent London of the 1850s.

His debut novel, *Devoured* (2010), features forensic scientist Professor Adolphus Hatton and his assistant

Albert Roumande, whose efforts to unlock the strange death of Lady Bessingham lead to the discovery of a scroll of unpublished letters which, in the wrong hands, could have drastic consequences for Victorian society.

The second novel, *The Devil's Ribbon* (2014), concerns the Anglo-Irish problems of the Victorian era, which led to bombing campaigns in London. Set in the scorching summer of 1858, the book finds Hatton and Roumande investigating a series of vicious murders. All the victims have had a green Fenian ribbon placed on their corpse and when the duo investigate the Irish community, they find shocking conditions have led a proud group of people to consider previously unpalatable actions.

www.demeredith.com

Hal Meredith *et al*

Sexton Blake was originally created by Hal Meredith (real name Harry Blyth) in 1893 as a rival to Sherlock Holmes, who had just been killed off by Sir Arthur Conan Doyle. Like Holmes, he was portrayed as a bachelor detective working from a home in Baker Street, and his young assistant, Tinker, takes the place of Watson.

Since then Sexton Blake stories have been written by many different authors in many different formats, including comic strips, novels, and short stories. The tales have varied from crime and detection to spy stories, but London has always been the main backdrop.

www.thrillingdetective.com/eyes/blake.html

John Milne

John Milne is an experienced TV scriptwriter for crime series (*Silent Witness*, *Waking The Dead, Bergerac)* who has written three novels featuring London private eye Jimmy Jenner, an ex-police inspector who lost a leg in a terrorist bombing.

In *Dead Birds* (1986), he is hired to mind the wife of a boxing manager. When she is killed he is plunged into a world of crime full of contemptuous policemen and wealthy criminals.

In the final novel (*Alive and Kicking*, 1998), Jenner has to investigate his own past, and in particular the life of his brother, a minor criminal whose accidental death thirty years ago occurred while he was linked to a major south London gangster.

www.twbooks.co.uk/authors/johnmilne.html

Dreda Say Mitchell

Born in the East End of London, Dreda Say Mitchell has been a teacher and an educational consultant. She has written for several broadsheet newspapers and is a regular voice on BBC Radio 4 Arts Show *Front Row*. In 2004 her debut novel, *Running Hot*, won the CWA John Creasey Memorial Dagger for the best first novel. Since then she has written four more novels, all set in London.

In *Killer Tune* (2007), rap sensation Lord Tribulation is shocked when his father is murdered in an alleyway. In trying to understand the murder, he is drawn back to 1976, when Notting Hill was in open rebellion and music and politics were brought together in an incendiary mix.

Another host of colourful characters appear in *Hit Girls* (2011). When two children from a gangster family are killed outside their school, the family vows revenge. The culprit is thought to be the psychopathic Paul Bliss, and DI Ricky Smart, the most senior black policeman in the Metropolitan Police, is trying to keep control. However, when Bliss is finally arrested, it is Ricky's beautiful lawyer girlfriend, Daisy, who will defend him in court.

www.dredamitchell.co.uk

Arthur Morrison

Possibly best-remembered for his realistic East End novel *A Child of the Jago* (1896), which highlighted the poverty on the streets of Victorian London, East End-born journalist Arthur Morrison also wrote detective stories.

Though these are difficult to find now the search will be worth it.

His main protagonists were Martin Hewitt, Investigator — a sort of working-class version of Sherlock Holmes — and a dishonest private detective, Arthur Dorrington. The stories were originally published in various London magazines — including some in the *Strand Magazine*, famous for publishing Sherlock Holmes — and were then brought together in various books such as *The Chronicles of Martin Hewitt* (1895) and *The Dorrington Deed Box* (1897).

www.arthurmorrisonsociety.vpweb.co.uk

Barbara Nadel

Born in the East End of London, Barbara Nadel trained as an actress, and later worked in the field of mental health for many years. She used her knowledge and life experience in a short series of books featuring East End undertaker and World War I veteran Francis Hancock.

In October 1940, Francis becomes mixed up in murder and the world of Nazi spies and sympathisers when he is called out to the death of a young Gypsy girl (*After the Mourning,* 2006).

Francis's background as a World War I survivor is explored in *Sure and Certain Death* (2009), when his sister is linked to the deaths of several White Feather Girls — girls who approached men who had not joined up and gave them a white feather, the symbol of cowardice.

In 2012 Nadel launched a new series based on a private detective agency in the twenty-first century East End, run by an ex-policeman named Lee Arnold. In the first novel (*A Private Business*, 2012) the agency provides help for a controversial stand-up comedian who thinks she is being stalked.

www.barbara-nadel.com

G.F. Newman

BAFTA award-winner Gordon Newman has been the scourge of politicians, policemen, judges, prison officers and social workers in a writing career which has spanned forty years. He has challenged readers to think the unthinkable, and opened their eyes to police corruption with novels such as *Sir, You Bastard* (1970) and *Law and Order* (1983), as well as creating TV series such as Judge John Deed.

His first books followed the career of corrupt London policeman Terry Sneed, beginning with *Sir, You Bastard* (1970) and ending with *You Flash Bastard* (aka *The Price*) in 1973. In the original novel DCI Sneed, greedy for power, takes a bribe that brings him nothing but trouble. In desperation, he has to use all his dishonesty to save his career — and his life. The series was instrumental in changing the rose-tinted view that many had of the police at the time.

Later books also poured scorn on the Metropolitan Police and were brutally honest about social problems in the city. *Crime and Punishment* (2009), for example, follows draft-dodger Jack from his poverty-stricken East End upbringing in the 1950s to the height of Thatcherism.

www.fantasticfiction.co.uk/n/g-f-newman

Caro Peacock

This is the pen-name of former BBC correspondent Gillian Linscott, which she uses for a series of Victorian mysteries featuring precocious private investigator Liberty Lane. Set in the early years of the Queen's reign, they highlight Liberty's support of the underdog.

In *Death of a Dancer* (2008), an on-stage row between two performers at The Augustus Theatre in London's West End leads to murder, and Liberty is desperate to prevent the wrong person being sent to the hangman.

In *When the Devil Drives* (2011), Liberty is engaged to prevent a royal scandal involving Prince Albert's brother, and to find a young man's missing fiancée. To her horror she finds that the cases are linked.

See also: the West Country, London (Gillian Linscott)

Mark Pearson

A former TV scriptwriter who worked on shows such as *Holby City* and *The Bill,* Mark Pearson has now written five novels about hard-nosed London copper DI Jack Delaney.

In the first book, *Hard Evidence* (2008), Delaney is shocked when a prostitute is brutally murdered just hours after leaving a frightened message on his answerphone. She was a friend, and Delaney is determined to find her killer. Then a young girl goes missing, and Jack is charged with this case as well. But his tough and rough-edged attitude has annoyed many of his colleagues, and if he puts a foot wrong they will be only too pleased to bury him.

By the fourth book, *Murder Club* (2011), Delaney is more relaxed. He has settled down, and has a young daughter, but an old case comes back to bite him. Michael Robinson is a violent rapist who was attacked in prison and left for dead. Now he has recovered, and is accusing Jack. Somehow Robinson is freed, but when he is found dead everyone starts asking questions that Jack cannot answer.

In 2011 Mark Pearson collaborated with bestselling American author James Patterson to produce *Private London.*

Anne Perry

Born in London, Anne Perry spent part of her childhood in New Zealand, before returning to England in her twenties. Over the last thirty-five years she has written two exceptional series of novels set in Victorian London. The two series are set thirty years apart and are quite different.

One series features Inspector (later Superintendent) Thomas Pitt, a working-class Victorian policeman who has married above himself. The twenty-eighth book in the series was published in 2013. Pitt regularly investigates the crimes of the upper classes, never more so than in *Buckingham Palace Gardens* (2008), when Pitt is summoned to the Palace following the discovery of a mutilated body whose identity could threaten the Prince of Wales.

The other series features a much darker character, London detective William Monk, who loses his memory in a coach accident in the first book (*The Face of a Stranger*, 1990). In later books he has flashbacks which only serve to remind him how much of his past is a mystery to him.

Anne Perry's books often deal with class issues in Victorian society, and sometimes she writes about difficult subjects such as child prostitution and homosexuality. In *Execution Dock* (2009), Monk, now working for the River Police, captures wanted murderer Jericho Phillips but is frustrated when the case against him collapses. When he delves deeper into the case, he discovers that Phillips's tastes were darker than he had imagined.

www.anneperry.co.uk

Mike Phillips

Born in the West Indies, Dr Mike Phillips has lived in London for most of his life. He has been a BBC journalist and broadcaster, and a university lecturer. In addition to non-fiction books on various aspects of race, he has written a number of thoughtful crime novels. He has used his Sam Dean series to assess London, and British society generally, from the point of view of a black migrant. A strong, tenacious character in a harsh world, Dean is not afraid of upsetting the establishment.

In *Blood Rights* (1989), Dean, a streetwise black journalist, is asked to find the daughter of an old college friend, who is now a white Tory MP. When this leads him into the world of drugs and prostitution, Dean finds the world is very much against him.

An Image to Die For (1995) is set in the world of television, as Dean is offered a job as an investigative reporter looking into the murder of a woman and her child. When a member of the TV crew is attacked he is pitched into a terrifying urban nightmare.

www.fantasticfiction.co.uk/p/mike-phillips

Derek Raymond

If *crime noir* has a godfather, then Derek Raymond (the pseudonym of English author Robin Cook — not be confused with the American writer of medical thrillers or the Scottish politician) is probably the man. His five "Factory" novels, published between 1976 and 1993 reached into the darkest parts of the human psyche, and shocked even the most unshockable of readers.

All set in London, they were narrated by an un-named police sergeant working for the Metropolitan Police Department of Unexplained Deaths. His best book is considered to be *I Was Dora Suarez* (1990), in which a prostitute is hacked to pieces in gory detail, and further gruesome events suggest a psychopath may be at work.

www.fantasticfiction.co.uk/r/derek-raymond

Ruth Rendell

Baroness Rendell of Babergh (to give her full title) has had a fifty-year writing career. She has written twenty-four novels featuring solid, dependable Inspector Wexford and around the same number of stand-alone psychological crime novels, with more books under the pen name of Barbara Vine. She has won four CWA Gold Daggers and received the Lifetime Achievement Dagger in 1991.

She has regularly set books in London, chronicling life in the city in her own distinctive way. In *13 Steps Down* (2004), weird loner Mix Cellini moves to Notting Hill to continue his obsession with John Christie, the chilling murderer from 10 Rillington Place. Cellini is also obsessed by supermodel Narissa Nash, and as his fantasies become more startling he begins to resemble Christie in the most frightening of ways.

The Keys to the Street (1996) is set around Regent's Park. A corpse is found on the park's railings, a victim of a murderer who becomes known as The Impaler. It is identified as that of homeless Irishman John Cahill, and the police investigation centres on an elderly dog walker, Leslie Bean. But, as always with Ruth Rendell, there is more to it than meets the eye.

The Vault (2011) is a Wexford novel (this series is mostly set in Sussex), but the action takes place in St John's Wood. Wexford has ostensibly retired, and is spending some time with his daughter in Hampstead. A chance meeting with an ex-colleague leads to him acting as a consultant on a murder mystery when bones and jewellery are found in a drain. Meanwhile Wexford's other daughter has been wounded in a stabbing, and the unravelling of the two cases leads Wexford across the city, and into danger.

See also: the South and South East, East Anglia (Barbara Vine)

www.authors.simonandschuster.com/
Ruth-Rendell/62237729

Kate Rhodes

A Londoner by birth, Kate Rhodes been a university lecturer in Britain and America. She has set her Alice Quentin series deep in her home city. Alice is a psychologist, an attractive, if flawed, character, and her personal issues are a vital part of each book.

In *Crossbones Yard* (2012), Alice discovers a body while out jogging. When the police link the murder to a pair of imprisoned serial killers, they ask her to build a psychological profile of the man they want. Unfortunately he turns out to be far more closely linked to Alice than she would like to believe.

In the follow up, *A Killing of Angels* (2013), a banker is pushed under a tube train, one of a series of murders in a long, hot, London summer. When her friend DI Don Burns asks for help, Alice agrees, becoming involved in the hunt for a killer in London's Square Mile — the City itself, where money counts for everything.

www.katerhodes.org

Mike Ripley

Mike Ripley is a former book critic for the *Daily Telegraph* and lectures on crime writing at Cambridge University. His novels are critically acclaimed and very funny — he has twice won the CWA Last Laugh award. He also writes the Getting Away with Murder column in the *Shots* ezine.

Part private eye, part musician, Fitzroy Maclean Angel is an unusual character who drives a London black cab (called Armstrong) to avoid the congestion charge and gets mixed up in lots of strange adventures when called upon to help by various friends.

In *Angel Touch* (1989), Angel becomes involved in the world of financial scams at the London Stock Exchange, and in *Angels in Arms* (1991) he is entangled in an extraordinary case when an old friend inveigles him into hunting down a shipment of drugs — thus bringing him into contact with a heavy metal band and the unforgettable Lucinda Luger.

www.thedonotpress.com/authors/mikeripley.html

Michael Robotham

Australian by birth, Michael Robotham was a journalist in Australia and the UK (at one time he was senior features writer for the *Mail on Sunday*) before becoming a ghostwriter of celebrity autobiographies and then a fiction writer. Most of his fiction is set in and around London, though Bristol, Somerset and Liverpool have also featured.

He has two main characters, a clinical psychologist (Professor Joe O'Loughlin) and a London detective (Vincent Ruiz). Dark and powerful, the books feature one or the other and often both, and walk the line between crime and thriller (he has twice been shortlisted for the CWA Steel Dagger).

In *Lost* (2005), Ruiz is found in the Thames, lucky to be alive. He has been searching for a missing child, Mickey

Carlyle, but everyone knows that she is dead, and a man is in prison for her murder. Ruiz is under investigation by his own force, but is suffering from amnesia after his ordeal. The Professor has to unravel the story and help Ruiz clear the demons in his head.

In *Say You're Sorry* (2012), O'Loughlin is called in after a double murder takes place in London during a weather-induced blackout. Though a young man is in custody, he shows signs of schizophrenia and there are doubts about his ability to commit the murders. But if he didn't do it, who did?

See also: the West Country
www.michaelrobotham.com

Jacqui Rose

Born in Manchester and brought up in Yorkshire, Jacqui Rose has nevertheless lived in London long enough to allow her to bring the city to life in her contemporary gangland novels. Her first novel, *Taken*, was published in 2012.

Trapped (2013) is a sort of Soho love story, following the careers of Maggie Donaldson and Johnny Taylor, who grew up in different crime families but committed the cardinal sin — they fell in love. Maggie's violent father has always hated the Taylors, a vendetta based on a secret that could endanger Maggie and Johnny's lives.
www.jacquirose.com

Leigh Russell

After a career teaching English, Leigh Russell had her first crime novel, *Cut Short*, published in 2009. It was nominated for the CWA New Blood Dagger, and two more followed, all set in the Home Counties and featuring the wonderfully realistic DI Geraldine Steel.

In *Death Bed* (2011), Geraldine is reassigned to a job with the Metropolitan Police, and the series continued with a London backdrop. This novel features a gruesome killer nicknamed "The Dentist". Geraldine has to balance a difficult race-related case with the problems of settling into her new role.

Stop Dead (2012) has a very high body count, as Geraldine faces a baffling case where the only available DNA evidence points to two people — one who has been a prisoner for twenty years, and the other a woman who died two years ago.

See also: the South and South East
www.leighrussell.co.uk

Mark Sanderson

After his partner's death from cancer, journalist Mark Sanderson wrote a moving memoir called *Wrong Rooms* (2002). More recently he has written two crime novels set in late 1930s London.

In the first (*Snow Hill*, 2009), journalist John Steadman gets a tip-off about a missing policeman that leads him into a horrific world of homosexual brothels, rent boys and bodies on meat hooks. Steadman narrowly escapes with his life, and reappears in *The Whispering Gallery* (2012), which begins with him watching as a man falls to his death from the Whispering Gallery in St Paul's Cathedral.

www.harpercollins.co.uk/Authors/8284/
mark-sanderson

Lloyd Shepherd

Lloyd Shepherd is a journalist and digital product manager who has worked for a variety of organisations including the BBC, Yahoo, Channel 4 and the *Financial Times*.

The English Monster (2012) is an extraordinary story, moving from the Ratcliffe Highway Murders in London 1811 to an Elizabethan sea voyage to West Africa, and back again. At the heart of it is Thames River Constable Charles Horton, who spends his life policing the dark, twisted streets of Wapping, trying to solve the mystery of the horrific murders.

Horton reappears in the follow-up, *The Poisoned Island* (2013), investigating the ransacking of a ship full of botanical specimens, the murder of some of its crew, and the possible involvement of a senior member of the Royal Society.

www.lloydshepherd.com

Lynn Shepherd

While working for Guinness, Lynn Shepherd devised the "Water of Life" environmental programme which has brought clean drinking water to millions in Africa. She is also a clever crime novelist, giving a new twist to nineteenth-century literary characters and novels.

In *Tom-All-Alones* (2012), Charles Maddox, great-nephew of the detective from her first novel *Murder at Mansfield Park*, is hired by Edward Tulkinghorn (the formidable lawyer of *Bleak House*) to discover the truth behind a series of anonymous letters being sent to his most wealthy and influential clients. Unfortunately this turns into far more dangerous commission than had been expected, leading Maddox into the depths of a Dickensian underworld.

A Treacherous Likeness (2013) sees Maddox finding a new client — the only surviving son of Percy and Mary Shelley. Following a surprise revelation Maddox starts to query the suicide of Shelley's first wife, Harriet.

www.lynn-shepherd.com

Stav Sherez

When he was shortlisted for the CWA John Creasey Award for his first novel, *The Devil's Playground* (2004), it was clear that Stav Sherez was a writer to watch. He has recently been nominated for the 2013 Theakstons CWA Gold Dagger for *A Dark Redemption* (2012).

In 2012 the latter novel started a new series featuring two London detectives, the careless, undisciplined DI Jack Carrigan and recently demoted DS Geneva Miller, who have to delve deeply into London's immigrant communities when they investigate the rape and murder of a Ugandan student.

Carrigan and Miller return in *Eleven Days* (2013) to investigate an arson attack which killed ten nuns, and a mysterious eleventh victim. As it is just before Christmas, their superiors want the case closed before the holiday, but as the duo delve into the mystery they discover links to South America, which give a whole new slant to the affair.

www.fantasticfiction.co.uk/s/stav-sherez

Gillian Slovo

Gillian Slovo was born in South Africa but educated in Britain. She is best known for her acute political novels, but she also wrote a short London-based crime series early in her career featuring feminist detective/reporter Kate Baeier.

In *Death Comes Staccato* (1987), Kate is acting as minder for the musician daughter of a wealthy woman when a body is found after a performance. By *Catnap* (1994) Kate has become a war correspondent. Returning to London she is shocked to be the victim of a mugging. When she investigates it, she finds links to the death of a long-dead ex-lover.

www.fantasticfiction.co.uk/s/gillian-slovo

Simon Spurrier

On the one hand Simon Spurrier is a comic writer who has written stories for *Marvel*, *D.C.*, *Avatar* and *Judge Dredd*. On the other he is a crime novelist with a brash, cynical style all his own.

His first novel, *Contract* (2007) was the unusual, rather gory, story of a contract killer whose victims came back to haunt him, and his second (*A Serpent Uncoiled*, 2011) centred on wry, vulnerable, drugged-up ex-gangland enforcer Dan Shaper, whose efforts to go straight as a private investigator bring him to the attentions of his old masters, with dreadful results.

www.simonspurrier.co.uk

Linda Stratmann

Although born in Leicester, Linda Stratmann's main affiliation has always been with the city of London, where she now lives. She is the author of many true crime books,and has also written a series of fine crime novels set in Victorian Bayswater.

Central character Frances Doughty first appears as a nineteen-year-old in *The Poisonous Seed* (2011), becoming an unwilling sleuth when her father is unjustly accused of poisoning a customer of his chemist shop.

Frances then takes up the job full-time and her first case is *The Daughters of Gentlemen* (2012), when her investigations into strange events at the Bayswater Academy for the Education of Young Ladies leads to the early suffragette movement, political intrigue and murder.

www.lindastratmann.com

Andrew Taylor

Andrew Taylor is one of the great crime writers. His long career began in 1982 with *Caroline Miniscule*, which won the CWA John Creasey Award for that year, and in 2009 he was awarded the CWA Cartier Diamond Dagger for outstanding contribution to crime writing. He also won the CWA Ellis Peters Historical Dagger in 2001 and 2003.

The masterful Roth Trilogy uses a London setting for the first two books. In *The Four Last Things* (1997) it is a 1990s London of dilapidated churches, rain-spattered streets, weed-filled gardens and lost respectability. A child has disappeared, and the ensuing drama is both moving and somewhat horrifying.

In *The Judgement of Strangers* (1998), the setting moves to the London suburbs in 1970, and centres on a widowed, sexually obsessed parish priest who brings home a new wife, leading to seething passion and violence. The final part of this exceptionally powerful psychological work is

The Office of the Dead (2000), which moves outside the capital to the cathedral town of Rossington in 1958, and links the two central families from the previous novels.

Several of his stand-alone novels use London as a setting (at least in part). A good example is *Bleeding Heart Square* (2008), which is set in a crumbling London backwater, a place of sanctuary for Lydia Langstone. To help settle down after a disastrous marriage she has turned to the man lodging at Number Seven — Captain Ingleby-Lewis. But there is an air of mystery about the place, and Lydia soon finds that asking questions is dangerous.

See also: the West Country (Andrew Saville), Wales
www.andrew-taylor.co.uk

Josephine Tey

Back in 1990 the CWA proclaimed that *The Daughter of Time* (1951) by Josephine Tey (pseudonym of Elizabeth Mackintosh) was the greatest crime novel of all. It features Inspector Alan Grant of Scotland Yard, who is laid up following a spinal injury. While recuperating, to alleviate the boredom and depression to which he is susceptible, he becomes interested in the historical mystery of Richard III and the Princes in the Tower. Using his intellect and experience, plus the services of an American researcher, he decides to try to piece together the full story. In doing so Grant examines the physiognomy of the characters involved, and considers how truth and myth can become entwined, even when there is no evidence.

Inspector Grant appears in six mysteries altogether. In the first (*The Man in the Queue*, 1929), he investigates the apparently motiveless murder of a man in a London theatre queue.

See also: Scotland: Highlands and Islands
www.josephinetey.net

Leslie Thomas

Formerly a reporter who covered such major events as the funeral of Winston Churchill, Leslie Thomas has been a novelist since the publication of *The Virgin Soldiers* in 1966.

He has written four wonderfully funny crime novels about Dangerous Davies, known as "The Last Detective" because either he was the last person his superiors would want on a case, or the case was so risky that no one else would want it.

Davies is a lowly CID officer in Willesden (later a private detective) and in the original novel *Dangerous Davies: The Last Detective* (1976) he solves, with the help of his drinking companion Mod, an old murder which has been neglected for years. As with all of Thomas's novels it is full of wonderful characters and the descriptions of London in the 1970s are evocative.

By the last book in the series (*Dangerous Davies and the Lonely Heart*, 1998) Davies has retired and set up a business as a private detective in North London, investigating the death of a woman who replied to lonely hearts advertisements.

www.fantasticfiction.co.uk/t/leslie-thomas

Mark Timlin

In a long career, Mark Timlin has written more than twenty novels under various names. Once a roadie for T Rex and The Who, he is best known for the Sharman novels, which were adapted for television in the 1990s with Clive Owen in the title role. Sharman is an ex-policeman who is now working as a wise-cracking South London private eye.

In *Ashes by Now* (1993), he agrees to help a convicted rapist clear his name, only to find his past life as a copper catching up with him. Then, in *Falls the Shadow* (1993), he is hired by Sunset Radio to discover who is sending unpleasant presents to one of their DJs. The prime suspects are a group of neo-Nazis, but there is also an obsessive fan to contend with.

www.marktimlin.co.uk

Peter Turnbull

Yorkshireman Peter Turnbull has a writing career going back more than thirty years, and has written three series of police procedurals as well as a number of stand-alone novels.

He started his Harry Vicary series in 2009 with *Improving the Silence*, in which Vicary and his team investigate corruption and murder within their own ranks after an unearthed skeleton proves to be that of an undercover police officer who disappeared thirty years ago.

In *The Garden Party* (2012), Vicary and his colleagues are thrust into the vicious world of London gangsters when the charred bones of two men are found. There are links to an infamous gangland garden party where two men were known to have disappeared.

See also: the North East, Scotland: Glasgow and the West of Scotland

www.fantasticfiction.co.uk/t/peter-turnbull

Cathi Unsworth

Originally a music journalist on the celebrated weekly music paper *Sounds, C*athi Unsworth has used her knowledge of the music scene in London over many years to give a superbly evocative background to her crime novels.

The Not Knowing (2005) is set in the early 1990s, when film director Jon Jackson vanishes after giving an important lecture. His body is found two weeks later in a Camden lock-up, the murder site being eerily reminiscent of the final scene of his greatest movie. Alternative journalist Diana Kemp wanted to write about crime, but finds herself intimately involved with one, as she tries to make sense of the disturbing events that surround her.

In *Bad Penny Blues* (2009), a young policeman stumbles upon the body of a murdered prostitute, and his search for her murderer leads into the darkest corners of Soho in the Swinging Sixties. It was loosely based on real series of killings known as the "Jack the Stripper" murders.

www.cathiunsworth.co.uk

Edgar Wallace

One of the few writers to rival John Creasey for his output, Edgar Wallace was one of the great crime writers of the early twentieth century. He started his working life at the age of eleven, in 1886, selling newspapers on Ludgate Circus. When he died, aged fifty-seven, he had written bestsellers in England and America, as well as plays and screenplays — he even co-wrote the screenplay for *King Kong*.

His novels used a wide variety of locations, but several were set in London. In *The Crimson Circle* (1922) a league of blackmailers is terrorising the city, while in *The Gaunt Stranger* (1928) London is terrorised by a masked murderer.

When the Gangs Came to London (1932) is a sort of early version of the film *Mona Lisa*, with Chicago gangs taking over the city and shots being fired in Parliament.

www.edgarwallace.org

Tim Weaver

Successful magazine journalist Tim Weaver came to prominence with his first David Raker novel, *Chasing The Dead*, in 2010. Mary Town's son disappeared six years ago, and his body was found in a fatal car crash five years later. However, his mother claims to have seen him on the street, and asks missing persons investigator David Raker for help. Unfortunately he uncovers more than he bargained for.

In *Vanished* (2012), he investigates the case of Sam Wren, who got onto a London Underground train one morning and was never seen again. It seems that Sam

has another life, and as Raker reaches out for the truth, he must enter the depths of the Tube system to find it.
www.timweaverbooks.com

Kate Williams

Historian Kate Williams is a writer, TV and radio presenter who has appeared on many programmes such as *Newsnight, BBC Breakfast* and *Woman's Hour.*

Her first historical crime novel was published in 2012, and is set in 1840, a time when London was troubled by economic problems, disease and crime.

The Pleasures of Men (2012) tells the story of Catherine Sorgeuil, a young woman who lives in Spitalfields with her uncle, and becomes obsessed by the grisly murders being perpetrated in the city by a killer nicknamed The Man of Crows.
www.fantasticfiction.co.uk/w/kate-williams

Laura Wilson

Currently the crime fiction reviewer for the *Guardian* and editor of *Crime Review,* Laura Wilson has been nominated for many crime fiction awards, winning the Ellis Peters Historical Dagger for *Stratton's War* (2007). This was the first book in a series of London-based novels featuring policeman Ted Stratton, an intelligent, humorous father of two who works in the West End. In this novel, it is June 1940 and Stratton is called in when a silent movie star is found dead, having apparently committed suicide. Stratton's investigations lead him into the murky, impenetrable world of covert operations, gangsters and MI5.

The third in the series, *A Capital Crime* (2011), is set in the war-ruined London of 1949, when Stratton arrests a murderer, only to discover, months later, that he may have sent an innocent man to the gallows. A murderer is still at large, and Stratton is afraid that he will strike again.

Apart from the Stratton series, London is also the setting for a number of Wilson's stand-alone novels, such as *A Little Death* (1999), in which the death of three elderly people in an unexplained shooting incident opens up links to a notorious murder that took place many years before.

www.laura-wilson.co.uk

Jacqueline Winspear

Though she now lives in America, Jacqueline Winspear is English. She is the author of the Maisie Dobbs series, set in London and Kent between the wars. Maisie is a strong-willed, spirited woman who has set herself up as a private investigator. Many of her cases have links back to the horrors of World War I, in which she was a nurse.

In *Birds of a Feather* (2004), Maisie is in Dulwich in 1930, searching for a runaway heiress. As she delves into the case she discovers a link to a recent murder, and the shocking deaths of several of the heiress's friends. The truth starts to emerge, but it takes Maisie back to the Great War, and the appalling scenes that she has tried to forget.

Elegy for Eddie (2012) finds Maisie in Lambeth, investigating the death of horseman Eddie Pettit on behalf of the costermongers (sellers of fruit and vegetables from barrows on London streets). What had looked like a terrible accident proves to be anything but that, and there are powerful men in the city who will do whatever it takes to prevent Maisie from uncovering the real truth.

See also: the South and South East

www.jacquelinewinspear.com

P.B. Yuill

Gordon M. Williams was a Booker-shortlisted author and Terry Venables was an England footballer (and later England manager) who played for Spurs, Chelsea and Queens Park Rangers between 1960 and 1974. Together this unusual duo co-wrote three crime novels in the seventies under the pen name P.B. Yuill.

The novels were all set in London. They featured ex-cop

turned hard-nosed private eye James Hazell, and were later turned into a TV series (*Hazell*).In *Hazell and the Menacing Jester* (1976), Hazell becomes involved with gangster "Moneybags" Beevers and his gorgeous wife — a move which proves to be a dreadful mistake.

www.fantasticfiction.co.uk/y/p-b-yuill

Ten Recommended Reads

1: *Lifeless* by Mark Billingham (2005)

2: *Now You See Me* by S.J. Bolton (2010)

3: *Dead Innocent* by Stephen Davison (2011)

4: *Clubbed to Death* by Ruth Dudley Edwards (1992)

5: *Blood From A Stone* by Christopher Fowler (2008)

6: *A Damned Serious Business* by Graham Ison (1990)

7: *The Last 10 Seconds* by Simon Kernick (2010)

8: *Gideon's Day* by J.J. Marric (1955)

9: *Sir, You Bastard* by G.F. Newman (1970)

10: *A Dark Redemption* by Stav Sherez (2012)

REGION FOUR
England — East Anglia

Norfolk is a desolate and beautiful place. It is often said that its landscape is the sky because the flat, marshy terrain offers a spectacular view of the wide, ever-changing sky. Norfolk is extremely rich in archaeology, from Stone Age remains (4000–2500 years BC) to the Second World War graves recently uncovered through coastal erosion. Perhaps because it has been inhabited for so long, Norfolk is said to be full of ghosts.
ELLY GRIFFITHS, **from her website**
(www.ellygriffiths.co.uk)

Though it generally includes only Norfolk, Suffolk and Cambridgeshire, for the purposes of this book I have extended East Anglia to take in the northern part of Essex, which is so very different to the part that borders London. If the whole area has a defining characteristic, it is being flat. There are few hills of any note, and areas like the Fens and the Broads are very low-lying, with a considerable amount of water in one form or another — rivers, canals, and marsh-lands. Norwich and Cambridge are the only major cities, but there are the large towns of Ipswich and Ely, as well as smaller market towns and quiet, sleepy hamlets.

Authors whose work is synonymous with the area include P.D. James, who uses both Norfolk and Suffolk, Sophie Hannah (Cambridge), Dick Francis (Newmarket), Jim Kelly (Ely) and Elly Griffiths (Norfolk). Dorothy L. Sayers grew up in Huntingdonshire and died in Witham, Essex, Margery Allingham lived in North Essex at Tolleshunt D'Arcy, and several authors are graduates of Cambridge University, including Susanna Gregory.

Jane Adams

Once the lead singer in a folk-rock band, Jane Adams turned to writing after a variety of jobs and is now a Fellow of the Royal Literary Fund. She has written four distinct series, and her books are often set in either East Anglia or her native Midlands. Her style has a considerable psychological aspect with occasional overtones of the paranormal.

The first book in the DI Mike Croft series, *The Greenway* (1995), was her debut novel, and finds Croft investigating a child's disappearance from a mysterious area of East Anglian woodland. It transpires that, twenty years before, another child vanished from the same area, and that the only person to link the two cases can remember nothing, her memories buried deep in her mind. The book was shortlisted for the CWA John Creasey Award and is based on the author's recollections of an ancient sheltered pathway in the village of Happisburgh.

The third in the series, *Fade to Grey* (1998), finds Croft faced with a shocking case. A rapist is stalking blonde women on the streets of Norwich. The book is unusual in that it is told from the perspectives of a number of characters, including the rapist himself.

See also: the West Country (Jane A. Adams), the Midlands
www.janeadamsauthor.wordpress.com

Margery Allingham

A contemporary of Agatha Christie, Margery Allingham is acknowledged as one of the great names of the Golden Age. Her Albert Campion novels, mainly written between 1929 and 1965, were set all over East Anglia, and she often used Essex as a backdrop because not only did she live in the county, she spent much of her childhood there.

The island in *Mystery Mile* (1930) is based on the little-known Mersea Island off the north Essex coast (not far from where she lived), and Pontisbright, which crops up in several novels, is thought to be modelled on the village of Chappel near Colchester.

Suffolk is also a regular setting, as in *The Crime at Black Dudley* (1929), the novel that introduced amateur sleuth Albert Campion. The host of a house party dies in mysterious circumstances, and Dr George Abbershaw, a guest, is suspicious when asked to sign the death certificate. Campion is also a guest, and helps Abbershaw to discover the truth in a classic novel which features strange rituals, secret passages and a variety of suspects.

The Case of the Late Pig (1937) is set in the same county, as Campion investigates the odd circumstances surrounding the death of former school bully "Pig" Peters, who had made his life such a misery in their schooldays.
See also: London
www.margeryallingham.org.uk

Kate Atkinson

Kate Atkinson was already regarded as a writer of the highest quality when she turned her hand to crime fiction with *Case Histories* in 2004, which was nominated for both the Orange Prize and the Whitbread Prize.

Case Histories introduces the laconic former police inspector Jackson Brodie, now working as a private eye in Cambridge. During a long, hot summer he reinvestigates three old cases while coming to terms with massive changes in his own life. Though apparently disparate, the cases (a missing child, a violent unsolved murder and a shocking domestic death) become linked, and Jackson's work stirs up a stalker who becomes increasingly violent.

So far Atkinson has written three further Jackson Brodie novels, two set in Edinburgh and one in Leeds. All the books showcase her vibrant prose and humour, and her ability to observe and understand contemporary society. She was awarded the MBE in 2011 for services to literature.

See also: the North East
www.kateatkinson.co.uk

Jo Bannister

The editor of The *County Down Times* in Ireland until she retired to concentrate on writing, Jo Bannister is the author of over thirty crime novels, including four different series and a number of stand-alone novels.

The Castlemere series of police procedurals are based on the fictional city of Castlemere, located between Cambridge and Bedford. They consist of seven books featuring a regular team of police officers.

In *Broken Lines* (1998), DSgt Cal Donovan finds himself fighting for his career and even his life after he falls foul of a family of career criminals, while in *No Birds Sing* (1996) Donovan goes undercover to infiltrate a gang of thieves, only to find that it was far easier to get in than to get out alive. Meanwhile his colleague DI Liz Graham sets herself up as bait to trap a vicious rapist.

www.fantasticfiction.co.uk/b/jo-bannister

Simon Beckett

Sheffield-based Simon Beckett now has several successful crime novels to his credit, most featuring forensic scientist Dr David Hunter. The first of these, *The Chemistry of Death* (2006), is a high-class whodunit, and the authentic, if grisly, forensic detail is a hallmark of all this author's work.

Hunter, acting as a locum doctor while trying to forget a devastating personal tragedy, becomes involved with the disappearance and murder of a local woman.. The killing has baffled the local constabulary, and Hunter's expertise is called upon. When another woman vanishes, Hunter is drawn into a complex case — a serial killer is at work in rural Norfolk.

See also: the West Country, Scotland: Highlands and Islands

www.simonbeckett.com

Francis Beeding

A pseudonym used by co-writers John Palmer and former House of Commons librarian Hilary St George Saunders, Francis Beeding wrote a number of crime novels in the 1930s and 1940s.

Death Walks in Eastrepps (1931) is set in and around Cromer in Norfolk, and is one of the earliest novels to feature a multiple murderer (or serial killer, as we would call him today). It has an excellent courtroom scene and a very good twist.

www.fantasticfiction.co.uk/b/francis-beeding

S.J. Bolton

Lancastrian Sharon Bolton has set the other books in her Lacey Flint series in London, but *Dead Scared* (2012) is situated specifically in Cambridge. A series of bizarre student suicides (using methods such as self-decapitation and self-immolation) leads DI Mark Joesbury to conclude that there is a major problem at the university. He sends DC Lacey Flint undercover to investigate. The only person at the university who knows Lacey's secret is counsellor/psychiatrist Evi Oliver, and they both begin to experience frightening dreams and appalling visions as they get try to get closer to the truth.

See also: London, Scotland: Highlands and Islands

www.sjbolton.com

Alison Bruce

Alison Bruce's first DC Gary Goodhew book, *Cambridge Blue*, appeared in 2009. Goodhew is a young Cambridge-based policeman who is given the chance to work on a murder investigation for the first time after he stumbles upon the body of a young woman on Midsummer Common. When there is a second murder, Goodhew realises that he must go out on a limb to uncover the truth, even if it costs him his job.

The series has gone from strength to strength, as can be seen with the fourth book, *The Silence* (2012), in which Goodhew is faced with an unpleasant murder, a series of suicides and links to an early case in his career which had had a profound effect on him. The books make a feature of Cambridge, a real city of contrasts, with a mix of ethnicity and the clash of town and gown — vast wealth alongside real deprivation.

www.alisonbruce.dreamhosters.com

Tania Carver

The pseudonym of husband and wife team Martyn and Linda Waites, Tania Carver is the author of a series of gruesome, unflinching, gripping crime novels set in Colchester. An attractive town with a long history, it makes an excellent backdrop to this series of heart-stopping books.

With the help of criminal psychologist Marina Esposito, DI Phil Brennan deals with some horrific killers, including, in *The Surrogate* (2009), someone who murders pregnant women then removes the unborn child, and in *The Creeper* (2010), a stalker who has progressed to murder and torture.

See also: North East (Martyn Waites)

www.taniacarver.com

Kate Charles

American-born but a long-term anglophile, Kate Charles has used England as the setting for her books. A passionate lover of English churches, all of her novels are connected to religion in some way. Her series about Norfolk solicitor and amateur sleuth David Middleton-Brown were written in the 1990s, and featured topics which were relevant to the Church of England at the time.

In *The Snares of Death* (1992), the vicar of St Mary the Virgin is murdered, and when the police arrest a suspect, Middleton-Brown is convinced that they have arrested the wrong man, while in *A Dead Man Out of Mind* (1994) he becomes embroiled in the difficult topic of women priests when a local vicar chooses to appoint a woman to replace a curate killed in a robbery.

www.katecharles.com

Brian Cooper

Former Derbyshire schoolteacher Brian Cooper wrote nine crime novels between 1991 and 2006, all set in post-war Norfolk. The series features retired detective John Lubbock and serving policeman Mike Tench, who finds that the "copper's nose" of the older man is very helpful in cases that range from a botched robbery in the terrible winter of 1947 (*The Cross of San Vincente,*1991) to a double murder in the aftermath of the great storm of 1953 (*Out With the Tide*, 2006).

www.fantasticfiction.co.uk/c/brian-cooper

Ruth Dugdall

Former probation officer Ruth Dugdall has used her professional knowledge to great effect in two powerful psychological novels about probation officer Cate Austin. The novels are set in Suffolk, including locations such as Lowestoft and Felixstowe, and are unflinching in the way they deal with subjects such as rape, incest, suicide and even cannibalism.

She won the CWA Debut Dagger award for *The Woman Before Me* (2010), in which Cate has to decide the fate of a woman who is ready to be released into society. Rose Wilks was imprisoned for the murder of her best friend's child. Now she is due for parole — but is she psychologically ready, and how has she coped with the prison system? Cate must decide this, and in doing so must try to understand what really happened in Rose's past. The book pulls no punches in its descriptions of women's prisons, obsession and loss.

In the follow-up, *The Sacrificial Man* (2011), Cate has to recommend a sentence in a case of Alice Mariani, who has been arrested following the death of her boyfriend, who had advertised on the internet for help in committing suicide.

www.ruthdugdall.com

Malcolm Forsythe

Malcolm Forsythe wrote seven crime novels between 1991 and 2001, all featuring DCI Millson and DSgt Scobie of Essex CID.

In *The Book Lady* (1993), they investigate the strange case of a respectable librarian with the county's mobile library service, who has been found dead on a riverbank near Colchester. They find that she offered more than books on her visits, and that her lifestyle had led her into danger.

In *Only Living Witness* (2000), the pair are called in when a builder unearths a murder victim in a house at Great Yeldham near Halstead. The autopsy shows that the man was killed twenty-five years earlier, forcing Millson to delve deep into the past.

www.fantasticfiction.co.uk/f/malcolm-forsythe

Dick Francis

Former champion jockey Dick Francis made a second career as a crime novelist, with over forty books to his name written between 1962 and 2009. All set in the world of horse-racing, his novels have had international success. Newmarket in Suffolk is synonymous with flat-racing, and has featured in many of his books. The National Horse Racing Museum in Newmarket now runs "Dick Francis" tours.

In *Dead Heat* (2007, written with his son Felix), celebrity chef Max Moreton investigates foul play after food in his Michelin-starred restaurant is poisoned on the eve of the 2000 Guineas race, while *Bonecrack* (1971) tells the story of Neil Griffon, who is abducted and threatened by an international gangster who wants him to train his son (a jockey) to win the Epsom derby.

Whip Hand (1979) won the CWA Gold Dagger and is the second book to feature one-handed ex-jockey Sid Halley, who is on the trail of a syndicate of racehorse owners who will stop at nothing to win.

See also: the West Country, the South and South East
www.dickfrancis.com

Jonathan Gash

For over twenty years Bolton-born John Grant (in real life a doctor specialising in tropical diseases) used the pseudonym Jonathan Gash to write a popular series of crime novels featuring rogue antique dealer Lovejoy. Many of the early novels were set in the border country of Suffolk and Essex, as was the BBC TV series which featured Ian McShane in the title role. Later novels often see Lovejoy venturing onto foreign shores.

In the books, Lovejoy himself is a scruffy, unloveable rogue, working various antiques scams across East Anglia, assisted by various friends including Tinker and Eric. Though more bending the law than breaking it, he often finds himself involved with unsavoury characters who break the law with impunity, and threaten either Lovejoy himself or those close to him.

In *The Judas Pair* (1977) — which won the CWA John Creasey Debut Dagger — Lovejoy is approached by a client who wants him to buy a pair of rare duelling pistols, sending him on the trail of a callous murderer, while in *Spend Game* (1980) an old friend is killed in a car crash that turns out to have been no accident. It may have had more to do with some antiques that he had recently acquired.

Pearlhanger (1985) sees Lovejoy searching for an antiques dealer who has vanished while on a buying trip. With a host of minor characters and some fascinating information about the making (and faking) of pearls, it's a classic Lovejoy story.

See also: the North West

www.fantasticfiction.co.uk/g/jonathan-gash

Susanna Gregory

This is the pen-name of Liz Cruwys, a marine biologist and Cambridge academic who has a flourishing writing career to add to her previous work as a West Yorkshire police officer, environmental consultant, and expert on Arctic and Antarctic mammals.

As a novelist she has written three series of historical murder mysteries, the most extensive of which features Matthew Bartholomew, Physician of Michaelhouse College in fourteenth-century Cambridge.

The series begins in 1348 as the Great Plague arrives in Britain. *A Plague on Both Your Houses* (1996) opens with the death of a number of scholars, including the current Master of Michaelhouse. Bartholomew is determined to find out why, even against the wishes of the university authorities. With the arrival of the Black Death adding to his problems, Bartholomew finds he is embroiled in events which lead him to question everything, even the innocence of his own family.

In *A Vein of Deceit* (2010), the College is in turmoil, having been found to be bankrupt. When the Master of the College is attacked and a pair of valuable chalices are stolen, Bartholomew has to act fast to save the College's reputation.

See also: London, Wales (Simon Beaufort)

www.susannagregory.com

Elly Griffiths

The setting of the bleak, forbidding North Norfolk coast is central to most of Elly Griffith's superb series of novels

A Matthew Bartholomew Chronicle

Susanna Gregory

A Plague on Both Your Houses

featuring Ruth Galloway, Head of Forensic Archaeology at the University of North Norfolk, and DCI Harry Nelson. The landscape, including the isolated, eerie Saltmarsh where Ruth lives, is a constant presence in the books, and the author uses an interesting mix of real and imaginary locations.

In *The Crossing Places* (2009), Ruth is called in by DCI Nelson when a child's bones are found on a local beach. Nelson is wrong in his assumption that he has found the bones of a missing girl about whom he has been receiving bizarre letters, but when another child goes missing Ruth's archaeological knowledge proves that the letter writer may well be involved after all.

In *The House at Sea's End* (2011) a team from the University are investigating coastal erosion when they uncover six bodies. Ruth is called in to help, and proves that they are from the time of World War II. When an old wartime plan to stop German invasion is uncovered, and a German reporter is killed, it is clear that Ruth and Harry have stumbled on to a secret that someone is very anxious to protect.

www.ellygriffiths.co.uk

Sophie Hannah

Sophie Hannah is the daughter of the children's writer and novelist Adele Geras. In addition to her crime-writing career she is also a respected poet. Her first crime novel (*Little Face*) was published in 2006, since when her work has gone from strength to strength. She specialises in psychological crime, often involving ordinary people in unnerving situations which spiral out of control after some perfectly normal event.

Her books are set in and around Cambridge, with the involvement of various officers from the fictional Spilling CID. DC Simon Waterhouse and DS Charlie Zailer meet in the first book, and their relationship is a subplot in most of the others.

The plots revolve around awkward situations such as the mistaken identity of very young children (*Little Face*,

2006), confessing to a crime that hasn't happened (*The Other Half Lives* (2009), seeing a body during an online "virtual tour" of a house for sale (*Lasting Damage* (2011), and sharing a room with a terrified stranger (*The Carrier*, 2013). In all the books, the plots are carefully constructed, and the tension is ratcheted up with every chapter.

Perhaps the most powerful of all is *A Room Swept White* (2010), in which Fliss Benson is caught up in a murder enquiry when making a TV film about miscarriages of justice against women who have been accused of killing their children. One of the women central to the film is murdered, and both women have received a similar mysterious message. As the police investigate, the moral maze deepens for all concerned.

www.sophiehannah.com

John Harvey

Though best known for his Resnick series set in and around Nottingham, John Harvey has used Cambridge and the Fens as the main backdrop for two thought-provoking novels featuring the Cambridgeshire police officers DI Will Grayson, who is generally unsympathetic, and DS Helen Walker, who is more likeable if slightly strange.

In *Gone to Ground* (2007), Grayson and Walker have to track down the murderer of a gay Cambridge lecturer, Stephen Bryan. He is writing a biography of a 1950s film star, Stella Leonard, who was killed in a mysterious car crash. Stephen's sister is convinced there is a link between the deaths, but as she and the police investigate, they stir up a maelstrom of violence and fear as they uncover a web of old family secrets.

In the second book, *Far Cry* (2009), the duo face an emotional case concerning missing children, a recently-released paedophile and the rights of suspects where violence to children is concerned.

See also: London, the Midlands

www.mellotone.co.uk

Alan Hunter

The long-running George Gently series of police procedurals originally began in the 1950s with *Gently Does It* (1955). For the next forty years Alan Hunter continued to produce a book a year, all featuring Gently, and usually set in East Anglia, where the author was an antiquarian bookseller. Gently began as a Chief Inspector, and was later promoted to Chief Superintendent covering a much wider area — indeed later stories take him to London, Scotland, Wales and France.

In *Gently at a Gallop* (1971), Gently investigates the strange death of local brewer Charles Berney, who has been found savaged and trampled to death by a horse. The more he delves into the man's life, the more bizarre the case becomes.

In the penultimate novel, *Over Here* (1998), a party of American servicemen revisiting their old airfield discover a body which is linked to events of fifty years before, when life was so very different.

Some years after the author's death the BBC started to televise some books from the series with Martin Shaw in the lead role. Strangely, they moved the setting of the series from Norfolk to Newcastle, and changed many of the characters.

www.fantasticfiction.co.uk/h/alan-hunter

P.D. James

East Anglia features regularly in P.D. James's novels, as she has a long-standing affinity with the area, having holidayed in Suffolk as a child, and been educated at Cambridge High School for Girls. She also has a holiday home in Southwold.

Her books are inevitably elegant, intelligent and tightly plotted, with many surprises and red herrings. Both *Unnatural Causes* (1967) and *Death in Holy Orders* (2001) are set near Dunwich in Suffolk and are full of marvellous descriptions of the East Anglian countryside.

In the former, Superintendent Dalgliesh has his holiday plans shattered when a local crime writer is found dead in a dinghy, while in the latter, an older Commander Adam Dalgliesh is called in by the wealthy father of a theological student whose body has been found near St Anselm's Theological College. Though written more than thirty years apart, both are powerful examples of the author's best work.

Two other fine examples of her work are set in East Anglia. *Death of an Expert Witness* (1977) is set in a forensic science laboratory in the Fens where a disliked senior biologist has been found clubbed to death. When a second murder takes place during the investigation, Dalgleish has to use all his powers to prevent further bloodshed.

Dalgliesh returns to Norfolk in *Devices and Desires* (1989). Having retreated to the area for a break from London, he finds a body while walking on a local beach. Thus he becomes involved in the hunt for a serial killer known as The Whistler, which leads him to a nearby nuclear power station.

See also: the West Country, London
www.randomhouse.com/features/pdjames

Jim Kelly

Formerly a journalist (at one time he was the Education Correspondent for the *Financial Times*) Jim Kelly is now a respected crime novelist, with two series to his name. All his books are set in East Anglia: the Philip Dryden series in and around the beautiful cathedral city of Ely, and the Shaw and Valentine stories in Norfolk. His descriptions of the countryside, the small market towns, the remote hamlets and flat, featureless fens combine to provide a distinctive style for all his novels.

Philip Dryden is a local journalist in Ely who through his work on the local paper, *The Crow*, is drawn into investigating various murder mysteries, in which he is aided and abetted by his driver, Humph. The first in the series, *The Water Clock* (2002), was nominated for a CWA John Creasey Award. It begins with Dryden watching as a car winched out of a frozen river yields a badly mutilated body. This is soon linked to a second body found in Ely Cathedral, and then to a terrible event more than thirty years before. This linking of the present with the past is central to many of Jim Kelly's books.

In 2012 Kelly returned to Philip Dryden after a gap of six years. In *The Funeral Owl* (2013), Dryden is puzzled by the sighting of a rare Boreal Owl, and confused by a bizarre series of incidents including a murder. As the truth begins to emerge, it appears that sightings of the owl may be oddly prophetic.

In 2009 he introduced new characters DI Peter Shaw and DS George Valentine in *Death Wore White* (2009), which will freeze the blood of anyone who has ever been caught in a snowstorm on a remote country road. Equally disconcerting is *Death's Door* (2012), in which Shaw and Valentine investigate a crime which took place on a remote island off the Norfolk Coast in 1994.

www.jim-kelly.co.uk

Patrick Lennon

Patrick Lennon's nerve-jangling novels are set in East Anglia. The first, *Corn Dolls* (2006), is a powerful story that links post-Glasnost Russia to the brooding, bleak Cambridgeshire Fens. It has a particularly gory beginning, as Inspector Tom Fletcher is called to an industrial accident in which a man has been killed. When a security guard at the company is killed as well, Fletcher is led to the village of Thinbeach, which is full of strange characters and pagan rituals. A link to Russia is uncovered through a man who was sent to East Anglia as a tractor mechanic, but never returned. What starts out as a simple murder investigation becomes something much more sinister.

The second is the equally exciting *Steel Witches* (2008), which involves medieval history, a murdered student and an old American Air Force base. After a complex and satisfying storyline, the book ends with a thrilling denouement in a spectacular East Anglian thunderstorm.

www.patricklennon.wordpress.com

Phil Lovesey

Son of crime writer Peter Lovesey, Phil Lovesey has set two of his four rather gory crime novels in his native Essex.

His first novel, *Death Duties* (1998), is set in the town of Maldon on the Blackwater estuary, with the police investigating two vicious murders, thirty years apart. Back in 1969 a seven-year-old girl confessed to the murder of her father. In 1999 an elderly woman is killed, daubed in grotesque make-up. When another brutal murder follows, the three original officers have to bare their own insecurities and emotional secrets in order to unmask a deranged killer.

In *When the Ashes Burn* (2000), the chairman of Chelmsford Allotment Society is the victim of local vandals, and when local reporter Jack Latimer gets involved he finds a trail that leads to death, drugs and a hangman's grandson.

www.fantasticfiction.co.uk/l/phil-lovesey

Karen Maitland

Karen Maitland spent many years living in the historic city of Lincoln and her love of history is apparent in her writing. Medieval Norfolk is the setting for her evocative mystery *The Gallows Curse* (2011). King John is on the throne but has been excommunicated by the Pope, which leads to bodies being buried in unconsecrated ground and children remaining unbaptised. An uncompromising new Lord of the Manor arrives in the village of Gastmere, and when the beautiful Elena is falsely accused of murdering her child, she has to implore all of her friends to stand up to him.

www.karenmaitland.com

Nigel McCrery

Former police officer Nigel McCrery is the creator of several major television programmes including the BBC series *New Tricks* and *Silent Witness*. He is also the author of four novels featuring Silent Witness's original main character Dr. Sam Ryan, all of which are all set in the Cambridge area.

In *Faceless Strangers* (2001), Ryan helps the police in their investigations into the horrific murder of the wife of a local MP, while also reconstructing the face of a dead drug addict —these appear to be two separate cases. However, the reconstruction leads the police towards the awful truth about the addict's life and death, and onwards to uncover a frightening trail of corruption and female exploitation.

In 2007 McCrery started a new series about Essex policeman DCI Mark Lapslie, an interesting character whose life is hindered by a rare neurological condition. In *Tooth and Claw* (2009), Lapslie is brought into a shocking, high-profile investigation when a TV celebrity is tortured to death and a commuter is killed in a bomb explosion at Braintree Station.

www.fantasticfiction.co.uk/m/nigel-mccrery

Christine Poulson

A Cambridge academic with a love of murder mysteries, Christine Poulson has written three crime novels set in the city and university she knows so well. Her protagonist is lecturer Cassandra James, and in the opening novel, *Dead Letters* (2002), she is shocked to find her head of department dead in a swimming pool. When she stumbles across the head's private papers it is clear that it was no accident, and she herself may be next in line.

In *Stage Fright* (2003), Cassandra is involved with drama production at a local theatre. When the leading lady vanishes on the eve of the opening night, Cassandra is concerned, especially when it transpires that the actress has left her young daughter behind. As Cassandra delves further, she soon realises that she has put herself in grave danger again.

www.christinepoulson.co.uk

Ann Quinton

It is the area north of Felixstowe, replete with thatched cottages and small creeks, which is fictionalised in Ann Quinton's series of Suffolk-based novels featuring DI James Roland and his assistant, DSgt Patrick Mansfield.

In *To Mourn A Mischief* (1989), they investigate when a skeleton is found in a local river, and the excavation of a World War II plane causes discomfort in a nearby village.

Some Foul Play (1996) sees Roland and Mansfield called in when a paintball game ends in murder. The victim turns out to be a man with a chequered past.

www.fantasticfiction.co.uk/q/ann-quinton

Sheila Radley

Over sixteen years Sheila Radley (real name Sheila Robinson) wrote ten crime novels, ending with *Fair Game* in 1994. All bar one featured DCI Douglas Quantrill and they were set principally in East Anglia, around the fictional town of Breckham Market.

In *Who Saw Him Die?* (1987), Quantrill and his assistant Hilary Lloyd uncover years of hatred and dislike when the death of a well-known drunk in a hit-and-run leads to robbery and a vicious murder.

The disappearance of an elderly couple and the possible psychological motivation of a major suspect are the central features of *Cross My Heart and Hope to Die* (1992), which is set in the fictional Suffolk village of Byland.

www.fantasticfiction.co.uk/r/sheila-radley

James Runcie

The village of Grantchester near Cambridge is the setting for a series of gentle crime novels by James Runcie, who is the son of the former Archbishop of Canterbury Robert Runcie. He has been the artistic director of the Bath Literature Festival, and has worked as a theatre director, television producer and documentary film maker. The author intends to publish six books in the series, ending in 1981 at the time of the wedding of Charles and Diana.

The books follow the sleuthing exploits of Canon Sidney Chambers. In the debut novel (*Sidney Chambers and the Shadow of Death*, 2012) he is a thirty-two year old vicar at the church of St Andrew and St Mary in 1953. With his friend, Inspector Geordie Keating, he is drawn into the world of theft, forgery and death, and he finds that being a clergyman can lead to many moral dilemmas.

In the second book, *Sidney Chambers and the Perils of the Night* (2013), which is set in the late 1950s, Sidney delves into the mysterious poisoning of a Grantchester cricketer, and the fall of a don from the roof of King's College, all the while considering the crucial question of marriage.

The series will be televised in autumn 2014, with James Norton in the role of Sidney, and Robson Green as Inspector Keating.

www.grantchestermysteries.com

Ian Sansom

Originally from Essex, Ian Sansom found success as an author through his Mobile Library series of gentle crime stories, set in rural Ireland. In 2013 he set out the details of a new series, in which he plans to set a Golden-Age-style crime novel in every English county.

He began with *The Norfolk Mystery* (2013), featuring Stephen Sefton, a Spanish Civil War veteran down on his luck, and Professor Swanton Morley ("The People's Professor"). The Professor's latest project is a traditional history of England, and Sefton is employed as his assistant. They start in Norfolk, but are sidetracked when the vicar of Blakeney is found hanging in his own church.

See also: Northern Ireland

www.iansansom.net

Dorothy L. Sayers

One of the all-time greats, Dorothy Leigh Sayers was born in Oxford in 1893, and lived the last thirty years of her life in Witham, Essex. She wrote fourteen crime novels featuring the aristocratic Lord Peter Wimsey, though only one is set in East Anglia.

Having said that, it is the one often quoted as Sayers' best — *The Nine Tailors* (1934). When Wimsey and his butler Bunter are stranded in Norfolk following a minor car crash, they find themselves embroiled in an extraordinary mystery featuring an unexpected death, an unsolved jewel robbery and a mutilated body in another man's grave. The bleak countryside, the fear of flooding and the eerie old churches of the area are all vital ingredients in this ingenious classic.

See also: the South and South East, Scotland: Glasgow and the West of Scotland

www.sayers.org.uk

Michelle Spring

A Canadian by birth and upbringing, Michelle Spring is nevertheless an anglophile who has lived and taught in Cambridge for many years. East Anglia is the setting for her five Laura Principal thrillers, written between 1994 and 2001. Laura is a private investigator, an interesting, resilient, well-drawn character who works with two other women — Sonny, her lover, and Stevie.

In *Nights in White Satin* (1999), Laura is providing security at the May Ball when an angelic-looking student, dressed in a white satin dress, vanishes without trace.

In the Midnight Hour (2001) is a story of love and loss, beginning when a woman befriends a teenage busker on the streets of Cambridge, believing he is her son who disappeared from a Norfolk beach many years before. Laura is called in to settle the question of identity and finds herself involved in a chilling story with far-reaching consequences.

www.fantasticfiction.co.uk/s/michelle-spring

June Thomson

In a writing career that began in 1971, June Thomson wrote twenty novels featuring the quiet, persistent Essex policeman, Inspector Jack Finch (who was renamed Jack Rudd in American editions). They are ingenious mysteries, cosy by today's standards, but are none the worse for that. The author compellingly recreates the countryside of North Essex, which is so different from the better-known London environs. Sleepy villages, creeks and marshes, isolated hamlets and lonely mudflats abound around the River Crouch and the Blackwater estuary, give the stories a melancholy, eerie feel.

Deadly Relations (1978) is set in a small, isolated village, where the social structure has remained unchanged for decades. When university dropout Christopher Lawrence takes a room in the home of middle-aged spinster Maggie Hearn, the results are predictable. When a young woman that Lawrence was seeing is found murdered, Inspector Finch finds that he must understand the inner hopes and fears of all the main suspects in order to solve the case.

In *Rosemary for Remembrance* (1988), Finch is called to investigate the death of Jake Nolan, a creative writing teacher at Morton Grange Summer School. Then a mature student is found dead in a carbon monoxide-filled car. There is clearly a link between the deaths — the killer had strewn pansies across one body, and sprigs of rosemary across the other.

www.fantasticfiction.co.uk/t/june-thomson

Charles Todd

This is the pen-name used by the American mother-and-son writing team of Caroline and Charles Todd. Charles had a career as a business consultant, and his mother is a history graduate. Their shared love of history is evident in their clever, thoughtful novels featuring Inspector Ian Rutledge, a Scotland Yard policeman who has to pick up the pieces of his life and career after being wounded in World War I. He suffers considerably from shell-shock, and is traumatised by the memory of a field execution.

In *The Watchers of Time* (2001), it is 1919, and Rutledge is summoned to the marshes of Norfolk where the local bishop wants a Scotland Yard investigation into the murder of a priest. The local police have a convenient suspect, but as Rutledge edges closer to the truth, he finds that secrets within the community are linked to the great *Titanic* disaster several years earlier, and that someone will go to any lengths to protect them.

See also: the West Country, Scotland: Highlands and Islands

www.charlestodd.com

Barbara Vine

Ruth Rendell has won gold, silver and diamond daggers from the CWA in a fifty year writing career. In 1997 she was created Baroness Rendell of Babergh in Suffolk, and the county has often featured in her Barbara Vine books — the pen-name that she uses for her stand-alone psychological dramas, which often blur the definitions of crime, evil and truth. Her books are always powerful, even mesmerising, and will linger with the reader long after they are finished.

A Fatal Inversion (1987) is a haunting, gripping, melo-drama set at a remote East Anglian country house, where a group of young people live in a commune in the long hot summer of 1976. Ten years later, the bodies of a woman and a child are discovered in the animal cemetery at the house, but no one knows who they are. Three men, who now have little in common, are forced to think back to those far-off, heady days — and the terrible events that took place.

Gallowglass (1990), an extraordinary story of obsession and kidnapping, is set in and around Manningtree and Bury St Edmunds on the Essex/Suffolk border. Sandor, a terrifying character, is obsessed with Nina, an exquisitely attractive former model whom he had once kidnapped. When he saves the life of a young man, Joe, Sandor demands that Joe helps him to kidnap Nina again. However, even the best-laid plans can go wrong, and planning is not Sandor's strength.

See also: the South and South East (Ruth Rendell), London (Ruth Rendell)

www.fantasticfiction.co.uk/v/barbara-vine

Ten Recommended Reads

1: *Dead Heat* by Dick Francis (2007)

2: *The House at Sea's End* by Elly Griffiths (2011)

3: *Lasting Damage* by Sophie Hannah (2011)

4: *Devices and Desires* by P.D. James (1989)

5: *The Water Clock* by Jim Kelly (2002)

6: *Corn Dolls* by Patrick Lennon (2008)

7: *Sidney Chambers and the Perils of the Night* by James Runcie (2013)

8: *The Nine Tailors* by Dorothy L. Sayers (1934)

9: *The Watchers of Time* by Charles Todd (2001)

10: *Gallowglass* by Barbara Vine (1990)

REGION FIVE
England — The Midlands

"The Peak District has a huge range of wonderfully atmospheric locations for me to use within a small area, plus thousands of years of history – much of it visible right there in the landscape, from stone circles to abandoned lead mines and more recent industrial history."
STEPHEN BOOTH, from an interview with the *Scene of the Crime* blog, 2011

The English Midlands is a varied area, which runs from Bedfordshire and Buckinghamshire right up to the edge of Yorkshire and Greater Manchester, it has cities, moorland, leafy lanes and run-down estates. It is an area of great character, and in many ways is the heart of twenty-first century Britain.

In Birmingham it has a major industrial city, second in size only to London. Nottingham, Leicester, Derby, Coventry and Oxford are major cities in their own right, with great history and importance. The Peak District of Derbyshire is a National Park of considerable significance, including as it does the lower section of the Pennines — England's geographical backbone. The rural areas include the lush green fields of Leicestershire and the rugged peaks of Derbyshire. Overall it retains a charm and personality all of its own.

Great detectives policing the Midlands include Charlie Resnick in Nottingham (John Harvey), Ben Cooper and Diane Fry in Derbyshire (Stephen Booth), Inspector Morse in Oxford (Colin Dexter), and Brother Cadfael in Shropshire (Ellis Peters). Colin Dexter was once a Leicestershire teacher, Keith Wright was a Nottinghamshire policeman, and Veronica Stallwood worked in the Bodleian Library at Oxford University.

Jane Adams

Leicestershire-born Jane Adams (who also writes as Jane A. Adams) was once a vocalist in a folk rock-band, and has featured her home city of Leicester in several of her books.

The Angel Gateway (2000) uses a real place in central Leicester as the crux of a fascinating novel, which weaves a crime story and a ghost story together. DI Ray Flowers is recuperating after a bomb attack which has left him disfigured. Whiling away his time, he becomes interested a strange historical story with bizarre parallels to his own .

Two further Ray Flowers stories followed. In *Angel Eyes* (2002), Flowers is retired but is contacted by an old colleague about a former drug dealer who is now active again. Initially he wants little to do with the case, but when his old friend is attacked he is forced to change his mind — with drastic consequences.

See also: the West Country (Jane A. Adams), East Anglia
www.janeadamsauthor.wordpress.com

David Armstrong

David Armstrong has written a number of evocative crime novels set around the Midlands in different time periods. His first novel, *Night's Black Agents* (1993), was set on the Midlands canal system in the 1930s, as a cuckolded man pays a bargee to kill his wife, not realising that the hitman's inexperience will lead to a murder enquiry. The book won the CWA John Creasey Award for best first novel in 1993.

Later, Armstrong started a series featuring DI Frank Kavanagh and his lover, DC Jane Salt. *A Pact of Silence* (2010) begins in a small Shropshire town in 1969 when two young men are involved in an accidental death. They cover it up but leave behind a vital clue to what happened, which only comes to light forty years later.

Written Out (2009) is also set in Shropshire. A novelist disappears at the end of a week's tutoring at a writing centre in the county. When Kavanagh and Salt investigate, they find that the author's colourful lifestyle had given him many enemies, from offended novelists to cuckolded husbands.

www.fantasticfiction.co.uk/a/david-armstrong

Maureen Ash

The beautiful cathedral city of Lincoln in the early 1200s is the background to Maureen Ash's Templar Knight series. The author is English, but currently lives in Canada.

In the first book in the series, *The Alehouse Murders* (2007), Templar Knight Bascot de Marins is on a sojourn at Lincoln Castle, recuperating after eight years of captivity in the Holy Land, when he discovers that what appeared only to be a brutal fight is actually something much more sinister.

In *A Deadly Penance* (2011), Bascot is summoned to the Castle to investigate the murder of a servant engaged in an illicit affair, and finds that the victim had more enemies than expected.

www.fantasticfiction.co.uk/a/maureen-ash

David Belbin

An experienced writer of crime stories for children and young adults, David Belbin wrote twelve stories about young police officers in Nottingham under the series title "The Beat". In these he dealt with difficult topics such as paedophiles, gang membership and rape. This series finished in 2000 with *Fallen Angel*, which was a fitting dramatic conclusion to a high quality series. Loose ends were tied up cleverly, as all major characters had decisions to make regarding their future.

In 2012 he started a new crime series about Labour politician Sarah Bone and her ex-boyfriend Nick Cane, an unusual sleuthing duo with a radical past which led one into politics and the other into prison.

In the first book, *Bone and Cane* (2012), Sarah successfully campaigns for the release of one of Nick's fellow prisoners, Ed Clark, but his subsequent admission to her of his guilt puts her in a dreadful position — she is responsible for him being back on the streets. Somehow with Nick's help she must expose Clark's lies for what they are.

The follow-up, *What You Don't Know* (2012), finds Sarah as a Nottingham MP in 1997, appointed as Minister for Prisons. Nick, meanwhile, is out on probation following a drugs conviction and is tutoring an attractive student. However, he gets too close to her, and someone tries to kill him. Meanwhile Sarah's career is in ruins after her boyfriend is found dead. As they try to solve their respective problems, the worlds of Westminster and local Nottingham politics become intertwined.

www.davidbelbin.com

Helen Black

Miner's daughter Helen Black spent some years working with disadvantaged and troubled young people, and her experiences are put to good use in her crime novels, several of which have Luton settings. Her books are hard-hitting and realistic, as the author has no compunction about raising serious issues. The protagonist is Lilly Valentine, a tough talking Yorkshire lawyer who has come south to work in Luton.

In *A Place of Safety* (2008), Family Care lawyer Lilly Valentine is embroiled in a difficult case involving racism and rape. A fourteen-year-old asylum seeker is raped by privileged white boys at a Bedfordshire hostel, and Lilly feels that justice will not be done. When the victim and a friend take matters into their own hands events spiral beyond her control.

Blood Rush (2011) is the fourth in the series. Lilly's home life is as disorganised as ever, and professionally she thinks has moved on from defending damaged children. However, she is drawn into the world of girl gangs when a member of a particularly violent gang is charged with murder.

www.hblack.co.uk

Victoria Blake

Oxford is the setting for Victoria Blake's novels about flawed private investigator Sam Falconer. Falconer is a world judo champion who has been educated at Oxford University. When she retires from the sport she sets up a private investigation agency in London.

But the call of Oxford is strong, and she finds herself back in the city, to search for a missing woman (*Bloodless Shadow*, 2003), or to find a star rower who has disappeared before the Boat Race trials (*Cutting Blades*, 2005).

Further novels followed in 2006 and 2007, by which time Sam has moved her investigation agency to Oxford. Her knowledge of the University (she grew up there, as her father was Provost of Queen's College) allows the author to explore the university from an insider's point of view.

Skin and Blister (2007) is an uncomfortable story for Sam. A student is found dead, and Sam's brother disappears. When their mother receives a card announcing a funeral mass for her son, Sam knows she must find out the truth — and quickly.

www.fantasticfiction.co.uk/b/victoria-blake

Stephen Booth

Formerly a sports journalist, Stephen Booth made his fiction breakthrough with the novel *Black Dog* in 1999, and his series has since gone from strength to strength. In 2003 he won the CWA Dagger in the Library for the body of work that had given greatest pleasure to library users in the UK. He uses a combination of real places (such as Castleton, Wirksworth and Matlock) and the fictional town of Edendale to give an authentic backdrop to the gritty novels.

The books feature the chalk-and-cheese pairing of DC Ben Cooper — a likeable, dependable, locally-born officer whose father was a policeman killed in the line of duty — and the harsh, somewhat abrasive DSgt Diane Fry, an incomer from Birmingham who has never quite settled into the ways of country life. The bleak and imposing Peak District acts as an extra character; it is where Cooper is happiest, but it is anathema to Fry.

In *Blind to the Bones* (2003), two deaths around the decaying peak village of Withens focus Ben Cooper's attention on the Oxleys, a close-knit and difficult family. When Diane Fry comes to Withens on a separate case, the disappearance of a teenage girl, they have to work together to find a link in order to bring a killer to justice — and to understand the secrets of an insular moorland community.

In 2007 Cooper appeared in a novella, *Claws,* in which he is assigned to the Rural Crime Squad, whose prime function is the investigation of wildlife crime. In this unusual story the victims are not always human, though the criminals most definitely are.

Even in 2012 the relationship between Cooper and Fry is still fractious (especially as Cooper is now equal in rank), and in *Dead and Buried* (2012), a series of moorland fires lead to the discovery of a body in an isolated, abandoned pub. When links are found to two missing tourists it seems that the old pub has many secrets — and

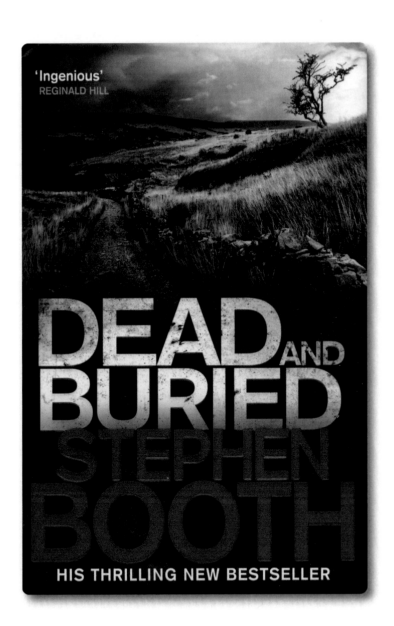

'Ingenious'
REGINALD HILL

DEAD AND BURIED

STEPHEN BOOTH

HIS THRILLING NEW BESTSELLER

someone does not want them divulged. Fire may be a good servant, but it is undoubtedly a bad master. The denouement is a shock, even to Booth's regular readers.
www.stephen-booth.com

John Buxton Hilton

Born in Buxton, John Buxton Hilton knew Derbyshire and the Peak District well, using them in many of his novels. He created three separate detectives in his writing career, which lasted nearly twenty years.

The short series of Derbyshire Mysteries featuring Victorian/Edwardian detective Thomas Brunt is set between 1870 and 1914. It is superbly evocative of old Derbyshire, with its lead-mining, superstitions, mills and abject poverty in some areas.

In *Slickensides* (1987), the title is not only the name of a farm in the High Peak, but also a cheese prepared at the farm and the name of the mines that run through the rock beneath it. The body of the local squire's son has been found in the mine, and as the Derbyshire mists descend Brunt is forced to use all his experience to bring a murderer to justice.
www.fantasticfiction.co.uk/h/john-buxton-hilton

Maureen Carter

A former journalist who worked at BBC Pebble Mill (the Corporation's Birmingham studios) for around twenty years, Maureen Carter writes about the city she knows so well. Her books pull no punches, though she leavens this with a good dose of sardonic humour.

She now has two separate series to her credit, both similar in style. The first centres on DS Bev Morris of the West Midlands Police, an outspoken, blunt and forceful character (to put it mildly), who has to deal with a number of unpleasant, if grimly realistic, cases. The second novel (*Dead Old*, 2002) is thoroughly uncompromising, as a gang of thugs targets elderly women on the city streets. When another elderly woman is murdered her colleagues assume it is part of the series of attacks, but Bev is not convinced. This annoys her boss, but Bev is certain that the woman's past has contributed to her death, and she is determined to prove it.

After seven books, Maureen Carter created a new series, highlighting the often difficult relationship between police officers and journalists. There is plenty of antagonism between hard-nosed DI Sarah Quinn (the "Ice Queen") and fiery TV reporter Caroline King, but they put their differences aside to find a kidnapped baby in *A Question of Despair* (2011).

www.maureencarter.co.uk

Jean Chapman

Originally a writer of romantic fiction (she is an ex-president of the Romantic Novelists' Association) Jean Chapman was also the President of the Leicester Writers' Club on three occasions. Recently she has turned her hand to crime fiction and has now written three crime novels featuring ex-policeman John Cannon, who has given up his career with the Metropolitan Police to run a country pub in the Lincolnshire Fens.

In *A Watery Grave* (2010), Cannon's early morning run is interrupted when he becomes entangled in a discarded fishing line, attached to a dumped body. Soon he is embroiled in a series of events which lead him into conflict with a Portuguese gangster, and his hard-earned life of retirement is put at risk.

Deadly Serious (2013) brings Cannon into conflict with a vicious gangland family from London when a local policeman receives death threats. The quiet waterways, lonely villages and gentle woodlands of Lincolnshire become the backdrop for hatred and gangland violence, and even John Cannon's pub is a dangerous place to be.

www.fantasticfiction.co.uk/c/jean-chapman

Chris Collett

Originally from Norfolk, Chris Collett is a lecturer in Birmingham, covering various aspects of special needs work and human rights. She has written a series of police procedurals set mainly in Birmingham, featuring DI Tom Mariner.

Written in Blood (2006) opens with a bang — literally — as there is a multiple murder, the centre of Birmingham is shattered by a bomb explosion, and a body is found in a sewer. Mariner is centre stage, and as the investigation deepens, he is desperately uncertain as to who he can trust.

In *Stalked by Shadows* (2009), Mariner has two difficult cases on his patch. The widow of a controversial policeman is viciously murdered, and a young woman called Lucy Jarrett has reported a stalker. When parallels between the two cases are found, Mariner and his team must consider a new motive — revenge.

See also: Wales

www.chriscollettcrime.co.uk

Edmund Crispin

Oxford in the 1940s and 1950s is the usual setting for the wonderfully funny Gervase Fen novels by Edmund Crispin (the pseudonym of composer Bruce Montgomery). The author was a graduate of St John's College and gave Fen the position of Professor of English Language and Literature at the University. His plots are intricate and the solutions imaginative, if sometimes unlikely. There were nine Fen novels altogether as well as a number of short stories.

The Moving Toyshop (1946) is often cited as a classic of comic crime fiction, as Fen investigates the bizarre story of young poet Richard Cadogan, who claims to have found the body of an elderly woman in an old Oxford toyshop. However no one will believe him, as he had then been knocked unconscious, to find on awakening that the corpse had vanished and the toyshop had become a grocers.

www.fantasticfiction.co.uk/c/edmund-crispin

A.J. Cross

Practicing forensic psychologist A.J. Cross knows the West Midlands well, and gives her books extra authenticity by using many real locations. Her main character, Kate Hanson, is also a forensic psychologist.

In Cross's first novel, *Gone In Seconds* (2012), the gruesome discovery of a body in woodland by a motorway near Birmingham is the starting point. Kate works with the Birmingham Unsolved Crime Unit to find the killer of a local teenager. When further human remains are found, Kate knows that she is looking at the work of a serial killer.

In *Art of Deception* (2013), Kate and the team have their New Year spoiled by the discovery of a mummified body in a deserted house. Evidence shows that the man had been student Nathan Troy, who disappeared twenty years ago. However, his old friends don't want to talk, and then a second death confirms Kate's greatest fear — the killer is still at large, and still looking for victims.

www.fantasticfiction.co.uk/c/a-j-cross

Judith Cutler

Born in the Black Country, Judith Cutler grew up in Birmingham and has used her home area as the backdrop for many of her novels.

Sophie Rivers is a college lecturer, sometime singer and amateur sleuth in Birmingham who gets mixed up in various murder mysteries. In *Dying to Score* (1999), she becomes romantically involved with an England cricketer, only for him to become a major suspect in the murder of one of his unpopular colleagues. The locations include Edgbaston Cricket Ground and parts of Smethwick. The series ended in 2003, with *Dying to Deceive*, and Warwickshire County Cricket Club is involved again, as

Sophie gets a job archiving some valuable memorabilia but finds herself up to her eyes in problems when the club archivist disappears.

A far grittier series is that featuring Birmingham detective Kate Power, which showcases the city's darker side. She is not from the area, so experiences all the problems associated with moving to a strange new city. In the first of the series, *Power on Her Own* (1998), she has just moved to Birmingham from London after a personal tragedy. Kate is thrown in at the deep end when investigating a series of offences against young boys, all the time getting used to new friends and colleagues. The sixth and final novel in the series is *Power Shift* (2003), in which Kate is promoted, and investigates the murky world of sex slaves.

See also: the West Country, the South and South East
www.judithcutler.com

Colin Dexter

Stamford-born Colin Dexter was originally a teacher, forced by deafness to give up his career in favour of an academic post at Oxford University. He took up writing almost by accident, and his first Inspector Morse novel was published in 1975. Many of the traits of the irascible, beer-drinking, crossword solving detective were based on his own enthusiasms (he even took the name of Morse from one of his favourite compilers of *Times* Crosswords).

The novels are high-quality police procedurals set in and around the dreaming spires of Oxford, and many have tentacles that lead in one way or another to the University itself, such as *The Daughters of Cain* (1994), where sexual obsession within the confines of a college eventually leads to murder. The novels often reflect the edginess between town and gown, and the importance of the University to the city.

Both *The Way Through the Woods* (1992) and *The Wench is Dead* (1989) won the CWA Gold Dagger, the latter being a throwback to Josephine Tey's brilliant novel *The*

Daughter of Time (1951), with Morse solving a Victorian murder mystery from his hospital bed.

The stories themselves were cleverly plotted and intelligently written. A fine example is *The Riddle of the Third Mile* (1983), in which Morse and his partner, DS Lewis, investigate the disappearance of an elderly Oxford don, and a savagely mutilated body found in the Oxford canal. A complex and convoluted story, it shows Morse and Lewis at their best as they uncover a long-standing hatred which had begun in one of the great battles of World War II.

The series also became a worldwide television phenomenon, with Morse being portrayed by the late, great John Thaw. The success had its drawbacks though, and the characters of Morse and Lewis are noticeably different in the later books of the series to those described in *Last Bus to Woodstock* (1975).

In 1997 Colin Dexter was awarded the CWA Cartier Dagger for lifetime achievement.

www.fantasticfiction.co.uk/d/colin-dexter

David Dickinson

David Dickinson is the author of a fine series of historical mysteries set in Victorian and Edwardian England. His main sleuth is the Irish-born aristocrat Lord Francis Powerscourt, whose considerable skills as a detective take him all over Britain and Europe at the turn of the nineteenth century.

In *Death in a Scarlet Coat* (2011), the fifteenth Earl of Candlesby has been killed, but only three people saw his body. One of them dies, a second vanishes. As Powerscourt investigates, he finds a trail of duels, robberies and adultery across Lincolnshire

See also: London

www.fantasticfiction.co.uk/d/david-dickinson

Stephen Done

The Great Central Railway (which ran from Nottingham to London between 1899 and 1966) is the main setting for

Stephen Done's series of books featuring Leicester-based railway detective Charles Vignoles. Done is a museum curator, and his grasp of history is evident in all the books, which are evocative of the dark, austere post-war world, and the difficult years for the railways that led towards the Beeching cuts. The novels will have particular appeal to railway buffs.

In *The Murder of Crows* (2008), Inspector Vignoles investigates when, during the big freeze of 1947, a woman's body is thrown from a train as it exits the huge Catesby Tunnel. As the weather gets colder still, Vignoles and his staff struggle to find a violent killer.

In *The Last Train to Brackley Central* (2012), a schoolteacher is woken when a young woman enters his compartment. She has a strange tale to tell, and a dangerous favour to ask. As the train reaches Brackley she disappears, and Vignoles becomes embroiled in an extraordinary case involving a jewel with a deadly reputation.

www.inspectorvignoles.ukwriters.net

Rod Duncan

Rod Duncan is an example to anyone who has ever felt held back by being dyslexic. Despite this apparent disadvantage, he has gained a degree in mining geology and written three gripping crime novels, all set in his adopted home city of Leicester. Each has the background of the same inner-city riot, but they follow the lives of different people as they experience the event from their own standpoints.

In the first novel, *Backlash* (2003), the discovery of a butchered pig in a city mosque turns the simmering flames of racial discontent into a full-scale riot — just what Leicester does not want ahead of a major political conference on racial harmony being held in the city.

In the follow-up, *Breakbeat* (2004), unemployed dyslexic drop-out Daz Croxley discovers the cash proceeds of a property fraud when he loots a store during the riot. Unfortunately for Daz, the perpetrators of the fraud want their money back.

The third book, *Burnout* (2005), sees Superintendent Shakespeare, the policeman who instigates the enquiry into the riot, targeted by a violent blackmailer. A junior officer is in danger, and the eventual climax in Western Park is both nerve-shredding and convincing.

www.fantasticfiction.co.uk/d/rod-duncan

Steven Dunne

A Yorkshireman by birth, Steven Dunne was a journalist writing occasional articles for the broadsheets before becoming a teacher in Derby, where he has taught English for many years.

The city of Derby is the backdrop to his series of books about DI Damen Brook, a former detective in the Metropolitan Police, who relocates to the Midlands to save his sanity but finds that there is no escape from serial killers or psychopaths.

Well-written, gruesome, and full of psychological tension, this series begins with *The Reaper* (2007). Brook encounters his worst nightmare — the killer that he had left London to escape is now on the loose in his new home city. Brook must use all his mental strength not to unravel again as he tries to end the killing spree once and for all.

By *The Unquiet Grave* (2013), Brook is seen as a maverick cop, and is farmed out to the cold case unit, where he finds a link in a series of unsolved murders that stretches back forty years. Unfortunately for Brook, the case leads him to examine the past of a close colleague, which makes him even more unpopular than ever.

www.stevendunne.co.uk

Marjorie Eccles

Having lived in the Midlands for a long time, Marjorie Eccles has used the area as the backdrop for most of her crime fiction. She has written a fine series of traditional crime novels featuring DI Gil Mayo, who is based in Lavenstock, a fictional market town located on the southern edge of the Black Country.

She uses the industrial heritage of the area in *Requiem for a Dove* (1990), in which the murder of a wealthy widow has links with her past as a factory owner. The changing times and the tensions between new and old communities can be seen in *A Species of Revenge* (1996), when a body is found on an allotment. No sooner is it identified than there is another local murder, forcing Mayo to focus very closely on people he thought he knew.

Eccles has also written a number of stand-alone novels, many of which are also set in the Midlands. An example is *Broken Music* (2009), in which a former policeman returns to his home area at the end of The Great War, determined to uncover the events that led to his daughter's drowning in 1914.

www.fantasticfiction.co.uk/e/marjorie-eccles

Raymond Flynn

Once an inspector with the Nottinghamshire Fraud Squad, Raymond Flynn used his knowledge of the law to good effect in his series of police procedurals set in the fictional Lincolnshire seaside town of Eddathorpe — sometimes described as Nottingham-by-the-Sea, a typical seaside town with a population that doubles in summer.

In *Over My Dead Body* (2000), someone is blackmailing the local supermarket chain. When this escalates to murder, DCI Robert Graham has to probe deep into Eddathorpe's seedy secrets.

Flynn's books always have a bit of humour, as in *Busy Body* (1998). Sir Jeremy Blatt, Eddathorpe's frozen vegetable magnate and local lothario, is found dead in a refrigerated lorry on a North Sea ferry. DCI Graham finds himself with too many suspects — and what he discovers will take his breath away.

www.fantasticfiction.co.uk/f/raymond-flynn

J.J. Franklin

This is the pseudonym of Bren Littlewood, a TV scriptwriter who started out writing murder mysteries for her own company, which ran murder mystery dinners around the UK..

Urge to Kill (2012) is the first in a series of novels featuring DI Matt Turrell of the Warwickshire Police. Turrell returns from his honeymoon to investigate the murder of a woman whose body was found in a spa in Stratford-on-Avon. Meanwhile the killer intends to continue his work, and when he sees Turrell as his main threat, he targets the policeman's most treasured possession — his wife.

www.bmlittlewood.com

Caroline Graham

Caroline Graham is a playwright, screenwriter and novelist. Though she once wrote for the TV soap *Crossroads*, she is far better known as the author whose books were adapted for the TV series *Midsomer Murders*. Though the locations in her books were entirely fictional, the series was filmed in Buckinghamshire and South Oxfordshire, and it is reasonable to suggest that the locations for the books were loosely based on this area.

Though the TV series has so far run to 95 episodes, there are only seven books, all featuring Inspector Jim Barnaby. The original novel, *The Killings at Badger's Drift* (1987), was well reviewed and won a Macavity Award for Best First Novel.

The plot concerns an elderly lady in the village of Badger's Drift who is convinced that her friend Emily Simpson did not die of a heart attack, but was poisoned. She is proved right, and then a second death occurs. As panic grips the village, Barnaby investigates and finds links to a much older crime.

Death in Disguise (1992) starts with a death at a country house which is being occupied by a New Age cult. It is put down as an accident. However, when a second death occurs a few weeks later suspicions are raised and Barnaby is called in. It is clear that the case is convoluted, and the suspects are somewhat strange. Barnaby will need all his experience to get to the truth.

www.fantasticfiction.co.uk/g/caroline-graham

Ann Granger

In just over twenty years Ann Granger has written over thirty crime novels, split into four different series – two of which are set in the Cotswolds.

The Mitchell and Markby village mysteries feature Chief Inspector Alan Markby and his inquisitive friend Meredith Mitchell. They began in 1991 and the last in the series (so far) was *That Way Murder Lies* (2004), in which poison pen letters sent to a middle-aged woman hint darkly at a murder for which she was acquitted in her youth. They are set in and around the fictional village of Bamford, which seems to be based on Burford and Chipping Norton. The plots are clever and the on-off romance between the two main characters is a strand which runs through the series.

Several years later, in 2009, Granger started the Campbell and Carter mysteries, in a similar setting. In this case both main protagonists are police officers — Inspector Jess Campbell and Superintendent Ian Carter. Inspector Campbell had appeared as a member of Markby's team in the previous series.

In *Rack, Ruin and Murder* (2011), family secrets come to light when the impecunious Monty Bickerstaffe, the last remaining member of a family which made its money from selling Victorian fruitcake, finds a body in his drawing room.

See also: London

www.anngranger.net

Martha Grimes

Martha Grimes may be American, but her novels are set all over England and her lead detective, Inspector (later

Superintendent) Richard Jury, is from Scotland Yard. The novels are all named after English pubs, and a map showing their locations can be found on the author's website — though the pub location is not necessarily that of the book.

In *The Dirty Duck* (1984), Jury is visiting Stratford when an American tourist is murdered. The only clue is two lines from a strange poem which are printed on a theatre programme. When Jury investigates he finds that there is a dark side to Shakespeare's home town.

The Case Has Altered (1997) features a double murder in the Lincolnshire fens. The prime suspect turns out to be Jenny Kennington, for many years the love of Jury's life. In order to uncover the real murderer Jury needs a helping hand, and he turns to his old friend, Melrose Plant.

See also: the West Country
www.marthagrimes.com

John Harvey

Once a writer of formulaic westerns, former English teacher John Harvey is now one of the most respected crime writers in the world. His long-standing series of police procedurals featuring the jazz-loving Nottingham-based policeman DI Charlie Resnick has won high praise, and in 2000 *The Times* listed the first in the series (*Lonely Hearts*,1989) as one of the greatest crime novels of the twentieth century. Harvey was awarded the Cartier Dagger by the CWA in 2007 for his lifetime achievement.

His books showcase Nottingham, and most of the locations are real. You can walk with Resnick from Canning Circus to the City Centre, and become immersed in the grey industrial city or the lighter suburbs.

In *Lonely Hearts* (1989), Resnick and his regular team of detectives battle to end the career of a sadistic killer who is targeting women using lonely hearts columns.

Having apparently finished the series in 1998 with *Last Rites*, Harvey brought Resnick back for an eleventh appearance in *Cold in Hand* (2008), in which he has to deal with a father who blames the police for his daughter's death in a gang war, while his colleague (and now partner) Lynn Kellogg takes on a murder case with tentacles leading to international crime. The consequences are horrific for all concerned.

In 2014 Harvey finally brought the series to a close with *Darkness, Darkness*, in which the discovery of the body of a young woman who disappeared during the miners' strike thirty years ago forces the virtually retired Resnick to return to the front line, and face up to his past —at the time of the strike he was a DI working at the very centre of the impassioned dispute.

Back in 2004 Harvey began a trilogy featuring retired Nottinghamshire policeman Frank Elder. The first book, *Flesh and Blood* (2004), won a CWA Silver Dagger, and the follow-ups, *Ash and Bone* (2005) and *Darkness and Light* (2006), are just as good.

In the latter, Elder returns to Nottingham at the behest of his ex-wife to look into the disappearance of a middle-aged woman. When she is found dead, Elder realises that to solve the crime he must delve deeply into his own past and face up to a shocking case from his police career — a murder that was never solved. In doing so he reopens many old wounds, a traumatic experience for the innocent as well as the guilty.

See also: London, East Anglia

www.mellotone.co.uk

Samantha Hayes

Having grown up in the Midlands, Samantha Hayes travelled widely, lived in Australia and America and had a number of jobs (including private investigator) before returning to the UK and settling in Warwickshire, where her new crime series is set. Her books have always been full of drama and suspense. After three stand-alone novels the first in the series was published in 2013.

Until You're Mine (2013) is an unsettling story about a pregnant woman with a young family and a creepy nanny. When her husband is away, the expectant mother finds the nanny in her bedroom rifling through her most personal possessions, and there is a series of attacks on local women. The attacks are investigated by married detectives Adam Scott and Lorraine Fisher, and they are horrified at what they find. The novel was long-listed for the CWA Crime Novel of the Year.

In *Before You Die* (2014), the village of Radcote is recovering from a spate of teenage suicides when two young men die in quick succession. Fisher finds herself caught up in the resultant police enquiry, and then her own nephew disappears, increasing her sense of unease. Are they all terrible suicides or something else — murder?

www.samanthahayes.co.uk

Reginald Hill

Reginald Hill died in 2012 after a writing career that lasted more than forty years. He is best known for his *Dalziel and Pascoe* series set in Yorkshire, but he also wrote a series of five witty novels set in Luton, featuring mild-mannered black private eye Joe Sixsmith. Very different from the Yorkshire books, they explore the perils of a small-time private eye in nineties Britain.

A former lathe operator, middle-aged and balding, Joe is an unlikely sleuth, and, through no fault of his own, often finds himself caught up in events beyond his abilities and expectations. In *Killing the Lawyers* (1997), he finds himself suspected of murder when a lawyer who has fobbed him off over a car insurance claim is found dead. Even when he is cleared he is still under pressure as another lawyer is murdered and a top athlete wants his help over a series of violent threats.

See also: the North East

www.fantasticfiction.co.uk/h/reginald-hill

Michael Innes

This is the pseudonym used by the Scottish novelist and academic J.I.M. Stewart for his long-running series of crime novels featuring DI (later Commissioner) John Appleby. The series began in 1936 and continued until 1986 — the author died in 1994.

The adventures are sometimes eccentric and take Appleby to exotic places such as South America (*The Daffodil Affair*, 1942), Dartmoor (*Appleby Plays Chicken*, 1957) and even a remote Atlantic island (*Hare Sitting Up*, 1959). However, many of the books have an Oxfordshire setting, though the exact location is often not clear. The books are full of literary allusions and are well worth seeking out.

The series began with *Death at the President's Lodgings* (1936), in which Appleby is called in to investigate the death of the an Oxford college president, and finds that the only suspects are the college fellows themselves.

Operation Pax (1951) is a thriller set in and around Oxford University shortly after World War II, and its climax takes place in the vaults of the Bodleian Library.
See also: Scotland: Highlands and Islands
www.fantasticfiction.co.uk/i/michael-innes

Christina James

Spalding-born Christina James uses her home territory of the Lincolnshire Fens as the backdrop to her crime novels featuring DI Tim Yates.

In her debut novel, *In the Family* (2012), Yates and his team are drawn into the complexities of the local Atkins dynasty when workmen discover the skeleton of a young woman. The detectives unravel a terrible crime at the heart of a dysfunctional family, and the story is full of powerful images and memorable characters.
www.christinajamesblog.com

Maureen Jennings

Maureen Jennings is originally from Birmingham, but at seventeen she emigrated to Canada. She went on to become the creator of the book and TV series *The Murdoch Mysteries*.

In 2011 she wrote *Season of Darkness*, a finely-crafted murder mystery sent in Shropshire at the height of World War II. With echoes of ITV series *Foyle's War*, it follows the life and career of DI Tom Tyler, the senior policeman in the small town of Whitchurch. It is summer 1940, and an internment camp for German nationals and undesirables has been set up in the area. When a young woman is found dead nearby, Tyler investigates, all the while worrying about his son, who is soon to be sent to France to fight.

In the follow-up, *Beware This Boy* (2012), it is November 1940 and Tyler's home life has fallen apart. He takes the chance to relocate to Birmingham to investigate an explosion at a munitions factory, and soon realises that it was no accident.

www.maureenjennings.com

Mary Kelly

Though rather forgotten now, Kelly was an excellent writer, who was nominated for the CWA Gold Dagger four times between 1961 and 1969.

The Spoilt Kill (1961) is an unusual novel, a Virago Modern Classic which won the CWA Gold Dagger — with John Le Carre coming second. Set in Stoke at the end of the 1950s, the book shows the Potteries area in its fading glory, warts and all. Nicolson, a private detective, is investigating the theft of designs from a pottery firm, which amounts to industrial espionage. When a body is found in a vat of clay, it is clear that the stakes have been raised. When Nicolson falls for the main suspect, an extra complication is added.

www.fantasticfiction.co.uk/k/mary-kelly

Mark Lawson

The journalist, presenter and critic Mark Lawson has been a commentator on crime fiction for some time, but *The Deaths* (2013) is his first novel for several years.

Set in leafy twenty-first-century Buckinghamshire, it features four couples who live a gloriously wealthy existence, sheltered from the recession that bites the rest of the country. However, undercurrents of tension result in a shocking, horrific act, and the reader is kept in suspense as to the victim, and even the perpetrator. As the police investigation continues, the author lays bare many of the worst aspects of middle-class life.

www.fantasticfiction.co.uk/l/mark-lawson

Clare Littleford

The city of Nottingham is the setting for Clare Littleford's two suspense novels, *Beholden* (2003) and *Death Duty* (2004). The author was working in Nottingham at the time and knew the city well, as is evident in the books.

Beholden is a taut psychological novel about Peter, an officer at Nottingham City Council, who picks up a notebook left on a bus by a girl he knows is a regular passenger. When she disappears he realises that, having read the notebook, he believes he knows what has happened to her. He also realises he must keep that to himself, despite the police interest.

In *Death Duty* (2004), social worker Jo Elliott is attacked, but thinks it was just a mugging until subsequent events lead her to think differently, and link it to a problem family she had long forgotten.

www.fantasticfiction.co.uk/l/clare-littleford

Val McDermid

One of the true greats of crime fiction, Val McDermid is best known for the *Wire in the Blood* series featuring Tony Hill and Carol Jordan. However, her first series features, "cynical socialist, lesbian, feminist journalist"

Lindsay Gordon, who is regularly involved with the police in one way or another.

In *Report for Murder* (1987) Lindsay is desperate for money, and agrees to cover a fundraising gala at a Derbyshire girls' school. When the guest attraction is garrotted with her own cello string, Lindsay is on the spot to unmask a vicious murderer.

Val McDermid has also written a number of stand-alone novels, the best of which is *A Place of Execution* (1999). It tells the story of a young policeman in Derbyshire at the time of the Moors Murders in the 1960s who investigates a difficult and harrowing case concerning the disappearance of a young girl. Years later, having agreed to tell the whole story to journalist Catherine Heathcote for a book, he suddenly refuses to communicate further. Catherine is determined to find out why, but only when she discovers a fresh clue can she begin to understand the horrific truth. The book was shortlisted for the CWA Gold Dagger, and won several awards in America.

See also: the North West, the North East, Scotland: Edinburgh and the Borders
www.valmcdermid.com

Iain McDowall

Iain McDowall is a Scot from Kilmarnock, but has set his books in the Midlands, as that was where he was living when he began to write them. The main setting is the fictional Crowby, an amalgam of various Midlands towns. This allows McDowall free rein to invent places at his own discretion.

The main characters are DCI Frank Jacobson, an old-fashioned beer and fags copper, full of cynicism and bile, and DS Kerr, a rough diamond who cheats on his wife. Tough and thick-skinned as they are, they are both good policemen, doing a difficult job to the best of their ability.

In *Killing for England* (2005) they are searching for the killer of two young black men, one an investigative journalist. The case leads them to investigate political extremism, and the racial hatred of the far right.

Envy the Dead (2009) revolves around three murders, two in the present day and one back in 1984. Martin Grove was freed after twenty years for a murder he didn't commit, but now he has been horrifically killed, and it looks like an execution. When another victim is murdered in identical fashion, clues lead Jacobson and Kerr to look back to 1984 for the solution to the mystery.

www.crowby.co.uk

Jill McGown

Jill McGown was born in Scotland, but lived most of her life in Corby, Northamptonshire. She used this area widely in her books, giving Corby the fictional name of Stansfield, and placing it in a fictional county, Bartonshire. However, she made no secret of the real locations that she used, including Rockingham Castle in *Redemption* (1988).

Her books were police procedurals, featuring DI (later DCI) Danny Lloyd and DS Judy Hill, who are romantically linked from the start. In all they feature in thirteen novels — the series was only cut short by Jill McGown's untimely death at sixty in 2007. McGown was not shy of dealing with difficult subjects such as kidnapping, rape and paedophilia.

In *Verdict Unsafe* (1996), a serial rapist is sent down, issuing vicious threats towards Judy Hill and others. When he is later released due to a legal technicality, she has to prove his guilt for a second time in the face of police corruption.

Plots and Errors (1999) opens with what appears to be a sad case of suicide. An unsuccessful private detective and his wife are found dead in their car, a tube leading from the exhaust. But DCI Lloyd knew the detective's wife as an ex-police colleague, and cannot believe that she would commit suicide, no matter how great her problems. Then a connection is found to the super-rich Easterbrook family.

Lloyd and Hill realise there is more to this case than meets the eye.

www.jillmcgown.co.uk

Leo McNeir

A linguist and dictionary compiler, Leo McNeir is the director of the European Language Initiative. He has compiled specialist dictionaries in many languages including Catalan, Danish and Scottish Gaelic.

The canals and waterways of the Grand Union Canal are the backdrop for Leo McNeir's series of crime novels featuring Marnie Walker.

Death in Little Venice (2001) is set partly in London and partly in Northamptonshire, as Marnie becomes involved with politicians and police, mystery and murder.

www.leomcneir.com

Rod Madocks

A senior professional in the world of mental health, Rod Madocks even worked for two years in a secure mental hospital. He has used this background for his only novel (so far) — the excellent *No Time To Say Goodbye* (2008).

The book serves as a salutary reminder that if you search for the truth, you must be ready to accept it, wheever it may turn out to be. Set in Nottingham and Retford, it tells the story of Jack Keyse, a worker in a mental hospital for the criminally insane, searching for the truth about his former girlfriend — who vanished without trace in 1986. To find it he must use (and abuse) his professional position to get close to those responsible.

www.rodmadocks.com

Faith Martin

Oxford-born Faith Martin uses her knowledge of the narrowboat community and the Oxfordshire countryside for her series of crime novels about DI Hillary Greene of the Oxfordshire Police.

In the first book (*A Narrow Escape*, 2004) Hillary is under internal investigation for corruption, and the only case she has been allocated is a straightforward case of accidental death — a drowning in a local canal. She discovers that there are depths to the case that no one could have imagined, and a killer needs to be stopped.

In *Down a Narrow Path* (2008), two cases combine to give Hillary the worst time of her career. A sniper is murdering police officers all across the country, and a much-disliked woman has been murdered in a quiet Oxfordshire village. As Hillary's search for the killer reaches its conclusion, a shocking act shakes her to her core.

www.fantasticfiction.co.uk/m/faith-martin

John Masterman

Sir John Cecil Masterman, to give him his full name, was an Oxford don and a member of the intelligence community in England before, during and after World War II (in which he chaired the Double Cross Committee). He was not a prolific fiction author but wrote two crime novels, set in the Oxford that he knew so well.

An Oxford Tragedy (1933) is set in the fictional St Thomas's College. An unpleasant Fellow of Classics has been murdered in the Dean's rooms, and all his colleagues are under suspicion. It is left to Ernst Brendel (a visiting lawyer about to give a lecture), and Francis Wheatley Winn (a senior tutor), to establish what happened. This was one of the first novels to use the setting of Oxford University to show the effects of violent death in a normally genteel setting, and it predated the works of Michael Innes and Colin Dexter.

The follow-up novel, *The Case of the Four Friends* (1957), again features Brendel. It is an unusual story in which Brendel recounts a tale of four companions, each of whom is considering committing murder.

en.wikipedia.org/wiki/John_Cecil_Masterman

Priscilla Masters

Staffordshire and Shropshire are the two principal areas used by Priscilla Masters for her various crime fiction novels. She comes from a medical family and has worked as a nurse at The Royal Shrewsbury Hospital, so the medical details of her books have the ring of authenticity.

She is best known for her series featuring the strong-minded Inspector Joanna Piercy. This is set around Leek in Staffordshire, and anyone familiar with the area will spot local landmarks such as the Winking Man rock formation and the Maer Hills.

In *Endangering Innocents* (2003), Joanna is faced with a traumatic case as she investigates a missing schoolgirl in a farming community while the an outbreak of foot and mouth disease is causing havoc.

The author's second series features Shrewsbury coroner Martha Gunn. In *Smoke Alarm* (2012) Martha is called to the scene of a fire which has claimed the life of three people. Her suspicions are confirmed when a second local fire is started deliberately, but there is no obvious connection between the two houses. As she delves further into the mystery with the help of the police, a tragic story of dementia and mental health issues unfolds.

Masters has also written a number of one-off medical mysteries, usually set in the Midlands. In *A Fatal Cut* (2000), a body is found in the grounds of a Birmingham Hospital. When pathologist Karys Harper examines it, she finds that the apparent surgical wounds were made after death. A bizarre killer is at work, and he hasn't finished yet.

www.priscillamasters.co.uk

Nicola Monaghan

Having gained an MA in Creative Writing from Nottingham Trent University in 2004, Nottingham-born Nicola Monaghan wrote her first novel, *The Killing Jar*, in 2006. The book deals with life on Nottingham's toughest estates. It is the story of Kerrie-Anne, a troubled child who is selling drugs at school by the age of ten. As a teenager she joins forces with her friend, Mark, in a life of drugs and crime. Eventually she wants to escape this world, but can she find the wherewithal to do so? The book won a Betty Trask award from the Society of Authors.

www.nicolamonaghan.com

Ian Morson

Oxford in the thirteenth century is the setting for Ian Morson's series of books about William Falconer, Regent Master at Oxford University in the very earliest days of its existence (Merton, Balliol and University Colleges were established between 1249 and 1264).

In the first book in the series, *Falconer's Crusade* (1994), Falconer is concerned when his students are suspects in the murder of a servant girl. As he tries to ascertain the truth, he is frustrated by the poor relationship between town and gown, and becomes embroiled in a murky world of violence and heresy.

In *Falconer and the Ritual of Death* (2008), a body is found when old University buildings are pulled down, and Falconer's subsequent investigations lead him towards the Jewish community, and to hidden details of his own past.

Ian Morson is also a member of The Medieval Murderers, that small group of crime writers who have joined together to create books based around their own characters, so William Falconer sometimes appears within their titles.

www.ianmorson.co.uk

Frank Palmer

The late Nottinghamshire-based Frank Palmer gave up a career in journalism (he worked for various newspapers including the *Daily Express* and the *Daily Mirror*) to write two crime series set in the East Midlands. His first series consisted of police procedurals which featured career copper DI "Jacko" Jackson.

In *Unfit to Plead* (1992), Jacko is convinced he has the right man for the shocking murder of a girl who disappeared during the miners' strike of 1984. The young man has a mental disorder, and has a previous conviction for a similar offence. However when further unpleasant murders occur, he has to face facts — as a policeman under pressure he may have got it wrong.

Palmer's second series featured Chief Superintendent Phil "Sweeney" Todd of the East Midlands Combined Constabulary, who replaces the now retired Jacko, in *Dark Forest* (1996). Todd is an interesting character, a high-flying officer brought down by a series of dreadful events which included being on the wrong end of a shotgun blast. The resultant leg-wound leaves him with a severe limp.

However, he is a good policeman and is involved in some fascinating investigations such as *Murder Live* (1997), when a journalist is murdered on live television, and *Final Score* (1998), which sees Todd entering the big money world of professional football in a case that leads him to Pride Park, the home of Derby County.

www.fantasticfiction.co.uk/p/frank-palmer

Iain Pears

An art historian, novelist and journalist, Coventry-born Iain Pears is the author of a highly praised series of novels about art thefts and frauds, as well as several very clever one-off tales.

One of these, *An Instance of the Fingerpost* (1997), is a complex literary story set in seventeenth century Oxford, just after the restoration of Charles II to the English throne. A Fellow of New College, Robert Grove, has been found dead, and a young woman, Sarah Blundy, stands accused of murder. The story is narrated by four witnesses, each with their own point of view. Some of the characters are based on real people, some events are based on real events, and the city of Oxford is superbly defined — indeed it is a character in itself.

www.randomhouse.co.uk/authors/iain-pears

Ellis Peters

Edith Pargeter wrote under several different pseudonyms, of which Ellis Peters is by far the best known — thanks to her creation of medieval monk Brother Cadfael.

Pargeter won many writing awards, and the CWA set up the Ellis Peters Historical Dagger in her honour. She was awarded the British Empire Medal for her war work with the WRNS, and was made an OBE in 1994. Many local places are used throughout the series, which came to an end after twenty books when the author died in 1995.

One of the great historical sleuths, Brother Cadfael is a middle-aged member of the Benedictine Order based at Shrewsbury Abbey in the twelfth century. Though a gentle man, he has been a sailor, and a soldier in the Crusades, and death is no stranger to him.

One Corpse Too Many (1979) is based on the true story of the siege of Shrewsbury Castle in 1138, and finds Cadfael administering the last rites to the defenders, who had been hanged as traitors. However where there should be ninety-four corpses, he counts ninety-five...

The Rose Rent (1986) centres on the Shrewsbury street of Maerdol, which survives today as Mardol. The husband of a beautiful woman has died, and so she has put one of his properties out for rent to Shrewsbury Abbey, at the cost of a single white rose from the Abbey garden. When Brother Eluric is found dead next to that specific rose bush, Cadfael must uncover the complex truth.

See also: Wales

www.fantasticfiction.co.uk/p/ellis-peters

Ann Purser

Born in the town of Market Harborough, Ann Purser has lived most of her life in the Midlands, and her love of country life is clear in all her books.

The main setting for her cosy country crime novels is the fictional Midlands village of Long Farnden, which is where working-class mum, cleaning lady and amateur sleuth Lois Meade lives. Lois runs a cleaning business for houses in the area, both large and small, and regularly becomes entangled in criminal activities around the village which necessitate the presence of her friend Inspector Cowgill.

In *Fear on Friday* (2005), Lois is invited to take on the cleaning for the mayor of nearby Tresham. When she stumbles on the mayor's secret life, and murder intervenes, she has to ask the Inspector for help before it is too late.

Having exhausted the days of the week, the author began a second series of Lois Meade stories with *Warning at One* in 2008. This time nocturnal noises wake a nosy neighbour with serious consequences. Lois and Inspector Cowgill must find out the truth about the blind lady across the road, and the man she says is her son.

www.annpurser.com

Dorothy L. Sayers

One of the major names from crime fiction's Golden Age, Dorothy L. Sayers was born in Oxford, though she only set one novel there. *Gaudy Night* (1935) sees Harriet Vane, Lord Peter Wimsey's lover, returning to the university to attend a college ball, or Gaudy. Someone is attacking the college with poison-pen letters and graffiti, and Harriet tries to find out who, later inviting Lord Peter to join her as events build to their climax.

www.sayers.org.uk

Veronica Stallwood

At one time Veronica Stallwood worked in the Bodleian Library in Oxford, so perhaps it is no great surprise that she uses it in one of her Kate Ivory mysteries, all of which are set in and around the city.

In the second book of the series, *Oxford Exit* (1994), Kate, a historical novelist by trade, is asked by a friend to help investigate a number of thefts of valuable books from the Bodleian Library. When she is also told of the mysterious death of a member of the library staff a year earlier, she realises that there is more at stake than a few missing books.

In the final novel of the series, *Oxford Ransom* (2011), Kate is forced to investigate the disappearance of her own literary agent, Estelle Livingstone, and make some vital decisions in her personal life — will she finally settle down, and with whom?

www.fantasticfiction.co.uk/s/veronica-stallwood

Aline Templeton

Though she is best known for her Scottish series based around DI Marjory Fleming, Cambridge graduate Aline Templeton also wrote a number of stand-alone crime novels.

Shades of Death (2001) is a fascinating psychological story set in the Peak District of Derbyshire. When the long-buried body of a young girl is found deep in a cave system a police investigation begins, which leads DSgt Tom Ward to a strange group of adults, their bizarre childhood games, and secrets which have been buried for twenty years.

See also: Scotland: Glasgow and the West of Scotland
www.fantasticfiction.co.uk/t/aline-templeton

Peter Tickler

Although a graduate of Oxford University, Peter Tickler is more interested in town than gown. His crime novels centre very much on the streets and alleyways of the city, and are more likely to mention Oxford United FC than Oxford colleges.

In his first novel, *Death on the Cowley Road* (2008), the police investigate the apparent suicide of a woman who has jumped from a city car-park. When the last person the dead woman phoned turns up in the River Isis, DI Susan Holden realises she must act quickly to prevent more deaths.

In *Blood on the Marsh* (2009), a death in care leads DI Holden to the Sunnymede Care Home, and when there is evidence of drug misuse, the investigation widens. Murder follows, and Holden is faced with a vicious and ruthless killer.

www.petertickler.co.uk

Simon Tolkien

Though he is the grandson of the great J.R.R. Tolkien, Simon Tolkien's novels have proved him to be an excellent novelist in his own right. An Oxford graduate, he has written three novels about Inspector William Trave of Oxford police.

The Inheritance (2010) is set in 1959, when Trave is unconvinced about the conviction of a young man for the murder of his father, an Oxford historian and former war hero. Trave's work uncovers links to a incident in France in the latter stages of the war which casts long shadows, even fifteen years on.

The follow-up is *The King of Diamonds* (2011). In 1960, Trave heads a manhunt for escaped prisoner David Swain, who is thought to have murdered his ex-lover Katya Osman. His suspicions lead him to Katya's family — but then Trave's wife is linked to the case, and his enemies on the force seize their opportunity to take over. When Swain is recaptured and put on trial, Trave has no choice. He must discover the whole truth, no matter how shocking.

www.simontolkien.com

Colin Watson

The small town of Flaxborough in Eastern England is the setting for all of Colin Watson's crime novels, and though its exact location is never made clear it is generally thought to have been south Lincolnshire, possibly based on the town of Boston. Watson's novels are full of wit and sometimes wicked humour, with sex and violence where necessary, but never to excess.

The novels are generally police procedurals featuring Inspector Purbright and Sergeant Love, who investigate various shenanigans behind the doors and blinds of a supposedly genteel English town. In *Blue Murder* (1979), a fearless journalist publishes the truth about local involvement in pornographic films, but finds he has stirred up more passion than he expected.

www.fantasticfiction.co.uk/w/colin-watson

Charlie Williams

Brutal, gory and politically incorrect, Charlie Williams' series of crime novels is set in the backwater town of Mangel — which is (very) loosely based on Worcester, where the author was born — and has the power and style of writers such as Irvine Welsh. The anti-hero is Royston Blake, an arrogant thug for whom swearing and violence are second nature.

In *King of the Road* (2006), Royston has just been released from a mental hospital, cured after three years. Much has changed: his girlfriend has had a child and his old haunts have been replaced by an appalling shopping arcade. The pressure group opposing this new development want Royston's help to oppose it, in what might be called an old-fashioned way.

When, in *One Dead Hen* (2011), a series of headless bodies turn up in Mangel, the police are looking for a suspect — and Royston Blake fits the bill. However, after interrogation, the police let him go, and Blake decides that this time, he will help the cops. As usual, nothing goes quite according to plan. Blake is up to his neck in trouble yet again.

www.charliewilliams.net

Keith Wright

A serving Nottinghamshire detective in real life, Keith Wright wrote four little-known crime novels in the 1990s, all fittingly published by Constable.

Fair Means or Foul (1995) features the famous Nottingham Goose Fair as DI David Stark and his team desperately try to find the killer of a teenage girl.
www.fantasticfiction.co.uk/w/keith-wright

Ten Recommended Reads

1: *Black Dog* by Stephen Booth (1999)

2: *Dead Old* by Maureen Carter (2002)

3: *Burnout* by Rod Duncan (2005)

4: *Wasted Years* by John Harvey (1993)

5: *Place of Execution* by Val McDermid (1999)

6: *Envy the Dead* by Iain McDowall (2009)

7: *Smoke Alarm* by Priscilla Masters (2012)

8: *One Corpse Too Many* by Ellis Peters (1979)

9: *Oxford Exit* by Veronica Stallwood (1994)

10: *Blue Murder* by Colin Watson (1990)

REGION SIX
Wales and the Anglo/Welsh Borders

Why no Welsh noir? I mean, this isn't Burns country,
this is the land of R.S. Thomas, for heaven's sake.
Wales can out-noir Scotland any day of the week.
PHIL RICKMAN, BBC Wales blog, 3rd August 2011

Wales has a population of over three million people, and
its major cities are Cardiff and Swansea — both of which
are in the south. Much of the rest of the area is hilly or
even, in the north, mountainous, with over 750 miles of
coastline. It has maintained a cultural identity separate
to that of England, and is officially bilingual, with over
500,000 Welsh speakers.

The border with England runs for 160 miles from the
River Dee estuary in the North to that of the River
Severn in the South. For the purposes of this book I have
included several crime writers in this section who have
set series close to the English side of the border, such as
Phil Rickman, M.R. Hall, Ellis Peters and Andrew
Taylor. Many of the other authors included have set individual books in Wales, rather than whole series. Wales
can be seen as being a bit of a gap in the crime fiction
market at present, but surely it can only be a matter of
time before a major Welsh crime series appears. Ewart

Hutton and Harry Bingham are certainly names to watch.

Simon Beaufort

Simon Beaufort is the pseudonym used by husband and wife writing team Liz Cruwys (better known as Susanna Gregory) and her husband Beau Riffenburgh for their historical crime series featuring medieval knight and former Crusader Sir Geoffrey Mappestone. Set in the very earliest years of the twelfth century, the novels have a wonderfully authentic feel, as the authors are steeped in historical knowledge.

Sir Henry's ancestral home is Goodrich Castle in the Welsh borders, and Wales features in several of the books. In *A Head for Poisoning* (1999), Sir Geoffrey is forced to investigate his own family to uncover a traitor who is presenting a grave danger to Henry I, and in *A Dead Man's Secret* (2010) the King orders Sir Geoffrey to deliver mysterious letters to recipients in West Wales. His misgivings about the mission are compounded when the scribe of the letters is murdered before they set off, and when a further death occurs early in the journey Sir Geoffrey must unmask a murderer and discover the truth of the letters, or face disaster.

See also: London (Susanna Gregory), East Anglia (Susanna Gregory)

www.susannagregory.com/simon-beaufort

Harry Bingham

Formerly a banker, Harry Bingham now runs "The Writers Workshop" and writes full-time. His books following the life and career of DC Fiona Griffiths are set in contemporary Cardiff, where she is the youngest detective in the major Crimes Unit. Griffiths is an interesting character, smart, intense, erratic, slightly strange, and with a darkness in her past that gives her a vulnerable, mysterious edge.

In the superb opening novel, *Talking to the Dead* (2013), she is assigned to the case of a murdered prostitute and drug addict, found dead with her small daughter in a grotty Cardiff flat. The only clue is a platinum bank card for a long-dead businessman. When further investigations lead to another dead prostitute, Fiona is plunged headlong into a vicious world of crime and murder. All the time she must battle against her own psychological demons, and hold herself together for long enough to crack the case.

In the equally good follow-up, *Love Story with Murders* (2013), body parts are found scattered throughout a Cardiff suburb —in kitchens, garages and even a potting shed. Then more are found in the nearby countryside outside the city. Two bodies are involved, one male, one female, and Fiona is desperate to find the connection between them, all the time battling to keep her fragile mental state from disintegrating.

www.harrybingham.com

Rhys Bowen

Rhys Bowen (a pseudonym of Janet Quin-Harkin) is best known as the award-winning author of the Royal Spyness and Molly Murphy mysteries, but her first crime series described the Welsh-based adventures of Constable Evan Evans, set in the tiny village of Llanfair in Snowdonia. Like all her novels, these were particularly popular in America, and indeed the second book, *Evan Help Us* (1998), was nominated for a Barry Award.

In *Evan and Elle* (2000), a new French restaurant is opened in an old chapel, but it is not popular with everyone. One night it burns down and a body is found in the debris, forcing Constable Evans to accept that a murderer is at large in the village. *Evan Only Knows* (2003) sees the constable face-to-face with the killer of his father, only to become convinced that a dreadful error has been made.

www.rhysbowen.com

A CRIME YOU'LL
ALWAYS REMEMBER

TALKING
TO THE
DEAD

HARRY BINGHAM

Glyn Carr

The novelist and mountaineer Showell Styles was best known for his naval fiction, but he used the name Glyn Carr for fifteen mystery novels set on mountains and crags all around the world. Quite a few of the novels were set in the hills and peaks of Wales, which Styles knew well from his boyhood. All the books featured actor and climber Sir Abercrombie ("Filthy") Lewker.

In *Death on Milestone Buttress* (1951), a climber dies in a fall, but Lewker is not convinced it was an accident. *Death Under Snowdon* (1954) sees Lewker on the spot when an MP is killed on a booby-trapped footbridge.

www.fantasticfiction.co.uk/c/glyn-carr

Chris Collett

Birmingham is the usual haunt for the DI Tom Mariner police procedurals, but in *Blood and Stone (2013)* he sets off on a walking holiday in Wales to recover from a terrible personal tragedy. Simultaneously a dying ex-con is released early from prison, and decides to get even with some of his old enemies. Tom stumbles upon a body and becomes a prime suspect. To clear himself, Tom must encourage the Welsh countryside to give up its secrets.

See also: the Midlands

www.chriscollettcrime.co.uk

David Craig

One of the pseudonyms for Welsh journalist James Tucker (also known as Bill James), David Craig is the author of a number of crime novels set in and around Cardiff Bay. Born and brought up in Cardiff, Tucker spent many years as a journalist in South Wales and his deep knowledge and affection for the area permeates the books.

DI Dave Brade is not exactly Morse or Wexford — neither of them would set up home with two Cardiff "working girls" or have the body tattoos that Brade does.

But the three Brade books are tough, grimly humorous and realistic. *The Tattooed Detective* (1998) is set at a time when Cardiff Bay was being developed, and the local crime lords wanted their cut. Then a prostitute is found murdered, and Brade (with his colleague Glyndwr Jenkins) must use all his local knowledge to find a vicious murderer.

There are also two books following DC Sally Bithron and Assistant Chief Constable Esther Davidson. In *Tip Top* (2005), a senior policeman is thought to have committed suicide, leaving Sally and Esther to ask some awkward questions — which are thwarted at a senior level.

M.R. Hall

Matthew Hall has been a writer and producer of drama for both BBC and ITV (e.g. Kavanagh QC). He is a law graduate who currently lives not far from where his books are set. The Jenny Cooper series is set in the Severn Valley (renamed Severn Vale) where newly-divorced Cooper is the Coroner. As might be expected from an experienced scriptwriter the stories are cleverly crafted and thought-provoking,

In Hall's debut novel, *The Coroner* (2009), Jenny inherits some old and forgotten files when she begins her new job in Severn Vale. A teenage death in custody and an unlikely suicide make her feel that her predecessor may have been searching for something, and soon Jenny is on the trail too. But her determined efforts to bring about justice prove to be incredibly dangerous.

The Flight (2012) revolves around Flight 189, a state-of-the-art passenger aircraft which crashes into the Severn Estuary, in Jenny's jurisdiction. In order to find out why the plane crashed, and secure justice for all those killed, she must ask the questions that the official investigation avoids — namely how could such a high-tech plane lose power and crash, and why did one passenger survive, only to die mysteriously soon afterwards? Both novels were shortlisted for the CWA Gold Dagger.

www.m-r-hall.com

Ewart Hutton

Already an award-winning playwright, Ewart Hutton's first novel, *Good People* (2012), introduced an excellent new character in crime fiction — DSgt Glyn Capaldi, a half Welsh, half Italian Cardiff policeman, who is exiled to mid-Wales after an investigation in the city goes badly wrong.

In *Dead People* (2013), a skeleton missing its head and hands is uncovered by excavations for a wind farm. Capaldi's superiors are convinced the body was murdered elsewhere and dumped, but Capaldi thinks the killer is more local. When more bodies turn up, the pressure on him to find a calculated, brutal murderer becomes intense.

At the beginning of *Wild People* (2014), the unfortunate Capaldi is recovering after a car crash. He had been bringing a suspect in for questioning when it happened, and she was killed in the accident. As he recalls the events that led up to it, he becomes suspicious — was there more to this than met the eye?

www.fantasticfiction.co.uk/h/ewart-hutton

Bernard Knight

Professor Bernard Knight had a forty-year career with the Home Office, performed a vast number of autopsies and was the main pathologist in many celebrated cases. Besides his Crowner John historical crime series set in Devon, he has written three mystery novels about a pathologist in the Wye Valley, set in 1955.

Where Death Delights (2010) is the first of these novels. Dr Richard Pryor and forensic biologist Angela Bray have set up a private forensic consultancy in the area. In a novel which in its wistful atmosphere is reminiscent of *Heartbeat* or the works of James Herriott, they must

determine the truth when two different women claim that human remains found locally are related to them.
See also: the West Country
www.fantasticfiction.co.uk/k/bernard-knight

Robert Lewis

Robert Lewis hails from the Brecon Beacons, and is the author of three novels about hard-drinking, hard-up, hard-living private eye Robert Llewellyn. Though the first book was set in the backstreets of Bristol, the remaining books in the trilogy have Welsh settings. If there was a crime genre called Welsh Noir, this series would be at the fore-front. Bleak, blackly funny and painfully honest, it describes Llewellyn's descent into the hell of cancer.

In *Swansea Terminal* (2007), he is in Swansea, sleeping on the beach and without a home to call his own. He is amazed when a woman hires him to find her missing boyfriend, but is still more interested in drink. Unfortunately she has links to local gangsters, and ignoring her is not a good idea.

In the final book, *Bank of the Black Sheep* (2011), Llewellyn is in a hospice awaiting the inevitable when he discovers that there is a fortune waiting for him in the depths of West Wales, if only he can stay alive long enough to outwit various pursuers.
www.robertlewis.com

Roy Lewis

Best-known for his Arnold Landon and Eric Ward crime novels, Welshman Roy Lewis has also featured his home-land in several well-written, thought-provoking books.

A Question of Degree (1974) is one of a series featuring Inspector John Crow. When a woman's body is found in a Welsh coalmine it is not long before her husband confesses to murder. Crow is unsure of the veracity of the confession, and decides to delve deeper. He must come to understand the history of a close-knit community in the Rhonnda in order to find the real story.

Lewis returned to the area for *Witness My Death* in 1976, where local doctor Taliesin Rees is shocked when one of his patients is arrested for the murder of a girl who is also on his register. Though the police think the case is closed, he is not so sure. His curiosity leads him into dangerous areas, as there are links to a major environmental dispute.

See also: the North East

www.fantasticfiction.co.uk/l/roy-lewis

Howard Marks

A convicted drug smuggler who served seven years in an American jail, Welshman Howard Marks is the author of the best-selling autobiography *Mr Nice* (2010). He has also put his knowledge of both sides of the law to good use in two interesting crime novels with Welsh settings.

Sympathy for the Devil (2011) is a clever, multi-layered story based around two characters — DSgt Catrin Price and rock singer Owen Face. Catrin has returned to Cardiff after years in London, and her ex-boyfriend, now a junkie but once a policeman, has turned up dead. He had been investigating the mysterious disappearance of Face, whose car had been found abandoned near the Severn Bridge (there are similarities to the real-life disappearance of Richey Edwards of The Manic Street Preachers). With the help of two friends she delves into an increasingly dark mystery.

Catrin returns in *The Score* (2012), with a dead girl in a remote mineshaft and an old friend hiding in the Brecon Beacons who leads her back to London's drug world.

www.howardmarks.name

Edward Marston

The prolific Welsh-born writer Keith Miles writes under various names. As Edward Marston he writes "The Railway Detective" series and the Domesday Books. Both series use locations from all over the country but two excellent titles feature Wales in particular.

"The Railway Detective" is Inspector Robert Colbeck, and the books are set in the heyday of Victorian railways. *The Silver Locomotive Mystery* (2009) takes place in Cardiff in 1855, when Colbeck is called to the Railway Hotel, where a young silversmith from London has been found dead. The immensely valuable silver coffeepot (in the shape of a locomotive) that he was carrying has been stolen, and wealthy ironmaster Clifford Tomkins wants it back. A group of touring actors (performing *Macbeth*) is also involved, and when a member of the group vanishes, Colbeck's case becomes ever more complicated.

The Domesday series, set in the late eleventh century, features Ralph Dechard and Gervase Bret, one a soldier who fought at Hastings and the other a talented lawyer. They are appointed Commissioners by the King, looking into irregularities in the compilation of the Domesday Book.

Each of the novels takes place in a different county. *The Dragons of Archenfeld* (1995) is set on the England/Wales border, where Dechard and Bret are due pass judgement on a land dispute, only to find that their main witness has been burned to death in a house fire.

See also: the West Country, the South and South East, London, the North West
www.edwardmarston.com

Gwen Moffat

The author and climber Gwen Moffat was heavily involved with the RAF Mountain Rescue Service in North Wales, and set several of her crime novels in the area.

She is best known for her novels featuring Melinda Pink, a tough, adventurous magistrate who loves climbing. The first of these, *Lady With a Cool Eye* (1973), sees Miss Pink searching for the real story when the wife of the director of the Plas Mawr Adventure Centre is found dead in her husband's car.

In *Persons Unknown* (1978), Miss Pink is visiting the isolated village of Abersaint when another visitor is killed in a fire. When it transpires that the visitor is a woman with shady links to prominent politicians, Miss Pink has a murder mystery to solve.

See also: the North West, Scotland: Highlands and Islands

www.fantasticfiction.co.uk/m/gwen-moffat

Ellis Peters

The novelist Edith Pargeter had had little success under her own name (or any of several previous pseudonyms), but the use of the name Ellis Peters and the creation of the Welsh-born monk Brother Cadfael led to a considerable upturn in her career. Wales featured in several of the twenty Brother Cadfael novels.

In *A Morbid Taste for Bones* (1977), Cadfael leads a delegation to a remote part of Wales to find the relics of St Winifred and transport them to Shrewsbury Abbey. The relics consist of holy bones, and not everyone is happy for them to be disturbed. When a man is murdered, Cadfael becomes involved in a complicated tale of scandal, love and jealousy.

The Summer of the Danes (1991) is set in North Wales, when Cadfael, a Welsh-speaker since his childhood, is sent as interpreter on a diplomatic mission to the Welsh coast. Unfortunately he becomes caught up in a long-standing quarrel between Prince Owen Gwenydd and his brother, which has led to a Danish fleet landing an army of mercenaries.

See also: the Midlands

www.fantasticfiction.co.uk/p/ellis-peters

Malcolm Pryce

Once an advertising copywriter for a major London Agency, Malcolm Pryce has written a series of unusual mystery novels set in a somewhat strange, alternative version of the town where he grew up — Aberystwyth. With a style that might be seen as "Chandleresque", and a combination of violence, very black humour, bizarre characters and Welsh folklore, the books have now developed a strong cult following. The protagonist is Louie Knight, famous as the only private eye in Aberystwyth.

Last Tango in Aberystwyth (2003) features the girls of the town's "What The Butler Saw" industry, and Dean Morgan from the Faculty of Undertaking. When Dean receives a suitcase intended for an assassin, he has to run for his life. Louie is persuaded to find him, and discover what was in the case — which is more shocking than he could possibly have imagined.

Don't Cry For Me Aberystwyth (2007) is set at Christmas, when a man wearing a red and white robe has been murdered. Soon Louie is on the trail of a legendary letter said to reveal the real fate of Butch Cassidy and his old mate, The Sundance Kid.

www.malcolmpryce.com

Stephen Puleston

Self-published author Stephen Puleston has started a series of books about Inspector Ian Drake, a police officer in beautiful and historic North Wales. In *Brass in Pocket* (2013), two police officers are called to a traffic accident on a lonely road in the dead of night — when their bodies are discovered the following morning Inspector Drake is called to a horrific scene. The killer taunts him by sending him a photograph of one of the dead men, with some song lyrics on the back. Recognising them, Drake knows the killings will continue, and that he must act fast to stop the killer, whatever the cost to himself, his family or his career.

The author has produced a second series featuring Cardiff Detective John Marco, whose first appearance in *Speechless* (2014) finds him on the trail of Polish gangsters.

www.stephenpuleston.co.uk

Phil Rickman

Formerly a journalist and news reporter for the BBC, Phil Rickman currently presents the Radio Wales book programme, *Phil the Shelf*. He has written several stand-alone novels as well as the Merrily Watkins crime series.

Deliverance Consultant for the Diocese of Hereford is hardly the sort of title you expect to see for a sleuth, but that is exactly what Merrily Watkins is. She is a parish priest and local exorcist, and after her husband is killed in a motorway crash, is left to bring up a teenage daughter on her own.

The books are all set on one side or the other of the Welsh border, and feature pagan or paranormal experiences to a greater or lesser extent. In *The Remains of an Altar* (2006), Merrily is called to the Malvern Hills to investigate the paranormal dimension to a series of road accidents. What she finds is an altercation between the defenders of "Olde Englande" and proponents of the new drug culture, which seems to be getting out of hand.

The Smile of a Ghost (2006) is set in the lovely town of Ludlow, as Merrily is called in to help in the mysterious case of a police officer's son who commits suicide by jumping from the castle ramparts.

In *The Magus of Hay* (2013), Merrily's policeman friend, DI Frannie Bliss, calls her in after a man is found dead in a waterfall near Hay-on-Wye. What follows is an extraordinary tale of tradition, murder and magic, set in the Welsh booktown.

www.philrickman.co.uk

Alison Taylor

Alison Taylor made headline news back in 2000 for her work exposing the shocking treatment of children in care in North Wales. She has also written five crime novels set in this area, featuring Welsh policeman Michael McKenna.

Her background in social care is used to good effect, especially for *In Guilty Night (1996),* a harrowing story of corruption and lies which are revealed when a teenage boy, who has run away from a care home, is found dead in a railway tunnel near Bangor.

Child's Play (2001) concerns The Hermitage, a girl's school on the coast near Anglesey. When one of the pupils drowns, McKenna and his team find that below the glossy exterior, the school is not what it seems.
www.fantasticfiction.co.uk/t/alison-taylor

Andrew Taylor

Though he grew up in East Anglia, Andrew Taylor has lived in the Forest of Dean for many years. He has a thirty-year writing career and has won many awards, including the CWA Ellis Peters Historical Dagger (three times) and the Diamond Dagger for his outstanding contribution to crime fiction.

The Forest of Dean and the Severn Valley act as the background to his clever Lydmouth series. The small town is described as being on the Anglo-Welsh border. The protagonists are DI Richard Thornhill, and journalist Jill Francis, and over the series, as the timescale moves from the 1950s to the 1960s, they investigate a number of emotional, complex murder mysteries. All the titles for the series are taken from the poetry of A. E. Housman.

In *The Mortal Sickness* (1995), the new vicar of St John's Church, Alec Sutton, is under pressure. A woman is found battered to death in the church, and he is under fire for not selling the Lydmouth Chalice to fund much-needed repairs. The police investigation then uncovers some very unpleasant secrets.

More secrets are exposed in *Where Roses Fade* (2000), when a young waitress is found drowned in the local river. Though there are doubts about the death, many prominent people in the town are anxious for the case to be closed. A further death occurs, and as Thornhill investigates, the whole town is beset by fear.

See also: the West Country (Andrew Saville), London
www.lydmouth.co.uk

Nicola Upson

The crime novels of Cambridge graduate Nicola Upson are unique, in that she uses real-life crime novelist Josephine Tey as her protagonist. The novels are a fascinating mix of fact and fiction, and a number of different settings are used, including Wales.

Fear in the Sunlight (2012) is a wonderful story, set in two time periods. In 1954 Chief Inspector Archie Penrose learns that a suspect for a terrible crime in America has confessed to three murders in North Wales eighteen years earlier. Back in 1936 Josephine Tey had been staying in Portmeirion to celebrate her fortieth birthday, when a famous actress was murdered nearby. Penrose led the police investigation at the time. In 1954 Penrose has to go back to North Wales to finally unravel the truth. The involvement of Alfred Hitchcock adds to the sense of tension.

See also: the West Country
www.nicolaupson.com

David Williams

After serving in the Royal Navy in World War II, David Williams completed a degree at Oxford and then worked in advertising before starting a successful writing career with *Unholy Writ* (1976). This was his first novel, and it featured banker and sleuth Mark Treasure — a clever and likeable detective.

The Treasure novels used many different locations, but *Divided Treasure* (1987) is set in Llanegwen, a fictional resort on the coast of North Wales which, once successful, has fallen on hard times. Treasure is using his accounting skills to uncover deceit and greed at a local sweet factory when there is a shocking double murder, and he has to act quickly to prevent more deaths.

Besides his seventeen Treasure novels, David Williams also wrote six books about DCI Merlin Parry and his colleague DSgt Lloyd. These well-constructed stories are set around Cardiff in South Wales. In *Death of a Prodigal* (1995), the duo investigate the murder of Mervyn Davies, whose severed head is found in a Tesco bag. It soon transpires that the dead man had left Wales in disgrace in the distant past, and had recently returned to collect a huge inheritance. With money involved, there is no shortage of suspects.

www.fantasticfiction.co.uk/w/david-williams

John Williams

Crime novels are not all straightforward whodunnits. The "Cardiff Trilogy" by John Williams (a former *NME* journalist) is a good example of the type of crime story that sets out to describe a subculture and lifestyle though characters and events — usually those who inhabit the lower reaches of society. With a wide-ranging cast of pimps, prostitutes and politicians, it is set in Cardiff during the regeneration of the late twentieth century and the new millennium.

Cardiff Dead (2000) sees Mazz, a musician, returning to Cardiff for a former band-mate's funeral. There is some doubt about his cocaine-related death, and in addition the band's former drummer has disappeared. In seeking answers, Mazz must think back to when the band was formed in the early 1980s, and understand the changes that have taken place in the city since, and their effects on the people who live there. Evocative and nostalgic, the novel brings together crime, music, and the city of Cardiff in all its glory.

The final part of the trilogy is *The Prince of Wales* (2004) which is centred around a pub of that name, and the characters whose lives are entwined with it.

www.theguardian.com/books/2001/jun/23/fiction

Ten Recommended Reads

1: *Talking to the Dead* by Harry Bingham (2013)

2: *The Tattooed Detective* by David Craig (1998)

3: *The Flight* by M.R. Hall (2013)

4: *Dead People* by Ewart Hutton (2013)

5: *Witness My Death* by Roy Lewis (1976)

6: *Sympathy for the Devil* by Howard Marks (2011)

7: *Last Tango in Aberystwyth* by Malcolm Pryce (2003)

8: *The Magus of Hay* by Phil Rickman (2013)

9: *The Mortal Sickness* by Andrew Taylor (1995)

10: *Cardiff Dead* by John Williams (2000)

REGION SEVEN
England — The North West

It is one thing to set a scene against a public background, such as the library, riverside or a castle in Kendal, quite another to dump a corpse in, say, a private house that actually exists. I try to ensure, so far as I can, that settings which are integral to the plot, such as Marc Amos's bookshop, and the 'coffin trail' over Tarn Fell, for example, have no direct counterparts in the real-life Lakes. In fiction, there has to be a limit to realism.

MARTIN EDWARDS, **www.martinedwardsbooks.com**

North West England includes the huge conurbations of Merseyside and Greater Manchester, as well as the beautiful Lake District. Its coast is dominated by Merseyside, but also includes the coastal section of the Lake District and the seaside holiday towns of Blackpool, Morecambe and Lytham St Annes.

Manchester was originally a major centre for the Industrial Revolution, when it was known as "Cottonopolis" due to its place at the centre of the cotton industry. Liverpool was an important centre for the slave trade and has a long history as a major port. The whole area has undergone considerable regeneration in recent years, and of course for many Liverpool will always be synonymous with The Beatles, the band who changed the course of musical history. Ron Ellis and Martin Edwards have used this period of the city's history extensively.

Lancashire has old mill towns such as Burnley and Blackburn, and a rural area to the north that borders the Lake District, which is England's largest National Park. An area of stunning beauty, it contains wild fells, picturesque villages and the famed lakes of Ullswater, Windermere and Coniston Water.

In recent years a number of new crime authors have emerged from this area, including Chris Simms, Nicholas Blincoe, Chris Ewan and recent ebook sensation Kerry Wilkinson. Martin Edwards has written a wonderful series of evocative novels set in the Lake District as well as a series set in Liverpool, Val McDermid was a journalist in Manchester, and Ron Ellis has been a Merseyside DJ.

Ray Banks

After a variety of jobs, including croupier and double glazing salesman, Scottish author Ray Banks established himself as a crime writer with his series of books about Cal Innes, a somewhat rough-and-ready private eye in Manchester. Banks has many influences, and the books follow in the hard-boiled tradition of authors such as Ken Bruen or Joseph Wambaugh. Punches are not pulled and political issues are addressed.

In the third novel, *No More Heroes* (2008), Innes is working for a slum landlord when he rescues a child after a firebomb attack on one of the landlord's buildings. The landlord then hires him to track down the arsonists, pitting Innes against various enemies, including a group of neo-Nazis. As the summer temperature escalates, Innes realises that heat has more than one source.

www.thesaturdayboy.com

Tom Benn

A graduate of UEA with a creative writing degree, Stockport-born Tom Benn received a Malcolm Bradbury bursary in 2009. Three years later his first novel, *The Doll Princess* (2012), was published to great acclaim. Hard-hitting and violent, it is set in an apocalyptic Manchester just after the shock of the IRA bomb attack in 1996.

The central character in this and the follow-up novel, *Chamber Music* (2013), is Henry Bane, a tough, quick-witted, sarcastic anti-hero. Bane is involved a full-scale turf war in a Manchester underworld where anyone might have a gun with a bullet meant for him. The dialect of the city is there in the spare prose, and the changing face of Manchester in the 1990s is exposed in all its glory.

www.randomhouse.co.uk/authors/tom-benn

Nicholas Blincoe

Lancashire-born Nicholas Blincoe has set two of his half-dozen crime novels in Manchester. At one point he even recorded for Factory Records, and his knowledge of the sleazy side of Manchester's music scene is reflected in his debut novel, *Acid Casuals* (1995). With gangland violence and lots of sex, it tells the story of a transsexual called Estella who is determined to kill her distinctly unpleasant boss.

The hard-hitting *Manchester Slingback* (1998) won a CWA Silver Dagger. It tells the story of Jake Powell, boss of a London casino, who had left the Manchester gay scene many years before when his best friend was killed. Now another friend has been murdered, and DI Davey Green is taking Powell back to confront his old life. Full of authentic descriptions of 1980s Manchester, and a world of drugs sex and violence, it is a gripping, if rather disturbing read.

www.fantasticfiction.co.uk/b/nicholas-blincoe

John Bude

Ernest Elmore was a founder member of the Crime Writers' Association, but wrote only a few novels under his own name. Under the pseudonym John Bude, though, he wrote around thirty novels between 1935 and his death in 1957.

The Lake District Murder (1935) was his second novel, and the second to be republished by the British Library in 2014. Like the first, it is redolent of the Golden Age, with the thought processes of the detectives (amateur and professional) as important as the location. A body is found at an isolated garage, and Inspector Meredith (a regular in the author's books) is called in, though it appears to be just a sad suicide. Meredith soon realises this is not the case and is drawn into a fascinating case involving illegal petrol and underground passageways.

See also: the West Country

www.fantasticfiction.co.uk/b/john-bude

Ed Chatterton

For twenty years or so Ed Chatterton was a writer and illustrator of children's books, but he has now turned to crime fiction with an accomplished, if rather grisly, debut *A Dark Place to Die* (2012) — which is set in Liverpool.

There are no holds barred from the moment that a body is found on the Liverpool shoreline, tortured and displayed as art. The body turns out to be the long-lost son of a former Liverpool detective, now living in Australia, who returns to the city to seek justice... or revenge.

The second novel, *Down Among the Dead Men* (2013), involves the extraordinary Williamson Tunnels, a bizarre Victorian labyrinth of underground passages under Liverpool which were only rediscovered in the 1990s. DCI Keane is desperate to find the missing son of a couple who died in a supposed murder/suicide pact. The boy was working on an film set in the city's underground tunnels and Keane will go to any lengths (or depths) to find him.

www.edchatterton.com

Deborah Crombie

Dallas-born though she is, Deborah Crombie is a confirmed anglophile who at one time lived in Chester. Her love for the area was confirmed by *Water Like a Stone* (2006), a book in the Duncan Kincaid series, which is set in and around Nantwich.

Superintendent Duncan Kincaid's family holiday in Cheshire is disrupted by three sudden deaths — two in the present and one from the past. Soon his idyllic childhood memories of Nantwich are replaced by far darker thoughts as he is drawn into a murder mystery on the Shropshire Union Canal that could put his whole family in peril.

See also: London

www.deborahcrombie.com

R.S. Downie

Back in 2004 Ruth Downie won the Fay Weldon section of a BBC writing competition called *End of Story,* and her first novel was published two years later.

Full of her irrepressible sense of humour, *Ruso and the Disappearing Dancing Girls* (2007) is set in Roman Britain, specifically in the Roman town of Deva (Chester), where Gaius Petreius Ruso is a doctor in the Roman Army. When someone begins murdering local dancing girls, his medical knowledge is required. However, he falls foul of the hospital administrator and falls in love with a slave girl after he has made the mistake of saving her from a dreadful fate. He really doesn't want to investigate the deaths, but someone has to.

See also: the South and South East

www.rsdownie.co.uk

Martin Edwards

As a lawyer, Martin Edwards has represented clients such as Alder Hey Hospital and Liverpool Football Club. He has been a crime writer since 1991 and is now the archivist of both the Crime Writers Association and The Detection Club. A prolific writer and blogger, he has written two superbly-crafted series of crime novels, and edited a number of anthologies.

The two series have separate settings, but both showcase the author's ability to evoke the character of the places about which he writes. The Harry Devlin series is set in Liverpool, where Devlin is, like the author, a lawyer. The novels are intricately plotted with subtle twists and turns to keep the reader interested. The city is brilliantly described, and the musical connections are as defined as the backstreet pubs and bars.

In *Yesterday's Papers* (1994), an amateur criminologist persuades Devlin to look into the case of a teenager killed in 1964 at the height of Merseybeat. When another more contemporary death occurs, it is clear that his investigations into the Beatles era must continue.

Waterloo Sunset (2008) continues the series of pop-related titles with a strong story which begins with Harry reading his own obituary in the press — apparently someone wants him dead. When Harry becomes a murder suspect and everything falls apart, he must use all his talents to save his career, and his life.

The second series is very different, in that the setting, rather than the resolutely urban Liverpool, is the Lake District in Cumbria. With an engaging detective, DCI Hannah Scarlett, and a historian with an eye for detection, Daniel Kind, the series deserves greater recognition than it has had so far.

*The Coffin Trail (*2006) introduces the pair, as Kind buys a retreat in the Lakes which has links to a cold case that Hannah is working on. As Hannah's investigations continue they uncover a crime with roots deep in the Lake District past.

In the most recent book in the series, *The Frozen Shroud* (2013), Daniel becomes interested in an old murder case and a link to similar case just five years ago, both in the remote community of Ravensbank. He goes to a Halloween party there, only to find that death has been brought up to date.

www.martinedwardsbooks.com

Ron Ellis

Ron Ellis grew up in 1950s Liverpool (he was born in the same year as John Lennon), and has used his first-hand knowledge of the city and the music of the period as a backdrop to his two distinctly different series of crime novels.

His first DCI Glass novel, *Murder First Glass*, was published in 1979, and three further novels followed in the next fourteen years. In *Snort of Kings* (1980), Glass investigates horse-racing scams around the country while his son-in-law, DCI Robin Knox, is working undercover as a pop promoter to trap a huge drug ring. The two cases come together in a dramatic finale at the Aintree Grand National.

In 1998 Ellis began a series of novels featuring the colourful Liverpool DJ and private eye Johnny Ace, who often finds himself involved in contemporary crimes that link to the past — usually the 1960s. In *The Singing Dead* (2000), for example, Johnny discovers some missing John Lennon tapes, only to find that others will kill to get their hands on them. The book ends with an extraordinary climax at a Beatles convention.

www.ronellis.co.uk

Chris Ewan

Having come to prominence through his excellent *Good Thief's Guide* series about writer and part-time burglar-for-hire Charlie Howard, Chris Ewan changed tack for

Safe House (2012), a well-written stand-alone novel set on the Isle of Man.

When Rob Hale recovers consciousness after a motorcycle accident on the island, no one will acknowledge the existence of his pillion passenger Lena. With the help of Rebecca, a private investigator hired to investigate the death of his sister, he sets out to discover what is behind this conspiracy of silence. As one twist follows another, it is clear that even in this apparently quiet backwater no one is quite what they seem.

www.chrisewan.com

A.D. Garrett

This is the pen-name used by two writers — a former Chair of the CWA and an eminent forensic scientist — Margaret Murphy and Professor Dave Barclay.

Their first collaboration, *Everyone Lies* (2013), is set in wintry Manchester, where DI Kate Simms is a struggling copper trying to recover her rank after a demotion for a professional error which affected a previous case — the disappearance of the daughter of an expert pathologist (Professor Nick Fennimore), who has now left the area to live in Scotland. Simms is handed a case no one wants, investigating the deaths of a number of local drug addicts, and she needs Fennimore's help — but has he forgiven her? Two further deaths add even further tension and Kate is faced with the worst case of her career.

www.adgarrett.com

Jonathan Gash

Best known for his Lovejoy novels, set in East Anglia, Jonathan Gash is in reality Lancashire-born doctor John Grant. When he moved away from the Lovejoy books he introduced a very unusual new sleuthing duo working in Manchester — Dr Clare Burtonall and her gigolo boyfriend Bonn.

They first appear in *Different Women Dancing* (1997), where Bonn witnesses a road accident in which a man is killed. When he proves to have suspicious links to Clare's husband, she needs to know more, and hires Bonn to help her. Far more sexually explicit than the Lovejoy novels, the five books in this series open up the grim streets of Manchester's underworld.

See also: East Anglia

www.fantasticfiction.co.uk/g/jonathan-gash

Elizabeth George

American writer Elizabeth George has used many different British settings for her Inspector Lynley novels. In *Missing Joseph* (1993), Lynley's friends Simon and Deborah St George are in Lancashire visiting an old friend, a local vicar. When they arrive, they find he has been poisoned. Suspicious of the method, Simon calls his old friend Lynley, who is on holiday nearby, and they uncover a complex web of sinister rural passions.

See also: the West Country, London

www.elizabethgeorgeonline.com

J.M. Gregson

A former teacher, Lancastrian J.M. Gregson has set his long-running DI Percy Peach series in the county he knows best. Peach is an old-style copper, a shrewd judge of character, clever and experienced. He has an attractive assistant in Sergeant Lucy Blake, and a somewhat unpleasant boss in the well-named Chief Superintendent Thomas Bulstrode Tucker. The setting for these traditional police procedurals is the fictional mill town of Brunton.

In *A Little Learning* (2002), two students at the University of East Lancashire plan to commit the perfect crime — stealing rare books from University Director "Claptrap" Carter. When they burgle his home they find him murdered. Peach's subsequent investigation uncovers all kinds of nefarious goings on in academia, including blackmail and drugs.

By 2012 Peach has been promoted to DCI, and in *Least of Evils* (2012) he investigates the shooting of a young man outside the estate of local benefactor and suspected gangster Oliver Ketley. It seems that Ketley has more than a police investigation to worry about...

See also: the West Country

www.fantasticfiction.co.uk/g/j-m-gregson

Mandasue Heller

Mandasue Heller has been a crime writer from a young age — her first book, *The Front* (2002), was published when she was just twenty-one. Her gritty, fast-paced novels are often set in the dark side of Manchester and portray a hard-working, hard-living city. She lived for some years in the Hulme Crescents area of the city, and her knowledge is crucial to the feel of the books, which reflect the toughness of both the area and the people. In many ways she is Manchester's version of London's Martina Cole or Jessie Keane.

In *The Game* (2005), Mary, a sassy and rebellious teenage girl, becomes involved in the world of prostitution and drug-dealing, which she can deal with until she is inveigled into providing two young men with alibis for a drug dealer's murder. Suddenly she is in desperate trouble. Years later she meets an old friend who is shocked by the changes that this world has had on Mary. Is there any way out?

In *Lost Angel* (2012), Johnny Conroy, a Manchester criminal, is trapped in a loveless marriage with the daughter of a major gangster, who has threatened to kill him if he ever leaves her. Conroy realises that if events take their natural course, a lot of family secrets will be brought into the open. He knows he must do something — and someone may get hurt.

www.mandasueheller.com

Frank Lean

Private eye Dave Cunane is the central character in Frank Lean's no-nonsense Manchester-based thrillers. An unpredictable, enigmatic character with a weakness for drink and women, he is often a disappointment to his father, a former senior policeman in the Manchester force.

With snappy dialogue and knockabout violence, the books follow the "hard-boiled" or "pulp" tradition.

Nine Lives (1995) finds Cunane in jail on Christmas Day for a murder he did not commit, and though he manages to extricate himself in due course he discovers that his enemies are many and varied. Not only that, but they want him out of the way — or worse.

In *Above Suspicion* (2001), Cunane is hired by a Premiership footballer whose daughter has been kidnapped. As he investigates, he finds that football, violence and blackmail make a deadly mix.

www.fantasticfiction.co.uk/l/frank-lean

Val McDermid

An Oxford graduate and national newspaper journalist, Val McDermid was the crime reviewer with the *Manchester Evening News* for four years. Her writing career started when she had a play performed in Plymouth, and her first crime novel was published in 1987, since when, with her full-on style that forces the reader to taste the blood, she has become one of the most popular crime writers in the world.

Her knowledge of Manchester was reflected in her Kate Brannigan novels. A Thai-boxing, tough-talking private eye, Kate Brannigan was the junior partner in a Manchester firm specializing in the investigation of computer fraud, and she featured in six books between 1992 and 1998.

Crack Down (1994) was shortlisted for the CWA Gold Dagger in 1994, and saw Brannigan dragged deep into the city's secret world — drug dealing, pornography and murder. Her boyfriend is in jail, and his young son proves to be as big a problem to Kate as his father.

In *Blue Genes* (1996), Kate is already having a bad time when the doctor responsible for her best friend's fertility treatment is murdered. To discover the reason she has to plumb the depths of the medical profession, where money rules and nothing can be taken at face value.

See also: the Midlands, the North East, Scotland: Edinburgh and the Borders

www.valmcdermid.com

Edward Marston

Few writers are as inventive as Keith Miles who, under a variety of pseudonyms, has about ten different mystery series to his name. As Edward Marston, he wrote the Domesday series, set (as the title suggests) in Norman England.

Ralph Delchard and Gervase Bret are commissioners looking into irregularities in the compiling of the Domesday Book, and the series takes them to many different locations. In *The Hawks of Delamere* (1998), they come to Cheshire to settle various disputes between church and state. When they discover the Prince of Gwynedd held prisoner in a castle by the Earl of Chester, they want know why.

See also: the West Country, the South and South East, London, Wales

www.edwardmarston.com

Andrew Martin

Gifted writer Andrew Martin combines a love of trains with an interest in Edwardian society for his series featuring railwayman Jim Stringer.

In *The Blackpool Highflier* (2004), Stringer is working on the Lancashire and Yorkshire Railway, driving a holiday excursion to Blackpool which is nearly derailed by a large stone that has been laid across the track. Determined to find the saboteur, he follows a trail from Blackpool Station that leads him into a very different world full of strange theatre acts, fraudsters, toffs and revolutionaries.

See also: the South and South East, the North East

www.jimstringernovels.com

THE BLACKPOOL HIGHFLYER

By the author of *The Necropolis Railway*

ANDREW MARTIN

Gwen Moffat

Born in 1924, Gwen Moffat has climbed all her life, and became Britain's first female professional rock-climbing guide. She is also a wonderful writer of mysteries, usually set in areas she knows well from her climbing background. The Lake District has featured in a number of her novels, including some featuring the redoubtable Miss Pink, Justice of the Peace and keen follower of outdoor pursuits.

Moffat's descriptions of the beauty and ruggedness of the Lakes can be seen in both early and late examples of her work. In *A Short Time to Live* (1976), Miss Pink is in the Lakes to investigate sheep-stealing, and when a dead body is found she is embroiled in murder too. In *The Lost Girls* (1998), Miss Pink is on the spot when a drought reveals the bones of a long-lost murder victim.

Gwen Moffat's last novel, *Gone Feral* (2007), may not feature Miss Pink, but the Lake District is still there in a classic story concerning a mysterious boathouse, a burnt-out caravan, and a long-dead murder victim whose watery resting place is disturbed by a passing Lakes steamer.

See also: Wales, Scotland: Highlands and Islands
www.fantasticfiction.co.uk/m/gwen-moffat

Margaret Murphy

A former Chair of the Crime Writers' Association, Margaret Murphy won the Short Story Dagger in 2012 and has written nine excellent novels set in North West England.

In *Weaving Shadows* (2003), the setting is the beautiful, historic walled city of Chester. Clara is recovering from the events of the previous novel (*Darkness Falls*, 2002) but is thrown into crime again when she takes on a new client who is a convicted killer.

The Dispossessed (2004) and *Now You See Me* (2005) are set on Merseyside. In the former, DI Jeff Rickman becomes embroiled in the world of Afghan asylum seekers when a young prostitute is murdered and the local community closes ranks. His life is turned upside down when he is framed for murder. In the latter, a woman with no past has gone missing, and a businessman with a dodgy past is worried when a hacker breaches his computer network.

www.margaretmurphy.co.uk

Nick Oldham

When Nick Oldham's first novel was published in 1996, he was still a serving police officer in the Lancashire Constabulary. He joined the force aged nineteen and retired in 2005 after a varied thirty-year career, which has enabled him to give his police procedurals a gritty realism and credibility that many others lack. Focusing regularly on places like Blackpool and Manchester, he peels away the outer skin of the cities to reveal the true picture underneath.

The series protagonist is DI Henry Christie, a tough, no-nonsense cop in the Lancashire constabulary. In *The Last Big Job* (1999), the blowing up of three police cars in Blackburn is just the start of an extraordinary case which involves the FBI, an undercover policeman in fear of his life and an attempt to rob the Royal Mint.

Blackpool is the setting for *Psycho Alley* (2006), in which Henry leads the investigation into a series of violent attacks on women, which have terrorised the city. The inquiry has a national profile, and Christie's reputation is under intense scrutiny.

www.nickoldham.net

Maurice Procter

Often seen as the originator of the British police procedural, Lancastrian Maurice Procter was a constable in Halifax, Yorkshire, for nearly twenty years. His knowledge of police work and his attention to detail was first seen in the semi-autobiographical novel, *No Proud*

Chivalry, in 1947, and his writing career lasted almost a quarter of a century.

He set most of his books in a fictional version of Manchester, which he called Granchester, with football teams called United and City, and a prison called Farways (as opposed to the real-life Strangeways). His main character was Chief Inspector Philip Martineau.

In *Hell is a City* (1954), Martineau is pitted against a escaped prisoner who he has known since childhood. During his escape the man killed a prison guard, and now he sets out to take revenge on Martineau, who he blames for sending him to prison in the first place. The book was filmed by Hammer in 1960 with Stanley Baker in the main role.

www.fantasticfiction.co.uk/p/maurice-procter

Sarah Rayne

A writer of fantasy novels under various pseudonyms, Sarah Rayne uses her own name for her crime and mystery novels. Her first crime novel, *Towers of Silence* (2005), was long-listed for a Dagger Award. Her interest in old buildings and atmospheric settings is obvious in all her books.

Her novels are set in various parts of the country including the Fens, London and Cumbria, which is the scene for *The Death Chamber* (2007). This novel centres on the fictional Calvary Gaol, a bleak and forbidding building in the Cumbrian Hills where a TV presenter wants to conduct an experiment in the old execution chamber. Meanwhile, Georgina Grey is investigating the work of her great-grandfather, who was a doctor at the prison in the 1930s. Unfortunately their curiosity unearths old secrets — secrets someone is desperate to keep hidden.

www.sarahrayne.co.uk

Imogen Robertson

Imogen Robertson is a TV and radio director whose series of Georgian mysteries features wealthy Harriet Westerman and reclusive anatomist Gabriel Crowther.

In *Island of Bones* (2011), Crowther and his friend Harriet return to Crowther's home town in the Lake District to investigate a mystery connected to his father's death. They discover that in Keswick, with its backdrop of fells and water, the past and present are due to collide. Modern justice is challenged by ancient methods, and rumours and suspicion are rife. A body has been discovered on an island in Derwent Water, and Crowther's family secrets are brought into the open.

See also: the South and South East

www.imogenrobertson.wordpress.com

Bill Rogers

Once the Principal Inspector of Schools for Manchester, Bill Rogers comes from a family of policemen which includes his father, grandfather and even his great-grandfather. He acted as a liaison officer between the Education Authority and Greater Manchester Police, setting up various initiatives to reduce crime. He has written a number of well-received crime novels set in his home city, all featuring DCI Tom Caton.

In *The Head Case* (2009), the Prime Minister's Special Advisor on Education is murdered in Manchester. The involvement of MI5 and Special Branch hinder Caton's investigation, and the family's reactions are strange, so he realises that something is wrong in the corridors of power — but will he be allowed to find out what?

Backwash (2013) sees Caton take on the might of the internet, as he follows up the killing of a young man in East Manchester. He finds that many dangers lurk online. Using social media will never seem the same again.

www.billrogers.co.uk

J.J. Salkeld

The pseudonym of journalist and photographer Richard Simpson, J.J. Salkeld's atmospheric Lakeland mysteries concentrate on the work of DI Andy Hall and his coll-eagues at Kendal CID.

Death on Account (2013) gives Hall and his team two cases to crack. A known supergrass has been killed, and Hall must find out if his identity was compromised by someone within his own team. Meanwhile, a woman and her disabled daughter are suffering horrendous threats on a run-down housing estate, and scarce resources mean that the police are struggling to provide help where it is most needed.

In *Riddled on the Sands* (2013), a fisherman vanishes while working out in Morecambe Bay. When a shocking discovery points to murder, Hall has a problem — the crime scene is cleansed with every tide.

www.fantasticfiction.co.uk/s/j-j-salkeld

Chris Simms

Back in 2007 Chris Simms was one of the twenty-five writers picked as the future of British writing by Waterstones. Now he is the author of a number of Manchester-based thrillers, usually featuring DI Jon Spicer. A thought-provoking writer, his novels are defi-nitely a cut above the norm. His settings are often bleak and mysterious, reflecting the underside of Manchester and the Peak District. He was shortlisted for the CWA Dagger in the Library award in 2011.

In *Outside the White Lines* (2003), a killer stalks the motorways of the North West, and when the police fail to catch him, a young traffic policeman takes matters into his own hands, with frightening consequences.

The Edge (2009) is the fifth Spicer novel, and sees him investigating the gruesome death of his wayward younger brother, who had links with the Manchester gangs that are threatening a small Peak District town.

In 2012 he began a new series, also set in Manchester, featuring the lively and likeable DC Iona Khan of the Manchester Police Counter-Terrorism Unit. In *A Price to Pay* (2013), she becomes a target when she investigates the case of a girl who jumped to her death from a motorway bridge.

www.chrissimms.info

Cath Staincliffe

Cath Staincliffe is a prolific writer, with books, TV series and radio plays to her name. Born in Bradford, she gained a degree from Birmingham University before working as a community artist in Manchester. She has three separate series of crime novels, with different themes and protagonists, but all are set in Greater Manchester.

In the first series, Sal Kilkenny is a private investigator trying desperately to balance her job with her role as a mother. She has featured in eight novels so far. In *Towers of Silence* (2002), she is persuaded to look into the circumstances surrounding the last hours of a woman who has fallen to her death from the Arndale Centre Car Park.

In the second series, Janine Lewis is a pregnant single mother who shakes up the Manchester Police Force by becoming its first female DCI. In *Blue Murder* (2004) she heads her first major enquiry, into a vicious attack on a local deputy headmaster. The book formed the basis of the TV series *Blue Murder* which starred Caroline Quentin.

In 2012 Staincliffe wrote a prequel to the TV series *Scott and Bailey,* called *Die to Me*, and a follow-up, *Bleed Like Me*, was published in 2013. The books follow the careers of two detective constables, DC Janet Scott and her best friend DC Rachel Bailey.

In *Bleed Like Me* (2013), three bodies are found in a pub on the Larks Estate in Manchester. The prime suspect has fled, and his two young sons are missing. Scott and Bailey are reeling from personal disasters, but must put these aside to find the missing man.

Besides these series, the author has also written several thought-provoking stand-alone mysteries, including

Witness (2011) — a powerful story about the human cost of being in the wrong place at the wrong time.
www.cathstaincliffe.co.uk

Rebecca Tope

Rebecca Tope is best known through her series of Cotswolds novels, but she has a new series of cosy Lake District mysteries about florist Simmy Brown.

In *The Windermere Witness* (2012), Simmy provides flowers for a wedding which ends in tragedy, and is soon a witness to a murder. The main suspects seem to be the groom's tough and volatile family and friends, but is there more to it?

See also: the West Country

www.rebeccatope.com

Alex Walters

Alex Walters is a management consultant working in the criminal justice sector. Under his real name, Michael Walters, he has written three unusual crime novels set in Mongolia.

His first novel as Alex Walters was *Trust No One* (2011), which centred on the character of Marie Donovan, a London-based detective who goes undercover in Manchester, living and working amongst some of the most dangerous criminals in the country, in order to bring down a major gangster. When her position is compromised she has nowhere to go for help, so must rely on her own abilities to extricate herself from a terrifying predicament.

The follow-up, *Nowhere To Hide* (2012), opens in spectacular style, as a hitman despatches four people, including a drug dealer and a police informant. The police believe that this is part of a long-running gang war, and Marie is sent to Chester in an undercover role. Things soon go wrong, and she finds herself caught between her complicated personal life back in London and her ever-more uncomfortable position in the North.

www.mikewalters.wordpress.com

Shirley Wells

Cotswold-born Shirley Wells has written a variety of books under a number of pseudonyms, but her crime novels are written under her own name. She has two series, both full of strong characters and set in the North West.

In the first, forensic psychologist Jill Kennedy has given up police work to live in rural Lancashire, but is often called upon to help by old colleague DCI Max Trentham. In *A Darker Side* (2008), they investigate the murder of a schoolboy in the village of Kelton Bridge, which has more secrets than any village should.

The second series features Dylan Scott, a disgraced ex-policeman now working as a private investigator in the dreary Lancashire backwater of Dawson's Clough. In *Dead Silent* (2011), Dylan is hired to find a missing girl who is considered dead by all but her father. As he digs into her past, someone tries to frighten him off, which only serves to prove that he is on the right track.
www.shirleywells.com

Neil White

A criminal lawyer by profession, Yorkshireman Neil White first appeared on the crime scene with *Fallen Idols* in 2007. Since then he has written four more books set in the fictional, grey-stoned, Lancashire cotton town of Blackley, all featuring DC (later DSgt) Laura McGanity and her journalist boyfriend Jack Garrett. Action-packed and occasionally very gory, they will appeal to fans of hard-hitting page-turners.

In *Last Rites* (2009), Blackley is rocked by a violent death. It appears to be just another tragedy, but Garrett becomes involved in the search for a suspect, and the facts don't add up. When Laura becomes caught up in the investigation, the town's grim secrets begin to unravel and they face a crazy killer who will stop at nothing.

In 2012 the author moved the action to York with the stand-alone novel *Beyond Evil*, but a new Manchester-set novel, *Next To Die*, was published in 2013.

www.neilwhite.net

Kerry Wilkinson

Self-published author Kerry Wilkinson became a literary sensation when he raced to the top of the Kindle charts in 2011 with his debut ebook *Locked In*. Following fantastic electronic sales he was then signed up by Macmillan in an extraordinary six-book deal.

The series features Manchester detective Jessica Daniels. In *Vigilante* (2011), the press are not too unhappy when a serial killer starts murdering hardened criminals, but when blood from a crime scene is matched to a man already in prison, alarm bells begin to ring.

In *Playing With Fire* (2013), Jessica is faced with protecting an arsonist whose actions led to a man's death, while investigating a series of teenage suicides. Meanwhile her boyfriend wants to set a wedding date, and the press are threatening to turn the public into a lynch mob.

www.kerrywilkinson.com

Ten Recommended Reads

1: *The Coffin Trail* by Martin Edwards (2006)

2: *The Singing Dead* by Ron Ellis (2012)

3: *Safe House* by Chris Ewan (2012)

4: *Lost Angel* by Mandasue Heller (2012)

5: *Psycho Alley* by Nick Oldham (2006)

6: *Hell is a City* by Maurice Procter (1954)

7: *The Edge* by Chris Simms (2009)

8: *Die to Me* by Cath Staincliffe (2012)

9: *Last Rites* by Neil White (2009)

10: *Vigilante* by Kerry Wilkinson (2011)

REGION EIGHT
England — The North East

*The officers of North End Division — Sullivan's
men — knew their own midden. They knew the bolt-
holes, the hideouts and the various gang
headquarters. They knew the cellars and the attics
and the half demolished houses... where a hunted
man might go to earth... under the railway
viaducts, the rat-runs behind the slaughterhouse...
they knew all the clubs, brothels, boozers, cafes,
dens and knocking-shops. They knew their patch.*
JOHN WAINWRIGHT, *The Last Buccaneer*,
Macmillan, 1971

The North East of England is an area full of contrasts,
from the great cities of Leeds, Newcastle and Bradford to
the glorious countryside of the Yorkshire Dales. Its cities
were crucial to the Industrial Revolution, its coal
producing power and its mills producing clothes for the
whole country and beyond, while its shipyards on
Tyneside built ships for the world. Now much of this has
changed, the mines and shipyards have closed and the
mills are empty, but the area is still vibrant — a hugely
important part of the UK.

Many great detectives police this area, for example,
DCI Alan Banks (Peter Robinson), Dalziel and Pascoe

(Reginald Hill), Vera Stanhope (Ann Cleeves), and DI Charlie Priest (Stuart Pawson). The *Red Riding Quartet* by David Peace is set in and around Leeds, Newcastle is the backdrop to several novels from Martyn Waites, and John Wainwright brought his extensive experience of policing in Yorkshire to bear in his excellent police procedurals. In recent years David Mark and Nick Quantrill have put Hull on the crime map, Daniel Ramsay has introduced us to Whitley Bay and Lesley Horton has painted a powerful picture of the urban and racial tensions of Bradford.

Kate Atkinson

Having made her name as a literary novelist with books such as *Behind the Scenes at the Museum* (1995), Kate Atkinson has written a series of superbly-observed crime novels featuring private investigator Jackson Brodie, each with a different setting

Started Early, Took My Dog (2011) is set in and around Leeds. The novel is witty and stylish, and concerns a group of people linked by various events. The central character (apart from Brodie himself) is retired police officer Tracy Waterhouse, who makes an extraordinary decision when she meets a drug addict and her daughter in a Leeds shopping centre. With a selection of wonderful characters like the elderly, dementia-affected Tilly and connections to a murder in the city in the 1970s, the novel weaves a powerful web of corruption, child abduction, and death.

See also: East Anglia
www.kateatkinson.co.uk

John Baker

A graduate of Hull University, John Baker has used Yorkshire as the setting for all of his crime novels. He was a founder member of The Crime Squad — a virtual collective of crime writers from the North of England.

The six novels featuring reformed alcoholic and rock music fan Sam Turner are set in the beautiful medieval city of York. Turner is a reluctant investigator. In *Death Minus Zero* (1996), he finds himself in deep trouble when he takes on a client who is an escaped psychopath. Then, in *The Meanest Flood* (2003), he has to investigate the murders of two his ex-wives while being a suspect himself.

John Baker has also written two novels set in the East Yorkshire port of Hull featuring ex-con Stone Lewis. *The Chinese Girl* (2000) involves a selection of social issues including mental illness, gang culture, drugs and racism.
www.murdersquad.co.uk/index.php?baker

Robert Barnard

In a career of around thirty years, Oxford graduate and distinguished academic Robert Barnard wrote over forty crime novels, and in 2003 he was awarded the Diamond Dagger by the Crime Writers Association for his lifetime achievements. Though he was born and brought up in Essex, he lived in Yorkshire and regularly used Yorkshire settings in his books. He died in September 2013.

Charlie Peace is a black Yorkshire policeman who has appeared in eleven clever and gently humorous novels since 1989. In *A Hovering of Vultures* (1993), Peace wonders why an internet entrepreneur should suddenly take an interest in the old case of a Yorkshire writer who committed suicide after murdering his sister with an axe.

The Corpse at the Haworth Tandoori (1998) sees Peace investigating a body found in a car park behind a Haworth restaurant — and discovering dark secrets amongst the local artistic community and in the forbidding countryside.

In addition, various stand-alone novels are also set in Yorkshire, such as *The Graveyard Position* (2004), in which Merlyn Cantelo returns to Leeds to claim his inheritance from an elderly aunt, a clairvoyant who had predicted a violent future for him. Sadly, she appears to be right.

www.fantasticfiction.co.uk/b/robert-barnard

Pauline Bell

Formerly a teacher in Halifax, Pauline Bell has family connections with the police, in that one of her grown-up children is married to a detective. She has created the fictional Yorkshire town of Cloughton (somewhat similar to Halifax), and the main protagonist is Benny Mitchell, a detective who, in the course of fourteen books, rises from DC to DCI.

In *Reasonable Death* (2001), an Asian schoolgirl is missing, and with his boss away Mitchell is in charge. When a drugs case deteriorates into a murder investigation unexpected depths are discovered in these complex cases.

Nothing But the Truth (2005) is a very personal story as far as Mitchell is concerned. His wife is the only witness to a hit-and-run, but the investigation is scaled down when evidence of intent is not forthcoming. Then it transpires that the victim is not only a known womaniser, but a former schoolfriend of his wife, who is seemingly prepared to break the law to help him.

www.fantasticfiction.co.uk/b/pauline-bell

Frances Brody

Having begun her writing career as a historical novelist under a pseudonym, Frances Brody returned to her own name in 2009 for a crime series set in the early 1920s featuring the spirited and energetic war widow Kate Shackleton.

The author is from Yorkshire, and her love of her home county is reflected in the novels. The books have an authentic feel with fine descriptions of the West Riding, the post-war world and the early Roaring Twenties.

A Medal for Murder (2010) is set in Harrogate, with a body in the town theatre's doorway and the kidnapping of the play's leading lady to keep Kate busy.

In *A Woman Unknown* (2012), a rich American, already facing ruin, is found dead in the Metropole Hotel in Leeds. He had recently employed Kate to investigate the mysterious actions of his wife, who is ostensibly visiting her sick mother. Kate tries to unravel the truth, and as she does so the case becomes much more personal.
www.frances-brody.com

Helen Cadbury

Helen Cadbury was one of the winners of the Northern Crime Writing competition in 2012, and her first novel, *To Catch A Rabbit* (2013), is set in her home territory of Doncaster and York.

Sean Denton is a young Police Community Support Officer (PCSO) in Doncaster, who is shocked when a dead prostitute is discovered on his patch. Meanwhile Karen Friedman is searching for her brother, who disappeared when running an errand for a local crime lord. So begins a complex tale of the sex trade in Yorkshire, human trafficking, and police work.
www.helencadbury.com

Ben Cheetham

Sheffield author Ben Cheetham is the writer of *Blood Guilt* (2012), a crime novel which has sold over 100,000 copies on Kindle alone. A fine novel set in the author's home city, it raises a major moral dilemma — how do you atone for causing a death?

DI Harlan Miller's son died in a freak accident, and in a drunken haze Miller killed a man, depriving a family of a husband and father. He is jailed for manslaughter, finally being released four years later. Then the dead man's son is abducted, and Miller is persuaded to investigate. The trail leads him into dark and evil territory, forcing him to question the very laws he used to enforce.

Moral questions are at the centre of Cheetham's follow-up novel, too. *Angel of Death* (2014) is again set in

Yorkshire. A Sheffield man on the verge of bankruptcy tries to kill his family. In Middlesbrough a prostitute known as Angel has unwillingly become a murderer. DI Jim Monaghan is on the verge of retirement, but is determined to see justice done in a case that connects the two events.

www.bencheetham.com

Ann Cleeves

Although she grew up in the south, Ann Cleeves has lived in the North of England for many years, and has set two fine series of crime novels there. She confesses to a love of Northumberland and the North East, and so it is no surprise that this area is the backdrop to many of her novels. She was inducted into the CWA Hall of Fame in 2012.

Between 1990 and 1997 she wrote a series of six novels set in Northumberland, featuring Inspector Stephen Ramsey. They are compelling stories with convincing storylines and characters, such as *Murder in My Backyard* (1991), in which Ramsay buys a cottage in the village of Heppleburn, only to find himself embroiled in local politics when uproar over a housing development leads to murder.

However, Ann Cleeves' most popular character is DI Vera Stanhope, a plain, overweight, middle-aged woman devised as the very antithesis of the glamorous detective often found on television. *Telling Tales* (2005) is set in a small East Yorkshire village, where Vera is reinvestigating the murder of a fifteen-year-old girl more than ten years ago. The woman originally convicted has committed suicide in prison, and new evidence proves her innocent and shows that the murderer is still at large.

By the publication of *The Glass Room* (2012), the series had become popular due to a TV adaptation with Brenda Blethyn as Vera. In this case, Vera becomes personally involved when one of her next-door neighbours goes missing. When she is found, Vera is shocked by a murder — and the neighbour's apparent guilt.

See also: Scotland: Highlands and Islands

www.anncleeves.com

John Connor

Formerly a barrister working on high-profile cases for the Crown Prosecution Service, John Connor is now a full-time writer. He has written five gritty and dramatic crime novels featuring West Yorkshire police officer DC Karen Sharpe, whose tangled personal life always seems to intrude into her equally complex professional career. The author uses his professional experience, as well the post-industrial decay and racial tensions of West Yorkshire, to give the novels a stark, realistic background.

Falling (2007) is a convincing novel, with Karen facing both personal and private problems. While recovering from a traumatic experience she tries to help a young child whose mother has been murdered. In addition, her relationships are in danger of collapsing, and then a series of race riots force her to confront her worst demons again.

In *The Playroom* (2008), the daughter of a Bradford judge is kidnapped. Left out of the police investigation, Karen pursues an allegation of rape against a local MP, but the two cases have links which result in violence and bloodshed — forcing Karen to re-examine a disastrous case which cost her former boss his life.

www.fantasticfiction.co.uk/c/jon-connor

John Dean

An award-winning journalist from Darlington, John Dean has used northern settings for both his series of crime novels

The fictional northern city of Hafton is the setting for books featuring DCI John Blizzard and his assistant DS Dave Colley. In *A Flicker in the Night* (2005), Blizzard investigates a series of arson attacks on elderly men which are reminiscent of attacks made twenty years ago by Reginald Marsh, who is now residing in a mental hospital. Blizzard must decide if there is a copycat pyromaniac at work, or whether the truth is even more improbable.

The second series is set in a rural area of the North Pennines and centres of the work of DCI Jack Harris. In *To Die Alone* (2010), the bodies of a man and a dog are found in the hills, and the ensuing enquiry leads Harris and his team into the world of organised crime and animal cruelty which threatens the rural community of Levton Bridge.

www.johndean.ning.com

Robert Edric

Robert Edric (real name Gary Armitage) is best known as a literary novelist, and has twice been long-listed for the Man Booker Prize (in 2002 and 2006). Between these nominations, he wrote a well-received crime noir trilogy, set in Hull, with fearless descriptions of the city early in the twenty-first century — faceless shopping arcades, unscrupulous second-hand car dealers, tired police stations, and a struggling population reeling from the unstoppable decline of the fishing industry.

The central figure is Leo Rivers, a private investigator who is reminiscent of Chandler's great detective, Philip Marlowe. The first book, *Cradle Song* (2003), is a powerful story of police corruption, child murder and violence, leavened by the vivid descriptions of Hull itself.

The final part of the trilogy is *Swan Song* (2005). The murder of two prostitutes indicates that there is a serial killer on the streets of Hull. An ambitious policeman is in charge of the investigation, and one of his senior officers is a long-standing adversary of Leo Rivers — who is working for the mother of a possible suspect. One way or another, they must unmask the killer.

www.fantasticfiction.co.uk/e/robert-edric

Kate Ellis

Originally from Liverpool, Kate Ellis has a long-standing love of York, and has based her DI Joe Plantagenet series in the city, using the fictional name of Eborby to give her a certain amount of freedom to play about with locations.

In *Kissing the Demons* (2011), Plantagenet is called in when a student is found murdered at 13 Torland Place, a house with a terrible history. Not only was it the scene of a multiple murder in the nineteenth century, it was linked to the disappearance of two girls twelve years ago. When further deaths are discovered, Joe thinks he has a serial killer to catch.

Watching the Ghosts (2012) centres on Boothgate House, once an asylum for the criminally insane. Solicitor Melanie Hawkes is investigating the strange events surrounding the death of serial killer Peter Brockmeister (once imprisoned at Boothgate House) when her daughter is kidnapped. A current resident of Boothgate House is burgled. When Joe Plantagenet becomes involved and links the events, his life is put in grave danger.

See also: the West Country

www.kateellis.co.uk

David Fine

Author and poet David Fine has one crime novel to his credit, *The Executioner's Art* (2002). Sheffield-based, it tells a brutal and often grim story of murder, intrigue and corrupt police officers. When a man is found in an empty factory, sand-blasted to death, it is shocking even for hardened policemen. When no obvious suspect emerges the police simply cover up and bury the case. However, a chance encounter at the victim's long-delayed funeral opens up a new line of enquiry for DI John Tilt, and the case is turned upside down.

www.tangled-web.co.uk/crimedigests/digests02/ tindalstwi02.html

Clio Gray

Though now living in Scotland, Clio Gray was born in Yorkshire. She is the author of a clever series of historical crime novels about a quiet, methodical Missing Persons Finder — Whilbert Stroop — which are set around the time of The Peninsula War, 1808–1814.

In *The Roaring of the Labyrinth* (2007), Stroop is called to Astonishment Hall in Yorkshire, where a number of macabre events have taken place, including arson and murder. Soon Stroop is battling against two different opponents — one seeking recompense for past misdeeds, and the other desperate just to survive.

See also: the South and South East, Scotland: Highlands and Islands

www.cliogray.com

Patricia Hall

For more than fifteen years Patricia Hall wrote for, and edited, the education pages of *The Guardian*, but she had always had a hankering to write crime fiction. Using a pseudonym (her real name is Maureen O'Connor), she has now written more than twenty high-quality crime novels. Most of her output is set in Yorkshire, though her recently-started Kate O'Donnell series is set in London.

Her long-running series of police procedurals featuring the are-they aren't-they couple of DCI Michael Thackeray and journalist Laura Ackroyd is set in the fictional West Riding town of Bradfield, which is loosely based on the author's birthplace of Bradford. The series deals with many prevalent social issues, including gang-culture, prostitution and corruption.

Dying Fall (1994) is set on a high-rise housing estate where tensions are high and joy-riding is the order of the day. The police are struggling to control a powder keg, and are stretched further when the joy-riding results in two deaths. Meanwhile local girls are the victims of a series of assaults, and Laura investigates a decade-old murder with an unsafe conviction. Before long the cases become closely entangled.

See also: London
www.patriciahall.co.uk

Mari Hannah

A Londoner by birth, former probation officer Mari Hannah now lives in the North East, which she uses as the setting for her series featuring DCI Kate Daniels. She makes her love of her adopted region clear.

When Kate first appears in *The Murder Wall* (2012), she is still emotionally affected by her failure to solve a double murder. A man is murdered on the Newcastle quayside, Kate is given the case, and she brings her professional and personal lives into conflict when she fails to disclose that she knows the victim. *The Murder Wall* won the Polari First Book Prize for a debut work which explores the LGBT experience, Kate being an openly lesbian detective in a typical male environment.

The A1 in Northumberland is the scene of a shocking road accident in the third book in the series, *Deadly Deceit* (2013). When an appalling fire is linked to the crash, Kate realises there is more to the case than meets the eye.
www.marihannah.com

Reginald Hill

Unquestionably one of the great British crime writers, Yorkshire-born Reginald Hill was a graduate of Oxford University, and worked for many years as a teacher before becoming a full-time writer. By the time of his death in 2012, he had written more than fifty high-class, ingenious novels and many short stories. He won the CWA Gold Dagger for *Bones and Silence* (1990), and the Diamond Dagger for Lifetime Achievement in 1995.

He was best known for his long-running series of intelligent, complex novels featuring mismatched Yorkshire policemen DSupt Andy Dalziel and Inspector Peter Pascoe. Whatever their ranks, the relationship between the gross, crude but higher-ranking Dalziel and the quieter, more liberal Pascoe is central to the success of the books.

Hill has covered many topical subjects, including the after-effects of the 1984–85 miner's strike (*Under World*, 1988), missing children (*On Beulah Height*, 1998), and terrorism (*The Death of Dalziel*, 2007).

In *An Advancement of Learning* (1971), Dalziel and Pascoe investigate a disinterred corpse at a local college, and their differing backgrounds give them opposite views of students. As the body count multiplies, they have to put aside their prejudices to catch a murderer.

By the time of *A Cure for All Diseases* (2008), a novel written in a highly idiosyncratic style, the pair are older and wiser. Dalziel is recovering from the events of *The Death of Dalziel* (2007) by convalescing in the coastal resort of Sandytown, but warring landowners and a shapely psychologist mean he has very little peace — and nor does DCI Peter Pascoe. A gruesome murder takes place and Pascoe is called in to investigate, helped (or possibly hindered) by the recovering Dalziel.

The series was televised by the BBC and ran from 1996 to 2007, with Warren Clarke as Dalziel and Colin Buchanan as Pascoe.

See also: the Midlands

www.fantasticfiction.co.uk/h/reginald-hill

Lesley Horton

Set in the mixed-race communities of twenty-first century Bradford, Lesley Horton's under-rated series of engrossing, convincing stories show the kinds of urban and racial tensions that exist under the surface of apparently respectable families. DI John Handford and DSgt Khalid Ali are highly credible as the policemen caught in the middle.

In *Devils in the Mirror* (2005), a young black girl has been murdered, and it transpires that she had been involved in a sexual harassment case at school and that the subsequent court case had collapsed. As they investi-

REGINALD HILL

ON BEULAH HEIGHT

A DALZIEL AND PASCOE NOVEL

'REGINALD HILL IS ON MAJESTIC FORM'
GUARDIAN

gate further, Handford and Ali find a variety of widely differing views of both the girl and the teacher concerned.

The Hollow Core (2006) follows Handford and Ali as they investigate a shooting with links to the BNP, while inducting a new detective into the team — DC Parvez Miah, the son of a powerful Muslim leader. When his wife is attacked, it appears that even he has secrets.

www.lesleyhorton.co.uk

Bill Kitson

Bill Kitson has always been a busy man. A former banker, he has many sporting interests which have included umpiring at Lords and running junior cricket teams. His first book, *Depth of Despair* (2009), was nominated for the John Creasey New Blood Dagger, and a later book, *Altered Egos* (2011), for the Ian Fleming Steel Dagger. The books focus on Yorkshire policeman DI Mike Nash of the Helmsdale force.

In *Minds That Hate* (2010), Nash has his hands full with extremist politicians stirring up unrest, and Gary Vickers, a convicted sex attacker, back on the streets proclaiming his innocence. When it appears Vickers has a point, Nash has to try to get to what really happened — and keep Vickers out of the hands of vigilantes.

www.billkitson.com

Sarah Lacey

A pseudonym of author Kay Mitchell, Sarah Lacey's novels focus on Leah Hunter, who is a tax inspector in Yorkshire when she first appears in *File Under: Deceased* (1992). She then becomes a private investigator in *File Under: Arson* (1994).

In *File Under: Jeopardy* (1995), Leah is still working as a private eye, and is surprised when, while waiting for her detective boyfriend, she sees an old schoolfriend bundled into the Bramfield police station, kicking and screaming. Leah remembers her only as a gentle girl, and when the friend subsequently disappears, she decides to investigate.

See also: the North East (Kay Mitchell)
www.twbooks.co.uk/authors/sarahlacey.html

Valerie Laws

Crime fiction is just one style of writing for Valerie Laws, who has written poetry, drama, and comedy, and performs it all live. She has written two crime novels set in the bleak atmospheric North East, featuring DI Will Bennett and his friend, alternative health therapist Erica Bruce.

In *The Rotting Spot* (2011), Erica's friend Lucy Seaton has vanished, just like her cousin many years before. When Erica cannot interest DI Bennett in the case, she begins her own investigation, which leads her to discover what the Rotting Spot really is.

The author has a scientific and medical background, and has used this to great effect in *The Operator* (2013), in which doctors and surgeons are being murdered by a sadistic killer who mutilates their bodies to reflect their medical specialities.

www.valerielaws.com

Roy Lewis

A former Inspector of Schools and a college principal, Roy Lewis is a long-standing crime writer whose first novel was published as long ago as 1969. Although a Welshman by birth, he has lived in the North East for many years and sets most of his novels there.

He has written more than forty crime novels, divided into three separate series. The first of these featured Scotland Yard detective John Crow, who in *Nothing But Foxes* (1977) is called in by the Chief Constable of Northumberland when the most prominent opponent of the local hunt is found murdered.

The second series featured former policeman turned Tyneside solicitor Eric Ward, who takes on a variety of cases including defending a serial killer in *Design for Murder* (2010), the hidden side of the foot-and-mouth epidemic in *Dead Man Running* (2003), and fraudulent marine insurance in *Premium on Death* (1986).

The author's third series began with *A Gathering of Ghosts* in 1983, which introduced Northumbrian archaeologist Arnold Landon, who appeared for the twenty-second time in 2012. Landon is involved in a variety of cases which bring him into contact with the local police, including murder on a local dig (*Angel of Death*, 2006), the death of a journalist (*A Short-Lived Ghost*, 1995), and a headless body in the Tyne (*Headhunter*, 2004).

In recent years Roy Lewis has also written a number of one-off novels with various settings, but returned to the North East in 2012 for two books featuring DCI Cardinal and DC Harry Grout (*The Paduan Conspiracy* and *Cardinal Error*).

See also: Wales

www.fantasticfiction.co.uk/l/roy-lewis

Ted Lewis

Brought up in Barton-on-Humber, Ted Lewis is best known as the author of *Jack's Return Home* (1970), the book on which the classic British crime film *Get Carter* was based. Though the film was set in Newcastle and on the Northumberland coast, the original novel sees Jack Carter returning to his home in Scunthorpe, not Newcastle. The premise is still the same, though, with Carter going home to investigate the death of his brother, and becoming involved in the seedy underworld of 1960s gangland. The author wrote two follow-ups and a few stand-alone novels, but nothing else with the same impact.

www.fantasticfiction.co.uk/l/ted-lewis

Howard Linskey

Once the marketing manager for a celebrity chef, Howard Linskey is originally from County Durham, and has set his compulsively readable, bleak, violent crime trilogy in the city of Newcastle.

In *The Drop* (2011), protagonist David Blake is a career criminal who dislikes violence, though he works for notorious gangster Bobby Mahoney. When another criminal goes missing with a wodge of his boss's money, Blake gets the blame, and sets out to clear his name. In the process he discovers that someone wants to take over from his boss, and that the police are closing in too. Throw in his interest in Mahoney's daughter and the fact that his girlfriend is a lawyer, and it is clear that Blake has some awkward decisions to make.

By *The Dead* (2013), Blake is running Newcastle himself, but when his crooked accountant is arrested and Serbian gangsters move in on his territory, he realises that the police net that is closing in on him is the least of his worries.

www.howardlinskey.com

Val McDermid

Widely recognised as one of the great crime writers, Val McDermid has won awards all around the world. She has written three separate series of crime novels, as well as a number of stand-alone books. Her writing is powerful and takes no prisoners, and her descriptions are gruesome and visceral if there is a point to be made.

The series featuring criminal profiler Tony Hill and DCI Carol Jordan is set in the fictional Yorkshire city of Bradfield. Gripping and gritty, it shows the author's humanity while still highlighting the havoc men and women can cause each other. The series was televised by ITV between 2002 and 2008, with Robson Green as Hill and Hermione Norris as Jordan.

In *Beneath the Bleeding* (2007), Bradfield's star footballer is murdered, then the club stadium is bombed. No one is quite sure whether terrorists are involved or whether it is a single murderer with a vendetta against the club. Hill and Jordan have to work together, but they are not always pulling in the same direction.

The Retribution (2011) saw them pitted against their old adversary, sociopath Jacko Vance, who has escaped from prison and is threatening vengeance on those who put him away. Knowing that he is coming for them is a terrifying ordeal, and Hill and Jordan know there will be no peace until he is caught.

See also: the Midlands, the North West, Scotland: Edinburgh and the Borders

www.valmcdermid.com

David Mark

For seven years David Mark was a crime reporter on the *Yorkshire Post*. He has used this knowledge and experience to great effect in his widely-praised novel, *Dark Winter* (2012), which is the first book in a projected series. It features DSgt Aector McAvoy, a relatively quiet, family oriented, Hull-based detective with an unusual name. The city of Hull is like an extra character in the books — damaged by the demise of the fishing industry, bruised by the general economic downturn, and generally somewhat bleak.

In *Dark Winter*, the city is reeling from a series of murders where each victim was a survivor of a previous tragedy. McAvoy is desperate to prove himself as a Detective Sergeant happier with a computer than a gun, and he knows that motive will be the key to the case — if he can only find it.

Sorrow Bound (2014) is set at the height of a sweltering summer. A new crime lord has taken over the local drugs trade, resulting in even more violence than usual. A series of murders are linked to old, badly mishandled, police investigations and McAvoy, working with DSupt Trish Pharaoh, has his work cut out to piece everything together. Then a blackmailer strikes, and everything McAvoy holds dear is threatened.

www.david-mark.co.uk

Andrew Martin

A qualified barrister, Andrew Martin won the *Spectator* Young Writer of the Year Award in 1988 and has written for several national newspapers. He is best known for his crime series about Jim Stringer, an Edwardian railway detective, who is often (though not exclusively) based in Yorkshire. The stories cover an evocative period in the history of British railways, and cleverly reflect the period up to and including World War I. Later in the series Stringer enlists in the Armed Forces, driving important munitions trains in France, and as far afield as the Middle East.

In *The Lost Luggage Porter* (2006), Jim finds himself in the dark underworld of the great city of York, searching for pickpockets and the like. Then in a dimly lit, smoky pub he meets a villain of much higher standing.

In *Last Train to Scarborough* (2009), Jim is sent to the seaside town to investigate the disappearance of a railway employee, but in the gloom of an out-of-season tourist resort he finds it is not only the charms of the man's landlady that he has to worry about.

See also: the South and South East, the North West
www.jimstringernovels.com

Kay Mitchell

Kay Mitchell wrote two Yorkshire-based crime series in the 1990s, one under the name Sarah Lacey and one under this, her real name. The series of five police procedurals is set in the fictional Yorkshire town of Malminster, and the central character is Chief Inspector John Morrissey.

In *Roots of Evil* (1993), Morrissey investigates the death of the local town planning officer, who is killed when his car crashes over a bridge. The inquiry uncovers more than Morrissey had bargained for.

See also: the North East (Sarah Lacey)
www.fantasticfiction.co.uk/m/kay-mitchell

Steve Mosby

Leeds-based writer Steve Mosby has a love of Stephen King and is not afraid to introduce a sense of terror into his novels, which are set in a variety of northern locations — un-named, but often fictionalised versions of Leeds and other parts of Yorkshire.

Clever, interesting and with an undercurrent of horror, his books are all very different. *The 50/50 Killer* (2007) is about two policemen, one an ambitious newcomer and the other a highly-decorated old hand, who are desperate to track down a killer who preys on young couples, asking them a terrifying question — what would you do to save the person you love? When a victim escapes and tells his story, the officers have to act quickly to save his girl-friend's life.

Black Flowers (2011) is an extraordinary story, which begins with a little girl appearing on a seaside promenade with a black flower in her hand and an unsettling story of her recent past. Meanwhile the lives of writer Neil Dawson and policewoman Hannah Price become linked when Hannah is assigned to investigate the suicide of Neil's father — a case with chilling ramifications for all concerned.

Though not yet the major name he ought to be, the author won the CWA Dagger in the Library in 2012.
www.theleftroom.co.uk

Rebecca Muddiman

Having gained an MA in Creative Writing from Teesside University, Rebecca Muddiman has set her first novel in that area.

Stolen (2013) begins with young mother Abby Henshaw being attacked and left by the side of a remote country road. Her baby daughter, Beth, is taken from her. The investigation is headed by DI Michael Gardner, who exposes various unpalatable truths about Abby. In time the case is dropped, but Abby cannot let it go. When Abby finally receives anonymous information as to Beth's whereabouts, she finds that Gardner's interest is limited, as he has another missing child to find. Therefore she must find Beth herself.

www.rebeccamuddiman.wordpress.com

Chris Nickson

Chris Nickson is an experienced writer who spent thirty years in America before moving back to his home town of Leeds in 1995. He has been a music journalist for many years, and has written a number of celebrity biographies as well as a crime novel set in the music industry in Seattle.

His crime novels are set in eighteenth century Leeds, where Richard Nottingham is the Constable, effectively in charge of law and order in the city. The author clearly knows the city well, has an eye for period detail, and has included streets and landmarks which are still recognisable today.

In *The Broken Token* (2010), Richard discovers a former housemaid's body, brutally murdered along with a man. It seems that the maid had been working as a prostitute. When he investigates, Richard finds that the truth is not only very complex, but unfortunately very close to home.

In *Come the Fear* (2012), a woman and her child are killed in a fire in a run-down district of Leeds. When he realises that it is murder, Richard follows a trail that leads from the poorest citizens to the rich cloth merchants who dominate the city..

www.chrisnickson.co.uk

Stuart Pawson

After careers as a mining engineer and probation officer, Stuart Pawson turned to crime writing, and his first novel was published in 1995. Set in the fictional town of Heckley in the Southern Pennines, somewhere between Huddersfield and Halifax, his high-class series of contemporary crime novels feature DI Charlie Priest of the town CID.

Charlie is basically a good guy, who believes in policing by the book. However, to quote the author, he sometimes turns two pages at once. He is an endearing hero, and his love of music is reflected in many of the jokey book titles (including *Shooting Elvis*, 2006; *Limestone Cowboy*, 2003).

In Pawson's debut novel, *The Picasso Scam* (1995), Charlie has suspicions about a local businessman with a dubious past whose current interests appear to involve art fraud. He has friends in high places, but Charlie is nothing if not persistent, and a link to drugs simply heightens his resolve to put the businessman behind bars.

In *Grief Encounters* (2007), Charlie is shocked when a murder victim turns out to be a woman from his past, and confused by a series of incidents which have left various high-profile local figures either embarrassed or dead. Charlie suspects a vendetta and, as usual, he is up to his neck in trouble.

www.meanstreets.co.uk

David Peace

The son of two teachers, David Peace is from Ossett, near Wakefield in Yorkshire. In 2003 he was named in *Granta*'s list of Best Young British Writers, just after the publication of the fourth and final part of what has become known as the Red Riding Quartet — his series of crime novels set in Yorkshire over the period 1974 to 1983. A thread of police corruption runs through them, as they chart the industrial and economic decline so prevalent in Yorkshire at that time. Gruesome, brutal and written in a his own individualistic style, they are not always an easy read, but they are wonderfully gritty.

Two of the books, *Nineteen Seventy Seven* (2000) and *Nineteen Eighty* (2001) are based on the real events surrounding the Yorkshire Ripper, Peter Sutcliffe. In the former, Bob Fraser, a policeman shown as less corrupt and brutal than most, is convinced that the murders of Leeds prostitutes are being committed by more than one man. A journalist agrees, but can they do anything about it?

In *Nineteen Eighty*, a new broom, Peter Hunter, is brought in from the Lancashire force to clean up the corruption and end the Ripper's reign. However, as the corrupt cops turn on him, his suspicions about the "Wearside Jack" tapes are the least of his problems.

www.faber.co.uk/catalog/author/david-peace

Nick Quantrill

Nick Quantrill had been a prolific writer of short stories for some years before his first novel was published in 2010. In 2011 he was appointed writer-in-residence for Rugby League club Hull Kingston Rovers. He has now written two novellas, as well as three fine full-length novels. His novels all feature Hull-based private detective Joe Geraghty.

In *Broken Dreams* (2010), he is struggling to make ends meet. He is asked to investigate case of staff absenteeism, but when the woman turns up dead in her bed Geraghty is thrust into the middle of a police investigation, which eventually leads back to the days when Hull had a thriving fishing fleet — now long gone.

In *The Late Greats* (2011), New Holland, Hull's popular 1990s band, is persuaded to reform, and Geraghty is employed to liaise between the various personalities. Then lead singer Greg Tasker disappears, leaving Geraghty to work out how and why.

www.nickquantrill.co.uk

Sheila Quigley

Sunderland-born Sheila Quigley rose to prominence as a writer in 2001 when there was a bidding war for her first two novels featuring DI Lorraine Hunt. All the Lorraine Hunt books are set in Houghton-le-Spring, County Durham, where Sheila has lived for many years, and feature the fictional Seahills estate. Lorraine has an off-on relationship with her detective sergeant, Luke

Daniels, and this gives the books an emotional hook to add to the crime story.

In *Every Breath You Take* (2007), Lorraine becomes worried when Luke's wilful, headstrong daughter is attacked, and it appears she may have been targeted by a deranged killer who leaves a white rose in place of the victim's heart.

In 2010 the author introduced a new trilogy featuring DI Mike Yorke and the beautiful setting of Holy Island, off the North East Coast. In *Thorn in My Side* (2010), Yorke returns to the island, where he was brought up as an orphan. He meets an abused street-kid called Smiler, and becomes involved in an extraordinary case which links a viciously flogged corpse, street drugs, disappearing children, and an explosive secret which could have appalling consequences.

www.theseahills.moonfruit.com

Danielle Ramsay

A Scot now living in Whitley Bay, Danielle Ramsay had an academic career before turning to writing full-time. Her first novel, published in 2010, was set in her home town.

Broken Silence (2010) was nominated for the CWA Debut Dagger, and introduced DI Jack Brady, a maverick damaged cop with a harsh outlook on life. When a young girl is found murdered in Whitley Bay, the subsequent investigation leads Brady into the town's underside, a dangerous mixture of corruption, under-age sex, drink and drugs.

The follow-up, *Vanishing Point* (2012), sees Brady dragged into the world of sex-trafficking and East European gangsters. A headless woman has been found on the beach, plunging Brady into a horrible case. Things go from bad to worse when his ex, DS Simone Henderson, is attacked. For his own sake, Brady must find the perpetrators — and quickly.

www.harpercollins.co.uk/authors/10534/danielle-ramsay

Danuta Reah

A former Chair of the Crime Writers' Association, Danuta Reah has written five chilling psychological dramas set in Yorkshire and Derbyshire.

In *Night Angels* (2001), a woman disappears after her car breaks down on her way to Sheffield, a prostitute drowns in the Humber, and a another woman is murdered in a Hull hotel. As the case unfolds, the investigating officers discover links to Eastern Europe, while unknown to them, a stalker is focusing on a linguist from Sheffield University, who may unwittingly hold the key.

Bleak Water (2002) centres on a new, innovative art gallery in Sheffield, which is opened in one of the warehouses on the old Sheffield canal, near where a small child was killed some years ago. The curator arranges an exhibition by controversial artist Daniel Flynn, and when a young woman is found murdered nearby, events start to spiral out of control.

www.danutareah.co.uk

Nicholas Rhea

Nicholas Rhea is a pseudonym of former Yorkshire policeman Peter Walker, who has written more than 130 books in a writing career that has spanned more than forty years. Having started as a beat bobby in Whitby in 1956, he eventually rose to the rank of Inspector before retiring in 1982. His *Constable* series was turned into the TV series *Heartbeat*. All of his crime series were set in Yorkshire, the county he knew best. The *Constable* series ran for over thirty years, from 1979 until 2011, though the TV series ended in 2009.

The novels were centred on rural policeman Nick Rowan, and followed his career as a village policeman in the fictional village of Aidensfield on the Yorkshire Moors. In more than thirty books Nick has to deal with all kinds of crime, from drunks to shoplifters, and from sheep-worrying to murder. The Yorkshire countryside is an important part of the books, and the author's humour and knowledge of the local people shines through from the first story to the last.

In *Constable Around the Park* (2004), Nick discovers a body in a remote house, and has to deal with a prowler at the local hospital, while in *Constable on View* (2007) he has to contend with a vanishing woman, a thief with a conscience and a drowned man whose family do not want to bury him.

Rhea also wrote another light-hearted series about Inspector Montagu Pluke, and a darker, more serious series about DSupt Mark Pemberton.

In *The Sniper* (2001), Pemberton suspects the work of a hitman when he is called to the murder of an elderly church-goer in the Yorkshire village of Robersthorpe. Pemberton becomes even more suspicious when two similar murders are committed elsewhere. It would appear that an assassin is at work, but Pemberton cannot work out why. A tiny clue leads to a big breakthrough.

www.nicholasrhea.co.uk

Candace Robb

Although she is American, Candace Robb is highly quali-fied to write about medieval England, as she holds a PhD in Medieval & Anglo-Saxon Literature. Her high-quality, atmospheric mysteries featuring the one-eyed Owen Archer are set mainly, but not exclusively, in fourteenth-century York. The historical accuracy is reflected in the descriptions of the old city and the lives of the characters, both major and minor.

The series opens in 1363 with *The Apothecary Rose* (1993), in which Archer, working for the Archbishop of York, is sent to the city to investigate a number of poison-ings. The main suspect is originally Nicholas Wilton, Master Apothecary, but as the deaths continue Archer realises the list of suspects is much wider, and even includes Lucie, Wilton's beautiful wife, with whom Archer is steadily falling in love.

In *The King's Bishop* (1996), Archer leads a deputation to Fountains Abbey whilst his old friend Ned Townley leads a similar venture to Rievaulx, both seeking support for the King's candidate for the post of Bishop of Winchester. But soon after leaving York there is trouble, and Archer finds himself dealing with some unpleasant enemies.

www.candacerobb.com

Peter Robinson

A Yorkshireman by birth, Peter Robinson has for many years divided his life between Yorkshire and Canada. He started writing in the mid-1980s and his first Inspector Banks novel was published in 1987.

The series follows the career of Alan Banks, from a newly transferred Inspector in *Gallows View* (1987) to his present position as a highly experienced DCI. He is based in Eastvale, a North Yorkshire town with a cobbled square and classic Yorkshire pubs — said by the author to be loosely based on the likes of Ripon and Richmond. Banks lives in a cottage in Gratly, a fictional rural area in the surrounding dales, and the local countryside is always a star of the books.

As a character Banks is humane and dependable, but his personal life is often laid bare. In the early novels Banks's declining relationship with his wife is an interesting sideline, and in later novels he is involved in an off-on relationship with his colleague DS Annie Cabbot.

Though in some ways traditional police procedurals, many of the novels show much more depth. *Aftermath* (2001) is a chilling story showing that the victims of murder are not just those who are killed. When two officers answer a call to a domestic dispute they discover a cellar full of unspeakable horror. A serial killer has been unmasked, but as Banks pieces together a story of untold evil, Annie investigates the fallibility of ordinary police officers placed in an extraordinary situation.

In a Dry Season (1999) sees Banks investigating a wartime murder which only comes to light when a local reservoir dries up in hot weather, and *Piece of My Heart* (2006) showcases the author's love of music in a brilliant story which links the contemporary murder of a rock journalist with a 1969 investigation into the death of a girl at a Yorkshire rock concert.

Only occasionally has the author moved away from Banks. He has written a number of short stories, and of his three non-Banks novels, two are set in Yorkshire. The first, *Caedmon's Song* (1990), is linked with the Banks novel *Friend of the Devil* (2007), though Banks does not appear in it.

The second, *Before the Poison* (2011) is a stand-alone book about a classical music composer who returns to his Yorkshire roots and becomes fascinated by the history of the house that he buys.

www.inspectorbanks.com

Roger Silverwood

Roger Silverwood uses the fictional South Yorkshire town of Bromersley as the setting for his novels featuring DI Michael Angel. Angel is unusual in that he seems to have a happy home life, living contentedly with his wife and various cats. The series began in 2004 with *In the Midst of Life*.

The plots are often quirky and different. In *Murder in Bare Feet* (2008), Angel investigates a strange case where both the murderer and the victim are shoeless, while in *The Dog Collar Murders* (2011), Angel and his colleagues are desperately searching for a murderer who is dressed as a priest.

www.rogersilverwood.uwclub.net

Peter Turnbull

Though born in Rotherham, Peter Turnbull spent many years working as a social worker in Glasgow. As well as six stand-alone novels he has written three different series in a thirty-year writing career, one of which is set in and around the beautiful, historic city of York.

These police procedurals feature the cases of DCI George Hennessey and his colleague DSgt Yellich. Whether facing biker gangs (*Once a Biker*, 2007), investigating the fate of underworld grasses (*Chelsea Smile*, 2007) or dealing with political extremism, (*No Stone Unturned*, 2008) the DCI is not one to be beaten.

In *Dark Secrets* (2002), Hennessey is forced to examine a tragedy from his own past after the discovery of a woman's body in a shallow grave helps to solve a series of unexplained disappearances, which had a link that he himself should have spotted.

Deliver Us from Evil (2010) is set in a harsh York winter. When a woman is found frozen to death on a bench by a canal towpath it appears to be misadventure. But it soon transpires that this is not the case.

See also: London, Scotland: Glasgow and the West of Scotland

www.fantasticfiction.co.uk/t/peter-turnbull

John Wainwright

Though largely forgotten today, John Wainwright was hugely popular in the 1960s and 1970s. His books depict police work as it was at the time, with no punches pulled. He could never be seen as a very literary writer, but his basic, uncomplicated style works extremely well.

Having spent World War II as the rear gunner in a Lancaster bomber (see his 1978 autobiography *Tail-End Charlie* for details), he joined the West Riding Constabulary in 1947. In the early 1960s he turned to writing, and his first novel, *Death in a Sleeping City*, was published by the Collins Crime Club in 1965.

Most of his works were set in fictional Yorkshire areas such as the city of Lessford or the rugged, rural moorland of Beechwood Brook, and he used his inside knowledge of policing to write several series of unsentimental, authentic crime dramas.

Using an array of recurring police characters, Wainwright's basic sympathy for a policeman's lot was always clear, but he was adept at detailing many different types of criminal, from gangsters and hitmen to those unfortunate people who become criminals through circumstances rather than breeding.

In the chilling *Freeze Thy Blood Less Coldly* (1970), two groups of men find themselves holed up in a farmhouse during a raging snowstorm. One is a jazz band returning from a concert, the other a group of highly dangerous gunmen making a getaway from a violent robbery. When the police arrive, the jazz band are held as hostages, with terrifying consequences for all concerned.

Brainwash (1979) is a powerful psychological drama, an extraordinary tour-de-force describing in detail the interrogation of a murder suspect in a Northern police station. The book was used as the basis for the film *Under Suspicion* (2000), which starred Gene Hackman and Morgan Freeman.

www.fantasticfiction.co.uk/w/john-wainwright

Martyn Waites

Probably the only crime writer (apart from Colin Dexter) to appear as an actor in an episode of *Inspector Morse*, as a policeman in *Dead on Time*, Martyn Waites turned from acting to writing, and his first novel was published in 1997. With his wife Linda he also writes crime novels set in Colchester, Essex, using the name Tania Carver.

Newcastle born and bred, Waites set most of his books in his native North East. He has written two series, featuring journalist Stephen Larkin and private detective Joe Donovan, and both have received excellent reviews.

Stephen Larkin is a former tabloid journalist who makes his first appearance in *Mary's Prayer* (1997), when he returns to his home city of Newcastle to cover a gangster's funeral. An ex-girlfriend asks him to look into the alleged suicide of a friend, and soon Larkin is immersed in the dark side of the city that he had tried to forget. The series ended with *Born Under Punches* (2003), a powerful drama which linked the Miners' Strike of 1984–85 to a contemporary crime in 2002.

Joe Donovan is an investigative journalist who, as the series progresses, works as a private detective with a small team of tough characters to help him. In *White Riot* (2008), Donovan becomes engaged in the dirty world of Newcastle's urban politics, and the race to find a killer who will even organise a race riot to ensure that a thirty-year-old secret with huge ramifications remains buried forever.

See also: East Anglia (Tania Carver)

www.martynwaites.com

Ten Recommended Reads

1: *Started Early, Took My Dog* by Kate Atkinson (2011)

2: *A Medal for Murder* by Frances Brody (2011)

3: *Deadly Deceit* by Mari Hannah (2013)

4: *On Beulah Height* by Reginald Hill (1998)

5: *Dark Winter* by David Mark (2012)

6: *Nineteen Seventy Seven* by David Peace (2008)

7: *Aftermath* by Peter Robinson (2001)

8: *No Stone Unturned* by Peter Turnbull (2008)

9: *Freeze Thy Blood Less Coldly* by John Wainwright (1970)

10: *Born Under Punches* by Martyn Waites (2003)

REGION NINE
Scotland — Glasgow
and the West of Scotland

Detective Catherine McLeod was always taught that in Glasgow, they don't do whodunit. They do score-settling. They do vendettas. They do petty revenge. They do can't-miss-whodunit.
CHRISTOPHER BROOKMYRE, synopsis of *Where The Bodies Are Buried*, 2011 www.brookmyre.co.uk

A vibrant and cosmopolitan city, Glasgow is full of great Victorian architecture, world-famous museums, and the work of Charles Rennie Mackintosh. It is the largest city in Scotland, and is now one of the top ten financial centres in Europe. Flowing through it is the River Clyde, and Clydeside was — at its peak in the early twentieth century — world-famous for shipbuilding. Now that this industry has declined the Waterfront has undergone huge regeneration.

The city is the background to many fine crime novels, and is home to numerous crime writers. Heading the list are the likes of Denise Mina, Alex Gray, Gordon Ferris and Craig Russell, but even they must bow to William McIlvanney, whose book *Laidlaw* (1977) is now considered by many to be the original Tartan Noir novel.

298

The West of Scotland includes towns such as Hamilton, Ayr, Dumfries and Paisley, as well as the port of Stranraer. Dorothy L. Sayers took Lord Peter Wimsey to Galloway, and that area is also the setting for Aline Templeton's relatively gentle series featuring DI Marjory Fleming.

Lin Anderson

Greenock-born Lin Anderson is a graduate of both Edinburgh and Glasgow Universities. She was working as a teacher of mathematics and computing when her first novel, *Driftnet*, was published in 2003.

This novel introduced Glasgow-based forensic scientist Rhona MacLeod, a strong, sassy, sexy woman who is brought in to a murder case to take samples from the teenage victim, only to find that the boy may be the son she gave up for adoption seventeen years before. In trying to find the boy's killer, Rhona becomes enmeshed in a frightening world of paedophile rings and influential men with everything to gain by her death.

Though the author does occasionally venture elsewhere, the series is mainly set in Glasgow, moving from art galleries to the Necropolis cemetery, from dark alleys to select independent schools.

In *Easy Kill* (2008), Rhona is called in when the body of a murdered prostitute is found draped over a gravestone in the famous Necropolis. When another girl is found secretly buried on the same spot and then a third girl goes missing, Rhona must use all her ingenuity to track down a cruel and brutal murderer.

www.lin-anderson.com

Campbell Armstrong

Glasgow-born writer Campbell Armstrong, who died in March 2013, is probably best known for his international thrillers about Special Branch officer Frank Pagan, but late in his career he wrote four excellent books set in his home city. The descriptions of Glasgow are immensely evocative and give the novels a bite and authenticity that adds to their power.

The Bad Fire (2001) was a return to form for the author. It is a gripping story that hints a little at *Get Carter*, featuring as it does a man returning home after the death of a close relative. Eddie Mallon, a New York policeman, returns to Glasgow for his father's funeral. His father, a powerful man with many friends and enemies, was murdered, and the less the local police say, the more Eddie pushes for answers. But in doing so, he finds himself caught in a series of uncontrollabe events.

Jewish Glasgow policeman Lou Perlman is the central player in three further equally-good novels. *The Last Darkness* (2002) is set in a vicious Scottish winter, when a man is found hanging from a railway bridge. Perlman investigates, only to find the case has links to his own family background in the Gorbals.

www.fantasticfiction.co.uk/a/campbell-armstrong

Christopher Brookmyre

Possessor of a fine wit and the best titles in crime fiction, such as *A Big Boy Did It and Ran Away* (2001) and *Attack of the Unsinkable Rubber Ducks* (2007), this Glasgow-born author has used Glasgow and Edinburgh as settings for his acerbic, satire-filled novels. Previously a journalist and film critic, he came to prominence in the 1990s and has retained his popularity ever since.

Where the Bodies Are Buried (2011) is a serious police procedural set in Glasgow, where young would-be actress Jasmine Sharp is helping out in her uncle's private eye business. When he goes missing, all leads point to a twenty-year-old murder mystery that he had been investigating, and vicious gang boss Glen Fallan. The problem is, Fallan is supposed to be dead. Meanwhile, local detective Catherine McLeod is investigating the murder of a drug dealer. The plot twists follow thick and fast as the two cases become entangled, threatening to expose a level of police corruption that could tear apart the entire city force.

Flesh Wounds (2013) finds Sharp and McLeod on opposite sides when someone very close to Jasmine is arrested for murder.

See also: Scotland: Edinburgh and the Borders
www.brookmyre.co.uk

Gordon Brown

Born and bred in Glasgow, Gordon Brown (not the politician!) has written two crime novels set in his home city. *Falling* (2009) is basically a chase novel, where three innocent people are faced with a stark choice on the Glasgow streets. Mild-mannered accountant Charlie Wiggs is fifty-four and working steadily towards retirement when he is asked to look after a package for a work colleague. Never in his worst nightmares did he consider being flung off a forty-storey building or being faced with a dreadful choice: run, die... or fight back.

The follow-up novel, *59 Minutes* (2010), follows the career of a Partick-born criminal as he rises through the Glasgow underworld to become one of the most powerful criminals in Britain, only to have it all ripped away from him. Jailed, then reduced to life on the street, he plans his terrifying revenge.

www.gordonjbrown.com

Karen Campbell

No one could ever say that Karen Campbell doesn't know what she is talking about. She spent five years as a policewoman in central Glasgow, and has used that knowledge to great effect in her series of crime novels, which began with *The Twilight Time* in 2008. The novels feature the career of policewoman Anna Cameron, and in this first novel she is a Detective Sergeant working on the Glasgow "Drag", an area frequented by prostitutes, drug dealers and other inhabitants of the seediest part of the city. With the added personal problem of working with her ex-husband, Anna has her work cut out to deal with the murder of an elderly man, a maniac who is slashing the faces of prostitutes, and increasing racial violence.

By *Shadowplay* (2010) she has been promoted to Chief Inspector and is working in another part of the city. With an abrasive boss who dislikes her, two major investigations, and her own family life being disrupted by her mother's illness, she is torn in all directions. Again, the city of Glasgow is to the fore, with the author's knowledge of its nooks and crannies clear for all to see.

www.karencampbell.co.uk

Gordon Ferris

After a career that led from the Ministry of Defence to Price Waterhouse, Gordon Ferris's rise to the top echelon of crime fiction was as quick as it was surprising to the author himself. His first foray into crime fiction was a two-book series set in London, and his first Douglas Brodie book, *The Hanging Shed*, was an ebook sensation even before it hit the bookshops in 2011. Ferris is superb at showing the hardship and the harshness of a major city struggling to cope with the aftermath of World War II.

The book follows the return of former soldier Brodie to his home city of Glasgow in 1946, and tells the story of his efforts to save the life of a childhood friend, unjustly accused of murder and rape. It is a time of turbulent change in the city, and the world in general. The Empire is finished, the war is over, and austerity is everywhere.

In the second Brodie book, *Bitter Water* (2012), Brodie is working as a poorly-paid crime reporter when he writes a small piece about vigilantes in Glasgow's post-war fight against crime. When the police blame the vigilantes for a local murder, Brodie disagrees with them and investigates, only to find the water is murkier than he realised. *See also: London*

www.gordonferris.com

Alex Gray

Born and raised in Glasgow, former teacher Alex Gray has featured her home city in all her novels, which feature the double-act of DCI William Lorimer and criminal profiler Dr Solomon "Solly" Brightman. Sharply realistic, these absorbing novels show both the light and dark side of the city and its people.

Never Somewhere Else (2002) is the first in the series, and sees Lorimer investigating the shocking murders of three young women in a Glasgow park. The investigation does not go well, and Lorimer is forced to use the services of Brightman, who provides a vital clue. A vagrant is arrested but released, and then disappears. More deaths follow, and then there is a frantic chase across the city to catch the perpetrator.

In *Five Ways to Kill a Man* (2007), someone is murdering elderly women at random, and a high-profile businessman and his wife die in a fire. With personal problems mounting as well, Lorimer asks Solly for his help, which becomes even more vital when the killer moves in on Lorimer and his family.

www.alex-gray.com

Bill Knox

Once the presenter for Scottish TV's *Crime Desk*, Bill Knox wrote two fine crime series set in his native country, one based in Glasgow and the other in more rural areas.

The Thane and Moss series started in 1957 with *Deadline for a Dream*, which introduced DCI Colin Thane and DI Phil Moss of Glasgow's Millside Division. The excellent series is generally set in the city, although the two detectives do occasionally venture outside their comfort zone.

In *The Taste of Proof* (1965), they investigate a swindle based on a famous brand of whisky liqueur, which leads them from the city into the wilds of the bleak Scottish countryside.

The series continued until the author's death in 1999. The last book, *The Lazarus Widow* (1999), was actually completed by Liverpool-based crime writer Martin Edwards.

See also: Scotland: Highlands and Islands
www.booksfromscotland.com/Authors/Bill-Knox

Douglas Lindsay

Douglas Lindsay is the creator of Barney Thomson, the Sweeney Todd of Glasgow and the most misunderstood serial killer In Scotland. His bizarre and laugh-out-loud funny adventures are the pure antithesis of the serious crime novel, but are none the worse for that.

In *The Cutting Edge of Barney Thomson* (2000), the police are after Barney, so he takes refuge in a remote Scottish monastery. Unfortunately, as the weather closes in and the police realise where he is, Barney finds he has a more pressing problem — there's another serial killer living there, and he's already at work.

In *Murderers Anonymous* (2011), Barney is back at the Glasgow barber's shop. He had handed himself in to the police, only to be rejected as yet another imitation version of the real thing. In trying to come to terms with his murderous past, he joins Murderers Anonymous. Soon a serial killer is at work in Glasgow again, and Barney is confused by the grotesque deaths and strange musical references.

www.barney-thomson.com

William McIlvanney

Now widely recognised as the Grand Master of Scottish crime fiction, Kilmarnock-born William McIlvanney had already won awards for his more mainstream fiction when his epic first crime novel, *Laidlaw*, was published in 1977.

DI Jack Laidlaw is a tough no-nonsense copper in a harsh city, dealing every day with the Glasgow underworld. His method of getting close to the people of the city is to walk the streets, giving him access to the alleyways and cobbled closes that would be too narrow for cars McIlvanney shows the city as it was in the 1970s — gritty, grimy, prejudiced and violent but with a redeeming sense of humour. His books transport the reader there, allowing them to experience the city at first hand.

In *Laidlaw*, a girl is found murdered in a Glasgow park and Laidlaw is put in charge of the case. As he uses his knowledge of the city to find the murderer, another group, led by the girl's father, is working towards the same end. It is then a question of who will get to the murderer first, the forces of violence or the forces of law and order.

McIlvanney wrote two follow-up novels including *The Papers of Tony Veitch* (1983), which, like *Laidlaw*, won the CWA Silver Dagger. In this case, Inspector Laidlaw is summoned to the bedside of a dying man, and in his last messages Laidlaw discovers clues to two ongoing mysteries — the murder of a Glasgow gangster and the disappearance of a student. By working in the city and getting under its skin, Laidlaw can unravel the truth behind these events.

www.personaldispatches.com

Pat McIntosh

Pat McIntosh wrote an acclaimed series of historical crime novels set in fifteenth-century Glasgow. The author uses Gaelic, Scottish dialect and a high level of historical accuracy to bring medieval Glasgow to life. Her main protagonist is Gil Cunningham, a notary in the legal system of the time.

In *The Nicholas Feast* (2005), Gil returns to his old university for the Nicholas Feast, and is entertained by a group of actors. When one of them is later found dead, Gil is asked to investigate, leading him into a web of black-mail, intrigue and violence.

The Fourth Crow (2012) begins with a young woman, afflicted by madness, tied to St Mungo's Cross outside the

Cathedral, where it is hoped she will be cured overnight. Unfortunately, in the morning she is found strangled to death, and Gil must find out not only who she is, but who would desecrate the Cathedral in this way. When another death occurs, solving the puzzle becomes even more urgent.
www.fantasticfiction.co.uk/m/pat-mcintosh

Malcolm Mackay

Shortlisted for the John Creasey Dagger for New Crime Authors in 2013, Malcolm Mackay comes from Stornoway on the Isle of Lewis in the Outer Hebrides, though his trilogy is set in the criminal gangland of modern-day Glasgow.

The Necessary Death of Lewis Winter (2013) recounts the story of Calum MacLean, a Glasgow-based contract killer who undertakes a new assignment — to kill small-time drug-dealer Lewis, who has trodden on the toes of drug lord Peter Jamieson once too often. Full of dark streets, harsh language and doubtful morals, it does not let go of the reader until the end.

The follow-up, *How a Gunman Says Goodbye* (2013), concerns Calum's relationship with ageing gunman Frank MacLeod, who has been there, seen it all, done it all. However, he has now lost much of his old confidence and Calum is beginning to worry about him. Frank has had an operation, his senses are not as sharp as they were, and someone could end up dead. However, it may not be the intended victim. The novel won the Deanston Scottish Crime Novel of the Year Award in 2013.
www.panmacmillan.com/author/malcolmmackay

Reg McKay

Formerly a social worker working the toughest streets of Glasgow, Reg McKay turned to writing in 1998. He became a widely-respected investigative journalist and crime correspondent for the *Daily Record*, as well as writing true crime books. In 2001 he wrote *The Ferris Conspiracy* with convicted gangster Paul Ferris, and with input from Ferris he also wrote two Glasgow-based crime novels. He died in 2009.

In *Deadly Divisions* (2002), crime boss Andy Grimes will stop at nothing to find the killer of his brother. The suspect is the mysterious James Addison, wanted by the police for a range of crimes. Grimes pulls in all the favours he is owed by his police and criminal pals to catch Addison, but when bearer bonds worth millions are found by a gang member it changes the picture completely.

The second novel was *Dancing with Death* (2007).

www.fantasticfiction.co.uk/m/reg-mckay

Sinclair MacLeod

Glasgow-born and bred, Sinclair MacLeod spent many years working in the railway industry before becoming a writer. A lifelong crime fiction fan, he turned to writing to help get over the death of his son Calum. His novels have been electronic bestsellers, and paperback versions have followed. He has written two series so far, both using authentic Glasgow settings to great effect.

His debut, *The Reluctant Detective* (2010), introduces Craig Campbell, an insurance investigator who is hired to find the killer of a woman's son. Though he agrees to help, he is uncertain of his ability. Before long he is embroiled in the unpleasant Glasgow underworld — full of greed, corruption and death.

The second series is darker in style, and features DI Alex Menzies and her boss, DSupt Tom Russell. On Alex's first day in her new post the discovery of a burning body is the first intimation that a serial killer is at work — a man attempting to solve the riddle of what happens to a person's soul at the point of death. Before long the body count is rising and the killer gets too close for comfort.

http://www.reluctantdetective.com

Michael J. Malone

Poet and crime writer Michael J. Malone burst onto the Scottish crime scene in 2012 with his highly-regarded first novel *Blood Tears*. It is the first of a proposed series of novels to feature dysfunctional Glaswegian policeman DI Ray McBain, who finds himself on the run as a suspect in a murder case. He covers up relevant information because of links to his childhood in a Catholic children's home. Unsure of even his own past, but certain that the home is central to the investigation, he must both prove his innocence and understand his own history.

McBain appears again in *A Taste of Malice* (2013), in which, while on "light duties", he comes across two cases in Ayrshire of children harmed by a woman trusted to look after them. He thinks the cases may be linked, but as he delves further a disturbing truth emerges. His bosses don't want to know so McBain must go it alone.

www.inpressbooks.co.uk/author/m/michael-j-malone

Denise Mina

Glaswegian Denise Mina studied law at Glasgow University, and has taught law and criminology. She sets her books in her home city, and it is clear that she knows it well. Her three different series portray the city through lives of three very different women – Maureen O'Donnell, a former psychiatric patient who becomes an amateur sleuth to save herself from arrest, aspiring journalist Paddy Meehan, and the volatile DS Alex Morrow. In terms of time, place and atmosphere Denise Mina's novels compare favourably with the best. She has been shortlisted for the CWA Gold Dagger and has won the Theakstons Old Peculier Crime Novel of the Year twice.

Garnethill (1998) is the first in a trilogy, and introduces Maureen O'Donnell, who is a suspect when her boyfriend is murdered. When even her own family think she is involved, she realises that she must fend for herself. What she uncovers in the world of mental health institutions is shocking in the extreme.

DENISE MINA

THE FIELD OF BLOOD

STICKS AND STONES
WILL BREAK YOUR BONES

Resolution (2001) is the final part of this trilogy, and finds Maureen implicated in a major murder trial, while becoming deeply involved in a family feud that leads her into the dangerous world of so-called health clubs.

The Paddy Meehan books are based around the character of a young journalist. In *The Field of Blood* (2005), it is 1981 and Paddy is working in a lowly position for a Glasgow newspaper. A horrific crime is committed by two teenagers, and Paddy's boyfriend is related to one of the accused. Paddy tries to understand what has happened and why, but becomes embroiled in a course of events that endangers everything she holds dear — including her life.

The third series features Glasgow police officer DS Alex Morrow. In *God and Beasts* (2012), three apparently separate cases (a strange robbery, a theft and a politician's lies) are brought to a shattering conclusion, and a sinister political network in the city is forced into the open.

www.denisemina.co.uk

G.J. Moffat

In the real world G.J. Moffat is a company lawyer concentrating on civil litigation. As a writer he has written a series of thrillers featuring lawyer Logan Finch and security consultant Alex Cahill.

In *Daisychain* (2009), DC Rebecca Irvine is called to a murder scene and the victim turns out to be Finch's former girlfriend — the one that he has never forgotten. Now, with Cahill's help, he must avenge her death, find their missing daughter and unmask a murderer.

In *Fallout* (2010), Finch and Cahill are providing protection for a prospective Hollywood star who has returned to her Glasgow roots, while Finch's partner, DC Rebecca Irvine, is helping former boyfriend and drug-addled rock star Roddy Hale to sort his life out. Unfortunately a deranged stalker and a professional killer are about to blow Logan's world apart.

www.gjmoffat.com

Caro Ramsay

A practicing osteopath from Glasgow, Caro Ramsay is also the author of several high-quality, dark and psychological crime thrillers set in the city.

In her heart-stopping debut novel, *Absolution* (2007), a vicious murderer, dubbed "The Crucifixion Killer", is terrorising Glasgow. Alan McAlpine, a senior detective, is brought in to head the case and it reminds him strongly of a case early in his career, when he had to guard a young woman horrifically burned in an acid attack. Now he must solve both the previous case and the new one.

In *Dark Water* (2010), a wanted criminal is found hanging in a tenement block, his face cruelly brutalised. He was a suspect in an old case — the attempted rape and murder of a student. However, he was thought to have had an accomplice, and when another woman is attacked in similar fashion, it is feared that this partner has returned for more.

www.caroramsay.co.uk

Craig Robertson

A long-serving journalist who has interviewed Prime Ministers and visited Death Row, Craig Robertson has written several powerful crime novels including *Random* (2010), a horribly realistic story of a sinister serial killer who strikes with no apparent rhyme or reason and terrifies the whole of Glasgow.

In *Cold Grave* (2012), the central character from *Random*, DS Rachel Narey, sets out to solve a twenty-year-old murder mystery to help bring peace to her father, a retired detective who failed to solve the original case. All Robertson's novels show a clear love of Scotland, whether it be the dank and bitter streets of Glasgow or the little-known Isle of Inchmahome.

http://craigrobertsonbooks.com

Craig Russell

A former police officer, Craig Russell is the author of two superb series, one set in Germany and the other in Glasgow. He won the CWA Dagger in the Library award in 2008 and has been nominated for The Ellis Peters Historical Dagger.

The Glasgow series centres on the character of Lennox, a sharp if slightly shop-soiled private investigator in 1950s Glasgow. Never short of a word or a punch, he is a tough man working a tough city, which is only just recovering from the war years. The city is evocatively described, full of shipyards, gangsters, bent coppers and black humour.

In *The Long Glasgow Kiss* (2010), a crooked bookie from the city's greyhound track is battered to death with a statue of his best dog. Lennox is persuaded to help hunt for his killer, but discovers that the bookie had links to the Three Kings — the crime lords who oversee the whole city.

In *The Deep Dark Sleep* (2011), body parts are recovered from the River Clyde. They are thought to be the remains of feared armed robber Gentleman Joe Strachan. Meanwhile, Strachan's daughters are mystified, as they are sent regular sums of money on the anniversary of Strachan's biggest robbery.When Strachan's daughters hire Lennox to solve this unusual mystery, Lennox finds himself up against the Three Kings again, and this time his luck may run out.

www.craigrussell.com

Dorothy L. Sayers

One of the true greats from the Golden Age, Dorothy L. Sayers was born in 1893, and educated at Oxford University. She used Scotland as the setting for one of her best novels, *The Five Red Herrings* (1931).

This novel is set in Galloway, a part of Scotland loved by painters because of its landscapes. Lord Peter

Wimsey is on holiday when Sandy Campbell, a painter and well-known drunkard, is found dead in a stream. The police think it is an accident, but Wimsey points out that this cannot be so. In the small artists' community there are six people who could have wanted Campbell dead — the murderer and five red herrings. Wimsey and the police sift the evidence, and Lord Peter points the dreaded finger. A clever novel, it is in some ways reminiscent of the work of Conan Doyle. The Galloway setting adds an extra dimension, and Sayers herself makes it clear that the places are real, and can be visited by the reader.

See also: South and South East, East Anglia.

www.sayers.org.uk

Anna Smith

Award-winning journalist Anna Smith has had a lengthy career in newspapers, having covered major news stories from all over the world for papers such as the *Sunday Mirror* and the *News of the World*. Her third crime novel was published in 2013, and all three feature tabloid crime reporter Rosie Gilmour.

Not afraid of hard-hitting storylines, the author has covered topics never far from the news — drugs, child abuse, human trafficking and asylum seekers. In *Screams in the Dark* (2013), problems with housing and unemployment are leading to vigilantes on the streets of Glasgow, with asylum seekers and immigrants as the targets of their abuse. When Rosie interviews a protest group outside a block of flats, she finds clues to a story bigger than she could ever have expected.

In *Betrayed* (2014) Rosie comes up against her most dangerous opponents yet — the Glasgow branch of the Ulster Volunteer Force (UVF).

www.annasmithscotland.com

Aline Templeton

Galloway on the West Coast of Scotland is a fine setting for Aline Templeton's gentle but atmospheric murder mysteries featuring DI Marjory Fleming, a tough detective on the one hand but a farmer's wife with a young family on the other.

The series began with *Cold in the Earth* (2005), which is set during a major foot-and-mouth outbreak in the area. An American woman returns to her birthplace in Galloway to end her uncertainty about her sister's disappearance fifteen years ago. Animals are being culled and communities are threatened with disaster. When the digging of a pit for slaughtered bulls exposes a long-dead body, Marjory's investigation becomes horribly complicated. Links are found to the family of one of her own officers, and tensions in the community rise even further.

The seventh in the series, *Evil for Evil* (2012), is a complex story set in the area around Kirkcudbright. It concerns a body chained to rocks, an ex-military man who rehabilitates soldiers with post-traumatic stress disorder, and a reformed prostitute. Marjory is caught between the murder investigation and the family trauma of her daughter leaving home for university.

See also: the Midlands

www.alinetempleton.co.uk

Peter Turnbull

Peter Turnbull is a Yorkshire-born author who spent many years working as a social worker in Glasgow. He used the knowledge gained in this job as background for his excellent series of police procedurals featuring the "P" Division of Glasgow Police.

Based at Charing Cross Police Station, DS Ray Sussock and his colleagues patrol the streets of the city in the depths of winter (*Deep and Crisp and Even*, 1981) and the height of summer (*Fair Friday*, 1983), dealing with the after-effects of drugs, unemployment, vagrancy and abuse.

In the final "P" Division novel, *The Man with No Face* (1998), the body of a mystery man, his face blasted away, is found in a quiet city street. He turns out to be a small-time crook recently released from prison after serving time for a robbery. When the details of this robbery are investigated further, it is clear that it was part of a major conspiracy.

See also: London, the North East
www.fantasticfiction.co.uk/t/peter-turnbull

Ten Recommended Reads

1: *Easy Kill* by Lin Anderson (2008)
2: *The Bad Fire* by Campbell Armstrong (2001)
3: *Bitter Water* by Gordon Ferris (2012)
4: *Five Ways to Kill a Man* by Alex Gray (2007)
5: *Laidlaw* by William McIlvanney (1977)
6: *The Necessary Death of Lewis Winter* by Malcolm McKay (2013)
7: *Random* by Craig Robertson (2010)
8: *The Deep Dark Sleep* by Craig Russell (2011)
9: *The Five Red Herrings* by Dorothy L. Sayers (1931)
10: *Deep and Crisp and Even* by Peter Turnbull (1981)

REGION TEN
Scotland — Edinburgh and the Borders

There were those who said Edinburgh was an invisible city, hiding its true feelings and intentions, its citizens outwardly respectable, its streets appearing frozen in time... Glaswegians, who considered themselves more passionate, more Celtic — thought Edinburgh staid and conventional... But that was Edinburgh for you. Reserved, self-contained, the kind of place where you might never talk to the person next door... not long ago one stairwell resident out Dalry way had a contract taken out on him by someone else in the tenement because he wouldn't sign his name to a repair estimate.
IAN RANKIN, *Set in Darkness*, Orion, 2000

Edinburgh is just forty-six miles from Glasgow, and is the capital of Scotland, a striking city with spectacular sights such as Edinburgh Castle, Arthur's Seat and the Royal Mile. It is home to the biggest annual arts festival in the world, and attracts more than a million overseas visitors every year. It is a UNESCO City of Literature, and both the Old Town and the New Town are UNESCO World Heritage Sites.

In crime fiction terms it is home to Inspector John Rebus (Ian Rankin), Assistant Chief Constable Bob Skinner

(Quintin Jardine), and Victorian Police Inspector Jeremy Faro (Alanna Knight). Arthur Conan Doyle was born here in 1859, and Ian Rankin was born nearby in Cardenden, Fife, 101 years later. Among the new writers setting work in Edinburgh are Gillian Galbraith, James Oswald and the Mulgray Twins.

The Borders here refers to the area between Edinburgh and the English border, including towns such as Peebles, Selkirk, Hawick and Jedburgh. The area is heavily used as a setting by Gerald Hammond, and other writers use it for occasional scenes.

David Ashton

Actor, author and radio scriptwriter David Ashton had had a long career in film and television before his first novel was published in 2006. He has now written five full-length novels and an ebook novella set in Victorian Edinburgh, featuring Inspector James McLevy. They are all based on a real-life Edinburgh policeman whose diaries Ashton came across at the British Library. The stories began as a radio series (*McLevy*) which featured Brian Cox and Siobhan Redmond, before appearing in book form. Ashton knows the city well and this is apparent in the way he brings it to life, from the cobbled wynds and the tenements to the grandeur of Princes Street.

In *A Trick of the Light* (2009), Levy teams up with Edinburgh doctor Arthur Conan Doyle to investigate the murder of an American visitor to the city — who turns out to be a Confederate officer sent to Edinburgh to buy a warship from the Edinburgh shipbuilders.

In *Nor Will He Sleep* (2013), McLevy meets Robert Louis Stevenson during his investigations into the death of an elderly woman in Leith Harbour.

www.david-ashton.co.uk

Tony Black

An award-winning journalist, Tony Black has become a major force in Scottish crime fiction in just a few years. The Edinburgh he describes may not be that portrayed in the tourist brochures, but it is just as realistic. While they may not be for the squeamish, Black's high-quality novels about Edinburgh's dark side are gripping and compelling. They are Tartan Noir at its best.

He has so far written four books and two novellas about private investigator Gus Dury, and two books about DI Rob Brennan.

Dury was once a hard-hitting journalist with a happy marriage, but is now an ex-journalist with a drink problem and a wife looking for divorce. In *Paying for It* (2008), he is persuaded to investigate the cruel murder of a friend's son, and finds himself immersed in a harsh world of political corruption and people-trafficking, with violence and brutality never far away.

In *Truth Lies Bleeding* (2011), traumatised Edinburgh detective Rob Brennan investigates the murder of a teenage runaway, only to discover that her baby is missing. It soon becomes clear that relations between the girl and her strict Presbyterian father were poor, to say the least. The grim realities of the city's rough underbelly are exposed as Brennan struggles to find the missing child.

www.tonyblack.net

Simon Brett

Best-known for his books about thespian sleuth Charles Paris, Simon Brett has also written for the stage, radio and TV.

The Charles Paris series began with *Cast in Order of Disappearance* (1975), and the second book in the series, *So Much Blood* (1976), is set at the Edinburgh Festival. Charles is performing a one-man set of the poems of Thomas Hood, when an actor is killed by what should have been a fake knife. Add in a beautiful girl, a bomb scare, and a suicide leap, and Paris finds himself involved in a complicated murder case. The city and the theatre setting itself are central to the plot.

See also: the South and South East, London

www.simonbrett.com

Christopher Brookmyre

Though originally from Glasgow, Christopher Brookmyre was at one time a sub-editor for the *Edinburgh Evening News*. Famed for his ability to mix politics and humour, his work may be an acquired taste, but it is one certainly worth trying. With a heightened sense of black humour, a love of football and plenty of comments on religion, he ensures that once read, his novels will not be easily forgotten.

In *Boiling a Frog* (2000), the third book in the Jack Parlabane series, the investigative journalist is doing time at Her Majesty's Pleasure, after being caught breaking into the headquarters of the Catholic Church in Scotland. What follows is a coruscating, blistering commentary on both religion and Scottish politics, interspersed with scatological references and an Edinburgh-based plot.

See also: Scotland: Glasgow and the West of Scotland

www.brookmyre.co.uk

Carol Anne Davis

To write was a long-held ambition for Dundee-born Carol Anne Davis, and she now has around a dozen books to her credit. In addition to her crime novels she has a written a number of books about real life murderers, including *Women Who Kill* (2001) and *Doctors Who Kill* (2010).

She often writes about difficult people, or challenging subjects. Unusually, she does not have a detective or private eye as a lead character in her fiction, preferring to give a voice to a victim or indeed, a murderer. Not for the squeamish, and uncomfortably descriptive in places, her novels are psychological and powerful.

In *Noise Abatement* (2010), a couple move into a new flat in Edinburgh and are slowly driven to distraction by appalling neighbours. Eventually one of them cracks, with bloody, shocking consequences.

Safe As Houses (1999) is the story of David Frate, a sadistic killer living a double life in Edinburgh with a wife who has no inkling of his dark side, until she attends an assertiveness class and realises there is something seriously wrong with their relationship.

www.carolannedavis.co.uk

Gillian Galbraith

A Scot from Perthshire, Gillian Galbraith is a graduate of Edinburgh University, and had several jobs including "agony uncle" for a teenage magazine before changing track and becoming an advocate specialising in medical negligence. Her first novel was published in 2007. Her main character is DS Alice Rice, who works out of St Leonards Police Station in Edinburgh, and the city is central to the feel of the books.

In *Where the Shadow Falls* (2007), Rice investigates the murder of a retired sheriff (the equivalent of a judge in England), which is linked to the environmental battle about the development of wind-farms on the hills outside the city.

In *The Road to Hell* (2012), a naked clergyman and a semi-naked woman are found murdered in separate Edinburgh parks. Alice is struggling with personal and professional issues, including a misconduct charge, and does not always make the right decisions as the investigation continues.

www.gilliangalbraith.net

Allan Guthrie

Orkney-born Allan Guthrie is not only a literary agent, but also a writer of hard-hitting, bone-crunching

American noir-style crime fiction. He has written novellas, short stories, and several full-length novels, all set in Scotland — mainly in Edinburgh. His storylines are tough and realistic, shot through with black humour. He won the prestigious Theakston Old Peculier Crime Novel of the Year Award in 2007 for *Two-Way Split* (2004).

In *Slammer* (2009), young prison officer Nicholas Glass is targeted and bullied by inmates and colleagues alike. Eventually, when his family are threatened, he agrees to a favour, but once that particular door is pushed open, it can never be closed. Eventually Glass will break, and broken glass is dangerous...

Killing Mum (2009) is a macabre novella about an Edinburgh gangster who arranges contract killings in gangland. When his usual hitman is imprisoned he takes on the job himself, but is horrified when his first target is revealed to be his own mother.

www.allanguthrie.co.uk

Gerald Hammond

An architect by trade, Gerald Hammond has written over fifty mystery novels since 1965, usually set in the Scottish countryside (often the Borders or the Highlands). He has written several series and many stand-alone books. His books are readable and enjoyable, especially for his knowledge of dogs (the John Cunningham series), guns (the Keith Calder series), and countryside pursuits such as hunting, fishing and poaching.

Give a Dog a Name (1992) features Cunningham, an amateur sleuth, war hero and dog breeder. He is shocked to be accused of animal cruelty, and though he proves the evidence to be faked, his beloved spaniel Stardust goes missing before he can work out who is threatening him, and why.

Thin Air (1993) sees gun expert and reformed poacher Calder helping the local police after a local farmer is

found dead of gunshot wounds. Calder's expertise helps them to reconstruct the killer's inventive methods.
www.fantasticfiction.co.uk/h/gerald-hammond

Joyce Holms

A teacher of creative writing who has written for the BBC and Mills and Boon, Joyce Holms is the creator of Fizz and Buchanan — Edinburgh lawyer Tam Buchanan and his lively legal assistant Fizz Fitzgerald.

The pair first appeared in *Payment Deferred* (1996), and there are currently nine books in the series which is generally set in Edinburgh, though other settings such as the Highlands are also used. The books are laced with humour, and this sense of fun is one of their great strengths.

In *Mr Big* (2000), Buchanan is drawn into the Edinburgh underworld when one of the city's top drug barons is murdered. He is sure that the police's main suspect is innocent, but when a clue leads to a retirement home for aged thespians he and Fizz discover that nothing is quite what it seems.

Hidden Depths (2004) sees the duo investigating strange goings-on at a local country house, when one of Fizz's friends disappears along with a Rubens painting worth £1.5 million.
www.joyceholms.com

Quintin Jardine

Once a media relations consultant, Quintin Jardine is author of a fine series of Edinburgh-set novels featuring Deputy Chief Constable Bob Skinner. A fearsome character, Skinner is one of the highest-ranking policemen in current crime fiction, and the stories reflect that.

He originally appeared in *Skinner's Rules* in 1993, and has fought to control the streets of Edinburgh ever since. Over the years he has faced murder at the Edinburgh Festival (*Skinner's Festival*, 1994), the murder of his in-laws (*Head-shot*, 2002) and the return to Edinburgh of a Scottish Pope (*Stay of Execution*, 2004).

Jardine is a lifelong fan of Motherwell F.C., and football plays a part in *Thursday Legends* (2000). The Thursday Legends are a group of friends, some of them policemen, who meet each week for a game of football. When one of the team, Alec Smith, is murdered Skinner is called in. Smith was the former Head of Special Branch, and had made many enemies in his career, so there is no shortage of suspects. However, it may be that there is more to the case than meets the eye.

In *Death's Door* (2007), Skinner's force is investigating the ritualistic killings of two young artists. The father of one of them is a powerful millionaire with connections in very high places. When the father's motives become blurred between business and family, Skinner starts to wonder about the abuse of power. Eventually, as they close in on the killer, there is a clear threat of violence, and collateral damage is inevitable.

www.quintinjardine.com

Paul Johnston

Edinburgh-born Paul Johnston is a graduate of Oxford University, where he studied Greek. Despite battling cancer three times he has written three separate series of crime novels since his first book was published in 1997.

The highly unusual Quint Dalrymple series is mainly set in a futuristic Scotland (the 2020s), where Edinburgh has become a bleak, independent city without television, pop music, cigarettes and even private cars, which are all prohibited, while Glasgow is a democratic city specialising in fashion and scientific research. Dalrymple is an irreverent, blues-loving part-time private investigator who, in *Body Politic* (1997), investigates a murder which is similar to those committed years ago by a vicious killer known as the Ear, Nose and Throat Man. To succeed he must unravel a web of corruption which leads to the heart of the city's governing body.

Water of Death (1999) is set in 2025, when global warming has led to water rationing. Life in Edinburgh is dominated by the all-year round tourist festival and the weekly lottery (first prize a weekly shower for a month). Quint is on the trail of a missing lottery winner when a body is found. Death was caused by poisoned whisky and the body count continues to rise as Quint finds conspiracy at every turn.

www.paul-johnston.co.uk

Doug Johnstone

Doug Johnstone may be one of the few crime writers with a degree in physics, and he is also a singer, musician and songwriter. He was writer-in-residence at the University of Strathclyde from 2010–2012 and is the author of five novels, all featuring his trademark black humour and sense of place.

Hit and Run (2012) starts with three young professionals, high on drink and drugs, who are driving back home to Edinburgh when they knock down and kill a pedestrian on Salisbury Crags. Desperate to cover up the accident, they dump the body over the edge. However, the driver was trainee reporter Billy Blackmore, and the following day he is told to cover the case. When it turns out that the murdered man was a crime lord with many unpleasant friends, Billy's life becomes a terrifying ordeal.

In *Gone Again* (2012) Mark Douglas gets a simple phone call saying that no one has picked his son up from school. Mark collects him and goes home, expecting his wife back at any minute. He's not too worried when she does.not appear immediately — after all she has vanished before. Then there is a terrible discovery, and his world is turned upside down.

www.dougjohnstone.wordpress.com

Alanna Knight

Alanna Knight was born on Tyneside but lives and writes in Edinburgh. She has a lifelong interest in history, is an authority on Robert Louis Stevenson and a founder member of the Scottish Association of Writers. In a writing career of over forty years she has written more than seventy books, including four series of crime novels.

She is best known for the long-running Victorian series featuring Inspector Jeremy Faro of the Edinburgh Police, and the seventeenth novel in the series was published in 2013. The Victorian city is brought to life in her novels.

A good example is *Blood Line* (1989), in which a Royal visit, a murdered man, a mysterious jewel and a child's mummified body lead to an investigation which places both Faro and his family in peril.

The Tam Elidor series is highly unusual, as Elidor is a time-traveller who solves murder mysteries at the court of Mary Queen of Scots (*The Dagger in the Crown*, 2001), at Falkland Palace in the reign of James VI (*The Gowrie Conspiracy*, 2003), and Regency Brighton (*The Stuart Sapphire*, 2005).

The author also wrote a short series of crime books for younger readers featuring Annie Kelty, a young Edinburgh woman who runs a bookshop with her father.
See also: Scotland: the Highlands and Islands
www.alannaknight.com

Frederic Lindsay

Frederic Lindsay was a writer for TV, radio and the stage as well as a novelist. He wrote a series of police procedurals set in and around Edinburgh, and his protagonist was DI Jim Meldrum of the Lothian and Borders Police.

The series began with *Kissing Judas* (1997), in which Meldrum is caught between the present and the past. An old case continues to haunt him, and when a convicted prisoner goes on hunger strike pleading innocence, Meldrum has to know the truth. Unfortunately his search takes him into another world, that of covert work in Northern Ireland, and the dangerous world he has entered could take its toll on his wider family.

In *A Kind of Dying* (1998), Meldrum is confused because the Chief Constable is on his back, taking an inordinate interest in what appears to be a routine missing persons investigation. When a murder in Oslo is linked to the missing man and to a dangerous group of neo-Nazis, Meldrum is submerged in a case which could have devastating consequences.

www.fantasticfiction.co.uk/l/frederic-lindsay

Alexander McCall Smith

Formerly a professor of medical law, Alexander McCall Smith is now a world-famous crime writer who was awarded a CBE for services to literature in 2007. He has honorary doctorates from nine universities in Europe and North America.

He is perhaps best known for his detective series set in Botswana (*The No. 1 Ladies Detective Agency*), but since 2004 he has written a superb series of equally classy stories about Edinburgh amateur sleuth Isobel Dalhousie. The books are full of McCall's natural wit and charm, and have wonderful, quirky titles such as *The Comfort of Saturdays* (2008) and *The Uncommon Appeal of Clouds* (2012).

In *The Comfort of Saturdays* (2008), Isobel is a new mother with all that that entails, when she overhears a chance conversation about a doctor whose career lies in ruins after allegations surrounding a patient's death and a newly-marketed drug . As she tries to unravel the plot, she must tread carefully while balancing life and work.

The Charming Quirks of Others (2010) is concerned with the title-tattle heard at dinner parties on a Saturday night. A successor is needed for a top boarding school, Bishop Forbes, but an anonymous letter has been received suggesting that one of the candidates has a murky past. Isobel is asked to help, but discovers that it is trickier than she expected.

www.alexandermccallsmith.co.uk

Ken McClure

Ken McClure has a PhD in molecular genetics, which he has put to good use in his long career as a writer of medical crime thrillers. Originally from Edinburgh, he has used the city as a backdrop to some of his finest stories, such as *Fenton's Winter* (1989) in which a body is found in the sterilizer at Edinburgh Hospital, and *Hypocrites' Isle* (2008), where a cancer breakthrough at Edinburgh Medical School leads to a terrifying realisation for the cancer research industry.

He has never been shy of including topical subjects in his books, and *Deception* (2001) is a perfect example. Featuring his series protagonist Dr Steve Dunbar, it focuses on the fears surrounding genetically modified crops. Dunbar is called to investigate a strange crop in a field outside Edinburgh, and when there is a threat to his life he realises that he may have stumbled onto something sinister.

www.kenmcclure.com

Val McDermid

Having grown up in a mining community in Fife, Val McDermid knows the area well, and has used the area in several of her stand-alone novels.

In *The Distant Echo* (2003), a twenty-five-year-old crime is at the centre of a double murder investigation in St Andrews, and Alex Gilbey knows that he must uncover the truth, or become a murder victim himself.

A Darker Domain (2008) is a powerful mix of fiction and recent history. During the Miners' Strike in the 1980s a wealthy heiress and her son were kidnapped. When the payoff went wrong, the heiress was killed and the child disappeared. More than twenty years later, a journalist finds a clue, and sets cold case expert DI Karen Pirie off on a trail that leads her into the heart of one of the most destructive disputes of modern times.

In 2014 Karen Pirie returns in *The Skeleton Road*,

when she investigates the discovery of bones in an old building in Edinburgh.

See also: the Midlands, the North West, the North East
www.valmcdermid.com

Grace Monroe

A pseudonym for the writing team of ex-lawyer Maria Thomson and ex-journalist Linda Watson-Brown, Grace Monroe is the author of four bloody and powerful novels set in and around Edinburgh, featuring unorthodox lawyer Brodie McLennan.

In the debut novel, *Dark Angel* (2007), a high-level lawyer is murdered outside a well-known gay haunt in Edinburgh, and Brodie is persuaded to defend the accused — a well-known dominatrix. At the end of the first day of the case Brodie is attacked and beaten up, and she soon realises the case she has taken on links back to a series of old unsolved murders and a possible paedophile ring.

The Watcher (2008) begins with a body found in a ditch near Edinburgh Castle, with the message "more will die" written in blood. As more murders take place, the city is left in the grip of a terrifying serial killer, soon dubbed the Edinburgh Ripper. Brodie McLennan becomes involved in the case, which then takes an even more horrifying turn.

www.fantasticfiction.co.uk/m/grace-monroe

The Mulgray Twins

Definitely different — the Mulgray Twins are indeed twins — identical twins to be precise. Helen and Morna Mulgray started writing after they ended their teaching careers (both teaching English) and won the Edinburgh Writers' Club novel competition in 2002. With humour to the fore, their clever, witty take on crime fiction centres on Revenue and Customs Officer D.J. Smith and her sniffer-cat Gorgonzola, and the settings are mainly in and around Edinburgh — though *Suspects All* (2011) is set on Madeira.

In *Above Suspicion* (2010), whisky and drugs make a volatile mix as D.J. Smith goes undercover as butler to the owner of the Sron Dubh distillery on Islay. When the girlfriend of a dangerous drug lord arrives, it seems that danger is everywhere, and the Firth of Forth makes a dramatic backdrop to the end of a deadly case.

www.the-mulgray-twinsonline.co.uk

James Oswald

If at first you don't succeed, try, try again. This should be the motto of Fife sheep-famer and newly-successful crime novelist James Oswald, whose first two novels became ebook sensations in 2012 and 2013, five years after they had been shortlisted for the CWA Debut Dagger award. When they were finally published in print form, the first story *Natural Causes (2012)* was chosen as a Richard and Judy Summer Read in 2013, which only added to its popularity.

The main character is Edinburgh policeman Anthony McLean, a newly promoted Detective Inspector. In *Natural Causes* (2012), he is given a low-priority case of a murdered girl, walled up in a sealed room as part of what appears to have been some sort of gruesome ritual sixty years ago. Meanwhile Edinburgh is reeling from a series of grisly killings, and Mclean becomes convinced that there is some kind of evil link.

The paranormal aspect is continued in the follow-up, *The Book of Souls* (2012), in which McLean's past is stripped bare by two murders and an arson attack, which seem to be very, very personal.

www.jamesoswald.co.uk

Ian Rankin

One of the most popular crime writers in the world, Fife-born Ian Rankin created the Edinburgh detective John Rebus in 1987. Edinburgh policeman, former paratrooper, rock fan and reactionary, Rebus is a wonderful character, and the novels have won praise and awards all round the world. In 2005 Rankin was given the CWA Cartier Dagger for Lifetime Achievement, and throughout his career he has brought Edinburgh to life by using real places in his books, such as the Oxford Bar (to which Rebus escapes for drink and conversation), Princes Street, Arthur's Seat and Salisbury Crags.

Rankin covers a wide range of subjects, including corruption in the Scottish Parliament (*Set in Darkness*, 2000), a serial killer on the run (*Black and Blue, 1997),* and corrupt police officers (*The Resurrection Men*, 2002). As a character, Rebus is generally good-natured and sympathetic, with an understanding of the real world and a hard edge if needed. He knows that like the world around him, he is not perfect. As time goes on he becomes slightly disillusioned, but never loses his basic humanity. However, unlike so many other fictional characters, Rebus ages in real time, and as he first appeared in *Knots and Crosses* (1987) aged forty, so in 2007 he is forced to retire, still raging against Edinburgh criminals and in particular his old enemy Ger Cafferty.

He heads off into the sunset in *Exit Music* (2007), when the killing of a Russian dissident brings him into contact with corrupt bankers and greedy politicians. Then Ger Cafferty is attacked — has Rebus gone too far?

After Rebus's retirement Rankin wrote a one-off novel about an art theft that went wrong (*Doors Open*, 2008), and then introduced a new character in *The Complaints (2009)*, Inspector Malcolm Fox of the Complaints and Conduct Department, the internal branch of the Edinburgh police which investigates grievances against the force.

In 2012 Rebus made a surprise return in *Standing in Another Man's Grave.* He is back to investigate cold cases, but when he falls foul of Inspector Fox many colleagues ask whether his many transgressions have finally caught

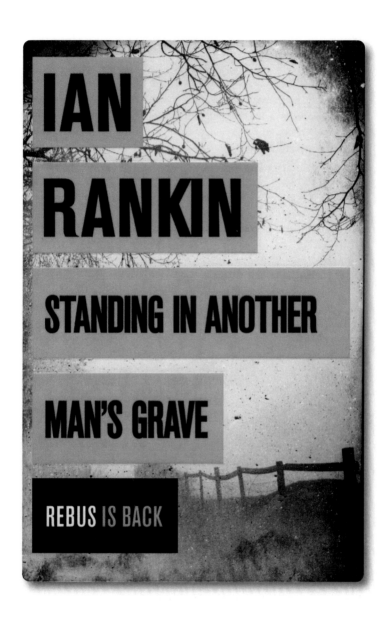

IAN RANKIN

STANDING IN ANOTHER

MAN'S GRAVE

REBUS IS BACK

up with him. As he battles to clear his name, he sets out to solve a series of unsolved diappearances.

www.ianrankin.net

Alice Thompson

Alice Thompson was the keyboard player for 1980s indie band The Woodentops, and is now an established author with six novels to her credit. One of them is crime novel *The Existential Detective* (2010), which is set in Portobello, Edinburgh, where private detective William Blake is persuaded to investigate the disappearance of a scientist's wife, and becomes involved in a shocking tale of prostitution, kidnapping and death.

www.fantasticfiction.co.uk/t/alice-thompson

Ten Recommended Reads

1: *Truth Lies Bleeding* by Tony Black (2011)

2: *Boiling a Frog* by Christopher Brookmyre (2000)

3: *Slammer* by Allan Guthrie (2009)

4: *Thursday Legends* by Quintin Jardine (2000)

5: *Body Politic* by Paul Johnston (1997)

6: *Blood Line* by Alanna Knight (1989)

7: *The Comfort of Saturdays* by Alexander McCall Smith (2008)

8: *Deception* by Ken McClure (2001)

9: *Natural Causes* by James Oswald (2012)

10: *Black and Blue* by Ian Rankin (1997)

REGION ELEVEN
Scotland — The Highlands and Islands and the North

On this storm-lashed island, three hours off the West Coast of Scotland, what little soil exists gives the people their food and their heat. It also takes their dead. And very occasionally, as today, gives one up.
PETER MAY, *The Lewis Man*, Quercus, 2012

The beauty and grandeur of the Scottish Highlands and Islands and the north of Scotland generally is matched only by its remoteness. Thurso, on the North Coast of Scotland, is 270 miles from Edinburgh, even more from Glasgow. Aberdeen is 150 miles from Glasgow. Roads are slow, and travel can be laborious. The islands are gorgeous, but the Shetlands are more than 100 miles from the North Coast, and a ferry to Lewis off the West Coast can take around three hours.

The area has been well used by crime writers. Peter May has set a fine series on Lewis, Ann Cleeves writes about Shetland, and the master of darkness Stuart MacBride gives DSgt Logan Macrae a hard time in Aberdeen. At the cosier end of the crime fiction spectrum, M.C. Beaton's Hamish Macbeth series is set in the fictional Highland village of Lochdubh.

Simon Beckett

Simon Beckett is a Sheffield-based crime writer who rose to prominence with his first novel *The Chemistry of Death* in 2006.

In his second crime book, *Written in Bone* (2007), forensic pathologist Dr David Hunter is sent to the Hebridean island of Runa after a gruesome discovery. Two feet and a hand have been found, the rest of the body being totally incinerated. A retired policeman living on the island is suspicious, but the local police think it is a case of spontaneous combustion, a rare but recorded phenomenon. Hunter realises this is not the case. As the investigation widens, an Atlantic storm shrouds the whole island in a dank, dangerous fog. When communication lines go down the island is cut off, and then the body count begins to rise.

See also: the West Country, East Anglia

www.simonbeckett.com

M.C. Beaton

Historical novelist Marion Chesney has used this pseudonym for her crime novels since 1985. As well as her Agatha Raisin stories set in England, she has written the long-running Hamish MacBeth series set in the Scottish Highlands. Police Constable MacBeth is the hero of these relatively gentle crime novels which are set in the fictional village of Lochdubh, Sutherland. The series was televised by BBC from 1995–97, with Robert Carlyle in the lead role.

The series began with *Death of a Gossip* (1985), and the twenty-eighth in the series, *Death of Yesterday*, was published in 2013. Hamish is a slightly lazy, laid-back character who asserts himself only if roused. Over the years he has solved some unusual crimes, often with the help of various locals. Though he is a good detective he enjoys living where he is and does not, under any circumstances, want a transfer.

In *Death of a Prankster* (1992), he thinks that the report of a death at the home of notorious prankster Arthur Trent will be just another of his little jokes, but on arrival discovers Trent really is dead, with a houseful of suspects all after the contents of his will.

By *Death of a Valentine* (2009), Hamish has been promoted and now has a constable to work with. Together he and Josie have to solve the murder of a local beauty queen who has been killed by a deadly Valentine's card. All the while Josie is desperate to make Hamish see her as more than just a colleague...

See also: the West Country

www.mcbeaton.com

S.J. Bolton

Sharon Bolton has set most of her spine-chilling crime fiction in and around London, but *Sacrifice* (2008) is different, being set on Shetland, where obstetrician Tora Hamilton has moved with her husband. When one of her favourite horses dies, she sets out to bury it (illegally) in the garden, but discovers the body of a young woman, wrapped in linen. When Tora tries to use her professional position to find out more details about the woman, she is warned off. Unable to let go, she delves further into the mystery, with horrifying consequences.

See also: London, East Anglia

www.sjbolton.com

Marten Claridge

Inspector Frank McMorran first appeared in Marten Claridge's debut novel *Nobody's Fool* (1989), which was nominated for the CWA Debut Dagger award. Reinstated after a fatal accident inquiry, McMorran is pitted against a serial killer known as The Hangman, and his search takes him from the mean streets of Edinburgh to the hills of Perthshire.

The exciting sequel, *Slow Burn* (1994), finds McMorran demoted to Detective Constable, trying to find the links

S. J. BOLTON

SACRIFICE

YOU'RE BORN. YOU LIVE. THEY DIE.

'A chilling, mesmerising thriller'
TESS GERRITSEN

between the slaughter of sheep on the Isle of Arran and a number of gory murders on the mainland. The body of an elderly man provides some answers, but more murders lead McMorran deeper into a dangerous mystery.

www.martenclaridge.com

Ann Cleeves

A crime writer for nearly thirty years, Ann Cleeves has always loved books and libraries, even becoming reader in residence for three different library authorities during the 2008 National Year of Reading.

She has written over twenty crime novels, including the successful Shetland Quartet — which was recently augmented by a fifth title. All the books in this series capture the loneliness and solitude of the Shetlands beautifully, enabling the reader to imagine life amongst the inhabitants and understand the island culture and a way of life that has almost disappeared. The series has been successfully televised by the BBC with Douglas Henshall as Jimmy Perez.

Raven Black (2006) introduced DI Jimmy Perez, the detective at the centre of all the Shetland novels. It won the CWA Gold Dagger. A sixteen-year-old girl has been found strangled and, for the first time in many years, suspicion reigns on the island. People shut their doors and look at each other suspiciously. Most suspect local recluse Magnus Tait, but Perez is not so sure. As he grew up on the island, he is ideally placed to find the truth.

The second novel, *White Nights* (2008), is set in high summer, when the sun never sets and daylight seems to last forever. A mysterious man appears at an artist's event, bursting into tears in front of a painting. When he is found hanging the next day, the police are called in. Jimmy's boss wants to take the glory of a quick solution, but Jimmy's local knowledge of the community takes centre stage in a slower but successful investigation.

See also: the North East

www.anncleeves.com

Caroline Dunford

A prolific short story writer in other genres, Caroline Dunford started a new crime series in 2009, set just before The Great War, when the Victorian era was over but life carried on much as before, no one knowing the horrors that were just around the corner.

A Death in the Family (2009) introduced Euphemia Martins, a well-brought-up young woman who is forced by family circumstances to take up the position of a maid. On her first day she is shocked to discover a dead body and, being curious by nature, she finds hidden family secrets, along with danger and romance.

In *A Death in the Highlands* (2013), Euphemia is promoted to housekeeper at the Stapleford family's new hunting lodge. A combination of unhappy locals and a group of strange house guests means that murder is not too far away.

www.carolinedunford.com

Barry Gornell

A graduate of the University of Glasgow's renowned Creative Writing course, Barry Gornell is an ex-firefighter and bookshop owner whose first novel was published in 2012.

The Healing of Luther Grove (2012) is set in the Scottish Highlands, where John and Laura, a wealthy young couple, replant themselves from the big city. They annoy local recluse Luther Grove, and when the latter finds himself drawn towards Laura, this provokes her husband. The arrival of John's brother proves to be pivotal, and as relationships crack, the events descend towards an inevitable, tragic, bloody conclusion.

www.freightbooks.co.uk/launches-of-the-healing-of-luther-grove-by-barry-gornell.html

Clio Gray

Clio Gray's love of books is reflected in the fact that she has worked for many years in her local library in Scotland. *The*

Brora Murders (2012) is a stand-alone historical crime novel set in Sutherland at the time of the Scottish Gold Rush (1869). When a panner is murdered Brogar Finn and Sholto McKay try to discover the truth behind his death. As that truth emerges, so the full heritage and history of this beautiful part of Scotland is laid bare.

See also: the South and South East, the North East
www.cliogray.com

Michael Innes

Michael Innes was the pseudonym of J.I.M. Stewart, the Edinburgh-educated Oxford professor who wrote academic titles (such as biographies of Kipling, Conrad and Hardy) under his own name and crime novels (or "entertainments", as he called them) as Innes.

The books were not generally set in his native Scotland, but the third in the Inspector Appleby series, *Lament for a Maker* (1938), sees Appleby called in when Ranald Guthrie, an impecunious Scottish laird, dies in a fall from castle ramparts on a bleak winter evening in the Highlands.

See also: the Midlands
www.fantasticfiction.co.uk/i/michael-innes

Bill Kirton

Though born in England, Bill Kirton has lived most of his life in Scotland. He is a lifelong writer and has been a Royal Literary Fund Writing Fellow at various Scottish universities. He is the author of a short series of books set in and around Cairnburgh, a fictional town near Aberdeen, featuring DCI Jack Carston.

In *Shadow Selves* (2011), Carston is immersed in hospital and university politics as he attempts to solve the post-operative murder of a university professor and track down the stalker of an attractive medical student. *Unsafe Acts* (2012) sees Carston investigating a double murder in Aberdeen which is linked to Falcon Alpha, an oil platform in the North Sea.

www.bill-kirton.co.uk

Alanna Knight

Novelist, biographer and playwright Alanna Knight has set most of her work in Edinburgh, but *The Seal King Murders* (2011) is set on Orkney in 1861, when Inspector Faro (her long-running series hero) returns to his birthplace to inquire into the death of champion swimmer and customs officer Dave Claydon. The backdrop of Orkney gives the book an added sense of character.

In 2000 she started a new series featuring Jeremy Faro's daughter, Rose McQuinn. In *An Orkney Murder* (2003), she too returns to the family home on Orkney, but her holiday is disrupted by the discovery of a recently buried corpse during an archaeological dig for a thirteenth century princess.

See also: Scotland: Edinburgh and the Borders
http://www.alannaknight.com

Bill Knox

A prolific author from the late 1950s onwards, Bill Knox wrote two excellent crime series. The first is set in Glasgow, but the second is very different. It features Chief Officer Webb Carrick of the Scottish Fishery Protection Service, and uses locations from all around the Scottish coast. The settings are authentic, the plots sharp, and the writing superb, as befits a former journalist.

Devilweed (1966) is an unusual story involving a fictional floating branch of the Bank of Central Scotland — a forty-foot boat called The Thrift. When it is found adrift in Hebridean waters it is thought to have been the victim of a violent robbery, but when Webb Carrick investigates, he finds that although three staff have gone missing the ship's safe is intact. It appears to him that the key to the mystery can only be found in the mysterious Hebridean islands themselves.

Stormtide (1972) finds Carrick thrust into danger when he intervenes in a dispute between a group of renegade shark hunters and Hebridean fishermen. When he finds a fishing boat wrecked and her captain dead, Carrick is faced with chaos.

See also: Scotland: Glasgow and the West of Scotland
www.booksfromscotland.com/Authors/Bill-Knox

Chris Longmuir

Chris Longmuir has written three Dundee-based novels featuring DSgt Bill Murphy. She knows the city well and the authenticity adds to the strength of the books.

In *Dead Wood* (2009), a young woman, Kara, goes onto the streets of the city to earn the money to pay off a debt to a gangster. She finds the victim of a serial killer and reports it the police, who begin an investigation. However, one of the victims is the gangster's daughter, and he wants revenge. It is just a question of who gets to the killer first.

www.chrislongmuir.co.uk

Stuart MacBride

Though born in Dumbarton, award-winning crime writer Stuart MacBride is a staunch Aberdonian and former project manager for an IT conglomerate (amongst other things). He is now one of the great names in crime fiction, and his dark humour and unflinchingly graphic style are reminiscent of authors such as Irving Welsh.

His main character is DSgt Logan McRae, a hard-working and constantly put-upon CID policeman, but it is the secondary characters such as the jelly-baby eating Inspector Insch and the flame-haired lesbian DI Steel who really stand out. Each book features scenes and language that are not for those of a delicate nature, but they are full of top-class, powerful crime writing, covering child murder, serial killers, pornographers, rapists, arsonists and more. They are all set in the Granite City of Aberdeen, and the author's knowledge of the city brings it to life — for better or for worse.

In *Flesh House* (2008), a container of human meat is found at Aberdeen Harbour. There is a concern that a serial killer nicknamed The Flesher, who was released on appeal seven years ago, may be up to his old tricks, especially when officers involved in the original case start to vanish. As panic grips the city, McRae starts to realise there may be more to this hellish case.than he had thought.

Dark Blood (2010) sees McRae and Steel responsible for the safety of convicted male rapist Richard Knox, who has now served his time, found God and wants to live in Aberdeen (under the taxpayer's protection) rather than his home city of Newcastle. Of course, this is by no means their only ongoing case, and soon they are up to their eyes in gangsters, jewel raids and missing money — and then Knox escapes from the safe house.

www.stuartmacbride.com

Russel D. McLean

Russel McLean works in the book trade, and has written short stories for a variety of crime magazines. *The Good Son,* the first in a set of novels set in the Dundee area, was published in 2009 and well-received on both sides of the Atlantic. All three books feature Dundee-based private eye J. McNee (enigmatically known only by his surname).

In *The Good Son* (2009), McNee investigates when a local farmer finds his brother's corpse hanging from a tree. The police put the death down as suicide, but McNee is not convinced. Unfortunately, digging deeper into the case brings him into conflict with a London gangster whose influence extends even to Scotland, and the danger becomes ever more personal.

In *Father Confessor* (2012), McNee has to delve into the life of his late mentor DCI Ernie Bright, whose career ended in disgrace. McNee has his own reasons for proving that Bright was not a bent cop — but in doing so he makes enemies and finds that justice and the law may be two separate entities.

www.russeldmclean.com

Shona MacLean

Inverness-born Shona MacLean is the niece of thriller writer Alistair MacLean, but her Alexander Seaton books show that she is perfectly capable of standing on her own as a writer. They are set in the seventeenth century, between 1620 and 1640, mainly in Scotland. The period setting is excellent, with the harshness, smells and brutality of life made clear.

The Redemption of Alexander Seaton (2008) takes place in Banff (North East Scotland) in 1626, when one of Seaton's friends is arrested for murder. The victim's dying words set Alexander, a disgraced divinity student and local schoolteacher, on a trail of cruelty, witch-hunting and prejudice that forces him to reconsider his belief in God.

Aberdeen in 1635 is the setting for *The Devil's Recruit* (2013). Locals are being press-ganged to board ships heading for the Thirty Years War in Europe, the son of a Highland chieftain disappears and a woman is found hanging in a garden. Seaton becomes involved in a conspiracy which becomes intensely personal as he realises that many of the events surrounding him are linked to his own past.

www.quercusbooks.co.uk/author/S.G._MacLean

Catriona McPherson

Dandelion Dahlia Gilver (Dandy to her readers) is the protagonist in Catriona Mcpherson's series of genteel crime novels set in Scotland in the 1920s. The settings are usually small towns rather than cities, and the tone and style of the books evokes The Golden Age of crime fiction perfectly.

The first novel, *After the Armistice Ball* (2005), is set in Perthshire, as Dandy sets out to discover what happened to the Duffy Diamonds, which went missing after the Armistice Ball. With a mysterious death, oddball characters and strange twists, there is much to enjoy in the classy period drama.

In *An Unsuitable Day for a Murder* (2010), Dandy is summoned to Dunfermline when a department-store heiress goes missing. Originally it seems that she has taken off in pursuit of forbidden love, but a dead body and ancient rivalry between two store-owning families leads to more trouble for Dandy than she had ever imagined. The book won an Agatha Award in America for Best Historical Novel in 2013.

www.sites.google.com/site/catrionamcphersonwriter

Peter May

Peter May has an unusual claim to fame in British crime-writing circles — he is an honorary member of the Chinese Crime Writers Association for his award-winning China Thrillers series. He is also a successful TV drama scriptwriter for the BBC and BBC Scotland (*Squadron, The Standard, Take The High Road, Machair*).The last of these was set on the Isle of Lewis in the Outer Hebrides, and his love of the area is clear in the wonderful Lewis Trilogy. The descriptions of the weather, the bleak yet beautiful scenery, and the culture of the small island communities bring Lewis to life better than any travel guide.

The books centre on the character of Fin MacLeod, an Edinburgh policeman who returns to the isle of his birth in *The Blackhouse* (2011) to investigate a murder on the island. His investigations turn up many links to his own childhood, so as well as catching a murderer he must lay to rest the ghosts of his past — especially the events behind a fatal visit to the gannet colony on the intimidating and remote islet of An Sgeir.

The Lewis Man (2012) begins with the discovery of a perfectly preserved body in a peat bog. It is a murder victim and is less than fifty years old, so when a DNA test links it to his childhood sweetheart Marsaili, Fin cannot stand idly by — he must find out the truth, for both their sakes.

The final part is *The Chessmen* (2013), in which Fin, now a security officer, investigates illegal game-hunting on an island estate. A local poacher turns out to be an old friend from his teenage years, whose knowledge of a long-buried secret could have disastrous consequences. When an extraordinary geological event on the island lays bare a light aircraft which crashed two decades earlier, the secret can no longer remain hidden and Fin's life is thrown into turmoil.

The Chessmen (2013) was shortlisted for the 2013 Theakston Old Peculier Crime Novel of the Year by the CWA, and the Lewis Trilogy has won no fewer than five fiction awards in France, where the author now lives.
www.petermay.info

Gwen Moffat

Gwen Moffat was a lifelong climber (she was the first woman to qualify as a British mountain guide) and loved detective fiction. She wrote over thirty crime novels, many featuring the hobnail-booted writer and amateur sleuth Miss Melinda Pink.

In *Miss Pink at the Edge of the World* (1975), two climbers are mysteriously killed on The Old Man of Scamadale, a huge rock stack off the coast of Scotland. One of them was assessing the climb for a possible television programme, to which the local laird is opposed. The laird persuades the local police to see the deaths as murder, but it appears that only he and his cronies have the climbing skills needed to commit it.

Snare (1987) is set in a quiet Scottish village where arson, anonymous letters and blackmail lead to murder. Other novels set in Scotland include *A Wreath of Dead Moths* (1998), *Quicksand* (2001) and *Man Trap* (2003).
See also: Wales, the North West
www.fantasticfiction.co.uk/m/gwen-moffat

T.F. Muir

Glasgow-born Frank Muir worked overseas for twenty-five years, but retained his love of Scotland. He is the author of a short (so far) series of fine crime novels set in the coastal town of St Andrews, where DCI Andy

Gilchrist lives and works. With its beaches, castle, university and world-famous golf course it makes an excellent and unusual setting for crime fiction.

In *Hand for a Hand* (2009), Gilchrist is called to a crime scene — a severed hand has been found clutching a note addressed to him. When more body parts are found with various one-word clues, he realises the identity of the next victim, and it dawns on him that the answer to the clues may be tied up in his own past.

Violence comes very close to home in *Life for a Life* (2013), as Gilchrist's son is brutally attacked. Then Gilchrist himself is targeted, and as he recovers, he starts to unravel a conspiracy that will lead him to Spain and America, and then to a frightening confrontation.

www.frankmuir.co.uk

Manda Scott

Veterinary surgeon Manda Scott is best known as a historical novelist, but she has also written a number of clever crime novels.

Hen's Teeth (1997) was nominated for the Orange Prize, and was the first of three books to feature psychologist Kellen Stewart. In *Stronger than Death* (1999), three people are dead, and pathologist Lee Adams knew them all. Stewart doesn't know whether he is next or whether, Lee is a suspect.

In *No Good Deed* (2001), Orla McLeod is a DI in charge of a Special Branch operation in Glasgow which fails spectacularly, and a young boy is witness to an act of pure brutality. Orla is able to move the boy in secret to a cottage in the Highlands, but the killer knows that to ensure his safety he must silence both of them.

www.mandascott.co.uk

Josephine Tey

One of the great writers from the Golden Age, Josephine Tey was a pseudonym, used by Scottish writer Elizabeth Mackintosh. Despite her Scottish background she did not normally use Scotland in her books, but *The Singing Sands* (1952) is an exception. Published in the year she died, the manuscript was found in her papers at her death. It features her regular detective, Inspector Alan Grant, who is on sick leave from Scotland Yard. En route to Scotland by train for a holiday, he finds a dead man in a nearby compartment. Intrigued by an enigmatic phrase written on the dead man's newspaper, he journeys on to the wilds of the Hebrides to uncover a mystery — which turns out to have been murder.

See also: London

www.fantasticfiction.co.uk/t/josephine-tey

Charles Todd

The American mother and son who write as Charles Todd have a created a fine character in Inspector Ian Rutledge, a brilliant Scotland Yard detective who gives up his career to fight as an officer in World War I. By the time he returns to the Yard in 1919 he is older, wiser, and suffering from the effects of shell shock, as well as the haunting inner voice of a young Scottish soldier he had ordered to be court-martialled and shot.

His boss tries to keep him out of trouble by sending him to take on awkward cases in out-of-the-way places, and every one of his adventures takes place in a different part of the country.

Legacy of the Dead (2000) was the fourth book in the series, and took Rutledge to the Highlands of Scotland, where not only does he have to investigate a body on a mountainside, but he also encounters people with secrets linked to his harrowing wartime experiences.

See also: the West Country, East Anglia

www.charlestodd.com

Louise Welsh

A former book dealer, Glasgow novelist Louise Welsh is a highly-rated author who has had excellent reviews for all her novels.

Naming The Bones (2010) finds university researcher Murray Watson on the remote Scottish island of Lismore, trying to restore the image of forgotten poet Archie Lunan, who died in mysterious circumstances thirty years before. The story is full of human interest, as Archie's artist brother, girlfriend and mistress are all involved in a strange tale of literature, obsession and intrigue.

www.louisewelsh.com

Ten Recommended Reads

1: *Written in Bone* by Simon Beckett (2007)

2: *Raven Black* by Ann Cleeves (2006)

3: *Shadow Selves* by Bill Kirton (2011)

4: *Live Bait* by Bill Knox (1978)

5: *Shatter the Bones* by Stuart MacBride (2011)

6: *Father Confessor* by Russell D. Maclean (2012)

7: *After the Armistice Ball* by Catriona McPherson (2005)

8: *The Blackhouse* by Peter May (2011)

9: *Hand for a Hand* by T.F. Muir (2009)

10: *Legacy of the Dead* by Charles Todd (2000)

REGION TWELVE
Ireland — Northern Ireland

Once upon a time, crime writers in Ireland were few and far between. These days it's not so much a case of "whodunnit", or even "who's doing it", as "they're all at it".
The Irish Times, November 21, 2013

Ireland, the third largest island in Europe, is divided politically into two — the Republic of Ireland, with its capital city of Dublin, and Northern Ireland, a part of the UK with its capital of Belfast.

Northern Ireland has a population of nearly two million people, and has been largely self-governing since the signing of the Good Friday Agreement in 1998. It was created in 1921, but its history has been somewhat fractious and included a thirty-year period generally known as The Troubles when conflict between Protestant Unionists and mostly Catholic Republicans erupted into violence, with British forces deployed on the streets.

All of this is great grist to the mill of crime fiction, and crime writers such as Brian McGilloway, Adrian McKinty, Colin Bateman and Stuart Neville are right at the forefront of the genre.

(Colin) Bateman

Formerly a journalist in Northern Ireland (he was the editor of *The County Down Spectator)*, Colin Bateman is now the author of more than thirty novels, as well as TV screenplays and a stage play. He is a proud Northern Irishman, and the city of Belfast plays a vital part in his novels. All his novels are laced with his trademark in-your-face style of humour, which is sometimes laid on with a trowel.

The Dan Starkey series, which began with *Divorcing Jack* in 1995, centres on the semi-autobiographical character of Starkey, a struggling journalist in Belfast with a penchant for swearing, drinking, dancing, ducking and diving. This tends to land him in trouble, as does his nose for a story.

By *The Horse with My Name* (2002), Dan is an ex-journalist, down on his luck and living in a grotty Belfast bedsit. Then another ex-journalist, who writes horse-racing gossip on the internet as "The Horse Whisperer", asks him to investigate Geordie McClean, the boss of Irish American Racing. Unfortunately this is not as easy as it sounds, as McClean and Starkey have met in the past. Soon Dan is up to his eyes in problems, and being shot at is the least of them.

I Predict a Riot (2007) is a stand-alone novel concerning Superintendent James "Marsh" Mallow of Belfast CID. He's nearing retirement, and before he goes he wants to take down crooked politician Pink Harrison. This could lead to trouble on the streets — and it does.

www.colinbateman.com

Gerard Brennan

Gerard Brennan's crime fiction is set in Belfast, and shows an unflinching picture of today's city, with the authenticity of a man who understands its sometimes difficult society.

Wee Rockets (2011) is about Belfast gang culture — harsh, brutal, and unforgiving. When a group of teenage tearaways are branded as scum by the local community, the involvement of a local vigilante only drives them to even greater violence.

www.gerardbrennan.co.uk

Paul Charles

Paul Charles has worked in the music business in London for many years, and is the author of a London-based crime series featuring Inspector Christy Kennedy. He has also written two quite different novels set in small-town Ireland. The main character in both books is Inspector Starrett, a gentle, middle-aged detective with a love of smart clothes and a pint of Guinness.

In *The Dust of Death* (2007), a man is found crucified in a church in the Donegal Heritage Town of Ramelton. When Starrett investigates, he finds that the dead man was having an affair with the church's pastor, and the town is by no means as quiet as it appears on the surface. *See also: London*

www.paulcharlesbooks.com

John Creed

This is a pseudonym for respected crime writer Eoin McNamee, for a series of Irish based thrillers featuring "deadbeat ex-spook" Jack Valentine.

In *Black Cat, Black Dog* (2006), dog tags belonging to a seaman missing for more than fifty years are washed up on a beach in County Antrim. Valentine becomes involved, and is thrust into an extraordinary conspiracy that links a World War II arms dump to a failed US mission in Iraq.

www.fantasticfiction.co.uk/c/john-creed

Brian McGilloway

Derry-born, Brian McGilloway is a graduate of Queen's University, Belfast, and is now Head of English at St Column's College in Derry. He is the author of a superlative crime series featuring DI Benedict Devlin of the

Garda, which has been nominated for many awards since it first appeared in 2007. He has more recently begun a second series with a new character, DS Lucy Black. The settings of both series are vital to their strength, with both Donegal and Derry portrayed honestly as areas where the past impinges on the present.

DI Devlin is a classic contemporary detective, human, fallible, methodical and determined, though unusually he has a happy home life. His patch is Donegal, near the Irish border, and it is impossible to police this area without politics playing its part. In *Borderlands* (2007), a girl's body is found on the border where Tyrone meets Donegal. There are few clues, but then a second teenager dies, and Devlin finds a link to a twenty-five-year-old case, which he fears may implicate one of his own colleagues.

In *The Nameless Dead* (2012), Devlin is involved in a moving case that involves both the sensitive history of the Northern Ireland conflict and the tragic death of a baby, whose body is found during a dig ordered by the Commission for the Location of Victims' Remains — a real organisation set up to locate the bodies of victims of the Troubles who disappeared prior to 1989.

Lucy Black is introduced in *Little Girl Lost* (2011), in which she is caught up in a case with wide-ranging ramifications when she rescues a young child found wandering in local woods. Set in contemporary Derry, the novel cleverly mixes Lucy's family struggles with a fascinating and ultimately personal case.

www.brianmcgilloway.com

Adrian McKinty

Though born in Carrickfergus, Adrain McKinty now lives in Australia. He still writes passionately about his home country in both stand-alone novels and the Sean Duffy series. This evocative, powerful series is set at the height of sectarian violence in the Northern Ireland conflict.

The Cold, Cold Ground (2012) is set in Belfast in 1981 with its hunger strikes, power cuts, and rioting on the streets. DSgt Sean Duffy is right in the middle of it — a Catholic police officer distrusted by everybody. There's a homophobic serial killer on the loose, and one of his victims is a suspected IRA man. When the wife of a hunger striker commits suicide Duffy is very worried. He suspects a link.

I Heard the Sirens in the Street (2013) is Duffy's second adventure. This time he is perplexed by a body in a suitcase. The only clue to its identity is a tattoo, and Duffy is determined to follow that clue... wherever it leads.

www.adrianmckinty.blogspot.co.uk

Claire McGowan

Born and bred in Northern Ireland, Claire McGowan has written two well-reviewed crime novels so far, and a third is due out in 2014. She set her first book in London, but returned to her Irish roots for her second.

Set in the fictional Irish border town of Ballyterrin, *The Lost* (2013) centres on Paula Maguire, a forensic pathologist who returns to her home town to help with the investigation into the disappearance of two teenage girls. What she discovers is a confusing mix of truths, half-truths and lies stretching back over twenty years, which even impinges on her own family history.

www.clairemcgowan.net

Matt McGuire

Another writer born and bred in Belfast, Matt McGuire taught English at the University of Glasgow before moving to Australia.

His first novel *Dark Dawn* was published in 2012. Set in Belfast in 2005, it is a hard-edged story of a recently promoted detective trying to find the murderer of a knee-capped teenager. Acting DSgt John O'Neill is in charge — his first murder detail, under a superior officer who disapproves of him. If it all goes wrong, he will end up back in uniform, and the case pits him against all the worst aspects of the new Northern Ireland, including vigilante justice, drug peddling and financial mismanagement.

www.literarybelfast.org/article/5116/a-dark-dawn-in-belfast

Eoin McNamee

Critically-acclaimed Eoin McNamee was born in County Down, and during his long writing career he has written for both adults and children. He was awarded the MacAuley Fellowship for Irish Literature in 1990, and his adult works have unflinchingly dealt with some of the most controversial subjects in Northern Ireland's recent history. As the books often used real-life figures and true events, it is sometimes difficult to know where the fiction begins — or indeed ends.

His short novel *Resurrection Man* (1994) was based on the career of the so-called Shankhill Butchers (a group of Loyalist paramilitaries), and it spotlights the politics of Belfast at that time, where sectarian loyalties meant that terrifying actions were carried out in the name of religion. The book was turned into the film *Resurrection Man* starring John Hannah and James Nesbitt.

In *The Ultras* (2004), he covered the extraordinary story of Captain Robert Nairac and his death in 1977, full details of which remain unknown even now. Nairac was a British army officer working undercover when he was apprehended by the IRA. He later received a posthumous George Cross. His body has never been found.

www.fantasticfiction.co.uk/m/eoin-mcnamee

Sam Millar

With several Irish fiction awards to his credit, Belfast-born Sam Millar is a highly-regarded writer of dark, controversial and unsparing novels. Four of them (so far) feature the psychologically-damaged Belfast private investigator Karl Kane. All are unstintingly violent, but they do have a powerful story to tell.

354

In *Bloodstorm* (2008), Kane has the opportunity to take revenge on the man who murdered his mother and sexually molested him as a child. But he doesn't take it. Two days later the killer rapes and murders two young girls, and Kane believes that he must then avenge their deaths as well.

Dead of Winter (2012) sees Kane on the streets of Belfast, enquiring into the mystery of a severed hand which has been found locally. The police have put it down to gangland warfare, but Kane is not so sure. When he becomes suspicious of his brother-in-law Mark Wilson — a man he detests — he finds that when it comes to breaking the rules, Wilson is an unsurpassed expert.

www.millarcrime.com

Stuart Neville

Armagh-born Stuart Neville has had a mixed career — he has been, amongst other things, a musician, a teacher and a film extra — but there seems little doubt that with the publication of his debut novel, *The Twelve* (2009), he proved that he had found his real calling.

The Twelve is a brilliant debut. Gerry Fegan is an IRA hitman from Belfast with a new-found conscience — he has the blood of twelve people on his hands, and he now wants nothing more than to take revenge on those who stood back from the conflict and pulled his strings, those who ordered his killing spree. When his vendetta threatens the fragile peace process, both friends and enemies want him removed for good. The result is bloodshed, and Fegan is determined it will not be his.

Collusion (2011) follows on from these events. Inspector Jack Lennon is searching Belfast for his daughter, and his former lover, who was a witness to the shootout that ended the first book. He is faced by a wall of secrets and lies, and as he nears the truth, his bosses intervene and order him to desist. The spectre of violence is never far away, and then Fegan is lured back from exile

in New York City to face another shocking confrontation.
See also: the Republic of Ireland
www.stuartneville.co.uk

Ian Sansom

Occupying the gentler end of the crime genre, along with the likes of Alexander McCall Smith and James Runcie, Essex-born Ian Sansom is the author of the Mobile Library series, set in Northern Ireland.

Full of quirky humour and wonderfully bizarre characters, it follows the career of Israel Armstrong — a diffident, vegetarian, Jewish, librarian-cum-sleuth who drives a mobile library around County Antrim, solving crimes and domestic tribulations as he goes. As unlikely detectives go, he is somewhere near the top of the tree.

The first book, *The Case of the Missing Books*, was published in 2006, and finds Israel, new to the area, somewhat concerned at the disappearance of 15,000 library books. While trying to locate them, he manages to solve the odd crime as well.

In *The Bad Book Affair* (2009), Israel has lent some books from the special "unshelved" section to the troubled daughter of a local politician, and she has now vanished. He is concerned that the books might have corrupted her, and has to find her before her father does, to prove that her disappearance was not his fault.

See also: East Anglia
www.iansansom.net

Ten Recommended Reads

1: *I Predict a Riot* by Colin Bateman (2007)

2: *Wee Rockets* by Gerard Brennan (2011)

3: *The Dust of Death* by Paul Charles (2007)

4: *Borderlands* by Brian McGilloway (2007)

5: *The Lost* by Claire McGowan (2013)

6: *The Cold, Cold Ground* by Adrian McKinty (2012)

7: *The Ultras* by Eoin McNamee (2004)

8: *Bloodstorm* by Sam Millar (2008)

9: *The Twelve* by Stuart Neville (2009)

10: *The Case of the Missing Books* by Ian Sansom (2006)

REGION THIRTEEN
The Republic of Ireland

Great storytelling knows no boundaries, such as oceans or borders. It is universal, and it is embedded in the twisting helix of our DNA. It is arguable that the Irish DNA is indeed different, that it has extra chromosomes for legend, metaphor and wit. For such a relatively small place its impact on the world of literature has been disproportionately huge.

MICHAEL CONNELLY, in the foreword to *Down These Green Streets*, edited by Declan Burke, Liberties Press, 2011

The Republic of Ireland was established as the Irish Free State in 1922, becoming Eire, or the Irish Republic, after 1937. It has become a relatively prosperous country, although, in common with much of Europe, it has suffered an economic slowdown since 2008. It has a population of about 4.5 million and Dublin is by far its largest city.

Irish crime fiction is currently buoyant, with many excellent writers. Ken Bruen is putting Galway on the crime map, and the likes of Declan Burke, Benjamin Black, Gene Kerrigan and Tana French are doing the same for Dublin.

Benjamin Black

Benjamin Black is the pseudonym of Irish writer and journalist John Banville. Born in County Wexford, he worked firstly for the *Irish Press* and then for the *Irish Times*, where he was the literary editor for eleven years. His novel-writing career began in 1971 with *Nightspawn*, and he won the Man Booker Prize for *The Sea* in 2005.

The following year he made his first foray into crime fiction with *Christine Falls* (2006), a brilliant, stylish crime novel mainly set in Dublin in the early 1950s. The central characters are Quirke, a world-weary, hard-drinking Dublin pathologist, and Inspector Hackett of the Dublin police.

In *A Death in Summer* (2011), a powerful newspaper magnate is found dead at his mansion, with a shotgun in his hands. Quirke and Hackett soon realise he was murdered, but the man had many connections, and many enemies. The deeper Quirke and Hackett dig, the more secrets of Dublin's elite are revealed, with shocking, violent results.

With *Holy Orders* (2013), Black takes a look at the power of the Catholic Church in Ireland in the 1950s. A body has been found in a city canal, and the investigation leads back to the Church — the all-powerful organisation that can censor newspapers and keep crimes hushed up forever. Just how far will the Church and its advocates go to protect its good name?

www.benjaminblackbooks.com

Ingrid Black

This is the pseudonym of Irish husband-and-wife team Eilis O'Hanlon and Ian McConnell. There are four novels, all set in and around Dublin and featuring DCS Grace Fitzgerald of the Dublin police's Murder Squad, and former FBI agent turned true-crime writer Saxon, who is Fitzgerald's partner.

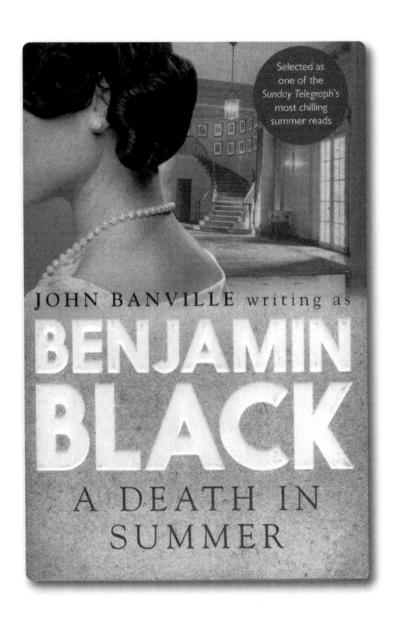

Selected as
one of the
Sunday Telegraph's
most chilling
summer reads

JOHN BANVILLE writing as

BENJAMIN
BLACK

A DEATH IN
SUMMER

In *The Dead* (2003), a letter to a Dublin newspaper suggests that serial killer The Night Hunter is prepared to strike again after five years. A body is found, but Saxon, who was writing a book about the killer when he disappeared five years ago, is convinced that the police are looking in the wrong direction. The truth is out there, but it may not be what the police expect.

The Dark Eye (2004) sees Saxon caught up in the hunt for The Marxman, a gunman whose apparently motiveless murders have terrified the whole city.

www.fantasticfiction.co.uk/b/ingrid-black

John Brady

Though originally from Dublin, John Brady emigrated to Canada while still a young man and trained as a teacher. He began his series of quality police procedurals back in 1988, and the eleventh in the series was published in 2011. All the books feature Garda detective Matt Minogue, middle-aged, fond of a drink and forever affected by a close call with a bomb explosion in his past. But those who consider him past it usually end up behind bars.

Unholy Ground (1989) sees Sergeant Minogue investigate the clinical murder of a quiet elderly man in Dublin. It is soon apparent that the man had connections to British Intelligence, and that they are desperate to gloss over the case. Despite being blocked at every turn, Minogue is determined to uncover the full story, no matter what the cost.

By *The Coast Road* (2010), Minogue is an Inspector. He is called in to examine the cold case of the murder of Padraig Larkin, a homeless Dublin alcoholic who was nicknamed "The King of Ireland". It will take all Minogue's ingenuity to unravel the dead man's complicated past.

www.johnbradysbooks.com

Ken Bruen

Ken Bruen is an extraordinary crime writer. He has PhD in metaphysics, yet spent twenty-five years as an English teacher in places such as Africa and Japan. He has been an award-winner in America, has won crime writing prizes in Germany and France, but has been criminally overlooked in the UK. Fans of classic crime noir need look no further.

As a writer, Bruen is at once stylish and brutal, funny and eye-wateringly moving. In Jack Taylor, Bruen has created one of the great characters in the genre — a hard man with a kind heart. When he first appears, in *The Guards* (2001) Taylor is a disgraced ex-cop working as a private investigator in Galway, where all the novels are set. His father has died, and he is immersed in drink. However, he still has an ability as a "finder". He is approached by a woman who is convinced that her teenage daughter has not committed suicide, which is the easy verdict the police have accepted. Taylor's methods are basically limited to straight questions and, if no answer is forthcoming, his fists. Slowly and painfully he uncovers a web of conspiracy and corruption that reaches to the highest levels in the city. As always, Galway is evocatively described, bleak, by no means romanticised, but still recognisable.

In *Sanctuary* (2008), Taylor is sober (just) and trying to help his close friend Ridge recover from surgery, when he gets a letter giving a list of proposed murder victims, including two Guards and a judge. It is believed to be the work of a crank, and the police dismiss it. When a Guard and a judge die mysteriously, followed by a child, Jack is compelled to investigate, with appalling repercussions for all concerned.

In 2010 *The Guards* was filmed for Irish TV, and its success has led to further episodes, all with Iain Glen in the role of Taylor.

See also: London

www.jacktaylorfilms.com

Declan Burke

Declan Burke is one of the current shining lights among Irish crime authors. He is a regular reviewer for newspapers and magazines, and edited (with John Connolly) *Books to Die For* (2012), a collection in which some of the world's best crime writers discuss their favourite crime novels. Rural Sligo is the setting he uses in his two novels featuring down-at-heel sleuth Harry Rigby. Chandleresque in style, they can be both rip-roaringly funny and unrelentingly bleak.

Slaughter's Hound (2012) begins with the horrifying description of a man diving from a high building onto a parked car, which immediately explodes. No one believes it was suicide, and the police think Rigby is the killer, as he had previously shared a cell with the dead man, and was a witness when he took his final leap. Various people want to know what made him jump, including Rigby. A rollercoaster ride into the dark soul of Sligo ensues.

www.crimealwayspays.blogspot.co.uk

Paul Carson

Born in Northern Ireland, Paul Carson works in Dublin, where he is a doctor specialising in children's allergies. Dublin is the main setting for all of his medical crime thrillers, the first of which was *Scalpel* (1997).

In *Cold Steel* (1999), a renowned American heart surgeon arrives in Dublin to head a new heart foundation at a major hospital. When his daughter is found murdered in a Dublin park, the police are under pressure to close the case quickly. Meanwhile, a consultant at the hospital is perturbed by two unusual deaths. When he delves further into them his whole life is put in danger and the two plotlines converge on a powerful denouement.

Inquest (2013) centres on Dr Mike Wilson, the Dublin City Coroner. When he has doubts about the suicide of a drug addict, he confides in a police contact. Suddenly he and his family are threatened, suggesting he is on the right track. What really happened in the addict's final hours?

www.paulcarson.ie

Rose Doyle

Rose Doyle is a writer in many different genres. As well as being a journalist she has written plays, TV documentaries, film scripts and about a dozen novels, though only a few could truly be listed as crime novels. Her books carry an air of romance and intrigue, and in several there is a murder mystery as well.

The Shadow Player (1999) concerns a young woman called Norah Hopkin. Separated from her boyfriend, she is horrified when his body is found in a car in the River Liffey. She cannot believe that he took his own life, but it is soon apparent that any attempt to uncover the details of his recent activities will put her life, and that of their child, in jeopardy.

www.fantasticfiction.co.uk/d/rose-doyle

Ann C. Fallon

American by birth, Ann Fallon was educated at Trinity College in Dublin before returning to America to teach. She has written six crime novels about Dublin solicitor and amateur sleuth James Fleming, all full of quirky characters and gentle Irish humour.

In *Dead Ends* (1992), Fleming is staying at Cromlech Lodge when a guest falls down the stairs and expires on the dining room carpet. Fleming is persuaded to discover whether he fell, or was pushed, and in doing so disturbs some unpleasant secrets.

www.fantasticfiction.co.uk/f/ann-c-fallon

Tana French

Though American by birth, Tana French attended Trinity College Dublin where she trained as an actress, and she has lived in the city since 1990. The city and the surrounding countryside act as the backdrop to all of her successful crime thrillers, and the author's love of the area gives a true picture of Ireland today.

Unusually, rather than having one protagonist, each novel is given a different voice, as each is narrated by a different member of the Dublin Murder Squad.

French's debut novel was *In the Woods* (2007), which won four different awards in America — the Macavity, the Barry, the Edgar, and the Anthony Award for a debut novel. Rob Ryan, detective with the murder squad, is shocked when he is called to the site of the murder of a little girl. It was on that same spot twenty years earlier that he had a terrible childhood experience, when two of his friends vanished and were never seen again. Rob keeps this to himself in order to stay on the case and solve a mystery that has dogged him all his life.

The second book, *The Likeness* (2008), is narrated by Ryan's partner in the first novel, Cassie Maddox. Having transferred out of the Murder Squad, she is horrified when she is called to another crime scene, only to find the victim not only looks like her, but has been using an identity that Cassie used when she was an undercover officer many years ago. Against her better judgement she is persuaded to go back undercover to solve the murder, and the danger to her becomes all too real.

Further novels have been narrated by Cassie's boss, Frank Mackay, and then one of his career rivals, "Scorcher" Kennedy. The latter is *Broken Harbour* (2012), which won the Ireland AM Crime Novel of the Year award.

www.tanafrench.com

Bartholomew Gill

The pen name of Irish-American journalist Mark McGarrity, Bartholomew Gill wrote a series of crime novels set in and around Dublin, where he had been a Trinity College student. The series ran for twenty-five years, and was only ended by the author's death from a fall in 2002.

The main character in the series is Chief Inspector Peter McGarr of the Dublin police, and the series is intelligent and evocative, depicting many different aspects of life in Ireland.

In *The Death of a Joyce Scholar* (1989), an acknowledged expert on Joyce is stabbed to death on Bloomsday, the annual Dublin celebration of the great man. McGarr finds many connections to Joyce in the case, and as the victim was a colourful man with a strong personality and a dissolute past, there is no shortage of suspects.

Death on a Cold Wild River (1993) sees McGarr suspended from the force, but forced to unofficially investigate the death of his former fiancée, Nellie Millar, who has been found drowned in a Donegal river.

www.fantasticfiction.co.uk/g/bartholomew-gill

Hugo Hamilton

Hugo Hamilton was born of German-Irish parents in Dublin, and grew up speaking three languages. Prior to writing novels, he was a journalist, and he has won various awards including, in 1992, the Rooney Prize for Irish Literature. Though not really known as a crime novelist, he wrote two books about "the Irish Dirty Harry" — Dublin policeman Pat Coyne.

In the first of these, *Headbanger* (1997), Coyne is an ordinary cop trying to take on the whole Dublin underworld in the 1990s. In the second, *Sad Bastard* (1998), he is at a low ebb, sitting alone in bars while on sick leave. When a body is found in the docks, the prime suspect is his son, Jimmy. Coyne decides to take matters into his own hands.

www.harpercollins.co.uk/Authors/2402/hugo-hamilton

Cora Harrison

Originally from Cork, Cora Harrison was a primary school teacher for twenty-five years. She has written many books for children (including a children's crime series, The Drumshee Chronicles) and also a series of historical crime novels for adults, set in The Burren on the West Coast of Ireland in the sixteenth century.

The Burren is very remote, and the novels are redolent of the place and its culture. The stories are set in the years when Henry VIII was on the throne in England, and the contrast between the Irish Brehon laws and those of England is distinct.

The main protagonist, Mara, is the investigating judge for The Burren. In *The Sting of Death* (2009), she must solve the strange case of a man found on the church steps, apparently stung to death by bees. In *Laws in Conflict* (2012), Mara visits the city of Galway, which is under English rule, to try to save a man accused of theft. When the mayor's son is charged with a shocking crime, Mara is suspicious. She sets out to prove that the case is not what it seems.

www.coraharrison.com

Erin Hart

Though she lives in Minnesota, USA, Erin Hart writes about the country she loves — Ireland. She has worked as an arts journalist and theatre critic, and has written four books about archaeologist Cormac Maguire and pathologist Nora Gavin. The books feature all the best elements of rural Ireland — the pubs, the bogs, the landscape, the archaeology, the culture and the mystery.

In her debut novel, *Haunted Ground* (2010), a severed head is found in a Galway bog. Uncertain as to whether the bog body is ancient or modern, Cormac and Nora investigate, uncovering long-buried secrets and stirring up the local residents. Soon the past infiltrates the present, and murder is in the air again.

In *The Book of Killowen* (2013), a ninth-century body is found in the boot of a car, with the body of a present-day TV personality beneath it. The investigation leads to a nearby artists' colony, where secrets are everywhere and no one is as innocent as they seem.

www.erinhart.com

Declan Hughes

An award-winning playwright and screenwriter, Declan Hughes was the co-founder of Dublin's Rough Magic Theatre Company. He has written several crime novels about Dublin private investigator Ed Loy.

In his debut novel, *The Wrong Kind of Blood* (2006), which was nominated for a Shamus award in the USA, Loy returns to Dublin after twenty years away for his mother's funeral. But the city has changed, with an economic boom meaning even the streets look different. When he is asked to find the husband of an old school-friend, he reluctantly agrees, and finds himself delving into the Dublin underworld inhabited by both the girl's father, and his own father many years ago. The closer he gets to the truth, the more he comes to understand that his own family history is steeped in blood.

In *The Colour of Blood* (2007), Loy investigates when a wealthy dentist asks for his help. His daughter is missing and he has received pornographic images of her and an accompanying blackmail threat. Within hours of accepting the case, the girl's ex-boyfriend and mother are killed, and Loy's client is in a cell accused of murder. Loy soon finds that their family history has more than its fair share of dangerous secrets.

www.declanhughesbooks.com

Arlene Hunt

Another of the new breed of Irish crime writers, Arlene Hunt's first novel was published when she was only in her late twenties. Her detectives are John Quigley and Sarah Kenny, a well-matched pair who between them run a detective agency in Dublin — QuicK Investigations. The novels are well-written and powerful, dealing with Dublin's darker side and keeping the reader interested.

In *Missing Presumed Dead* (2007), a toddler goes missing in 1980. Sixteen years later a woman appears at house in Dublin, shoots the man who opens the door and turns the gun on herself. The woman's family want answers, and soon John and Sarah are involved in a tale of deception and retribution, with a terrible price to pay.

Undertow (2008) finds John and Sarah with their own problems, which are exacerbated when they take on a case of a pregnant Slovakian immigrant whose boyfriend has vanished. They soon turn up a link to a vicious criminal, but their investigations have upset some very violent people who have no scruples at all.

www.arlenehunt.com

Gene Kerrigan

A successful and hard-hitting Irish journalist, Gene Kerrigan was Journalist of the Year in 1985 and 1990. He has written a number of non-fiction titles including true crime, and also four highly-rated crime novels, the latest of which, *The Rage* (2011), was chosen as the CWA Gold Dagger winner in 2012.

All four novels, written from 2005–2011, are set in contemporary Dublin, showcasing both sides of the city: the newly rich, the new buildings, the successful money men; and the downside of all this: the men with dead eyes, the gangs, the violence. His characters are perfectly drawn, and all too believable.

Dark Times in the City (2009) won the 2010 Ireland AM Crime Fiction Book of the Year award. The central character is ex-con Danny Callahan, who is drawn back into a world of violence and death when he steps in to save a stranger from a gangland hit.

The Rage (2011) centres on three characters — professional thief and ex-prisoner Vincent Naylor, hard-pressed policeman Bob Tiday, and retired nun Maura Coady. When the nun reports suspicious activities in the street, she sets in motion a train of events that bring Tiday and Naylor together in a welter of violence.

www.fantasticfiction.co.uk/k/gene-kerrigan

Jim Lusby

Jim Lusby was born in Waterford and is recognised as a dramatist, essayist and novelist. He has written for Irish radio, and two of his crime novels were turned into TV programmes by RTE.

The McCadden series features the atmospheric Waterford area, and the central character is DI Carl McCadden, an unorthodox detective whose laid-back attitude does not always sit well with his bosses.

In *Flashback* (1996), a murder at a popular guesthouse leads him into the world of the theatre and alternative comedy.

Crazy Man Michael (2000) finds McCadden expecting to lead a newly reformed Murder Squad. However, an old friend, who has been working undercover, comes to him with an extraordinary story about a dead man and the involvement of Special Branch. McCadden should stay out of it, but he has never been one to take the easy route.

www.fantasticfiction.co.uk/l/jim-lusby

K.T. McCaffrey

Having worked for various leading advertising agencies in Dublin, K.T. McCaffrey set up his own graphics practice in 1984.

He began the Emma Boylan murder mystery series in 1999, and the eighth in the series was published in 2012. The series is mainly set in and around Dublin, and Emma is an investigative reporter in the city. Unusually for such a reporter, she is not brash and pushy, but a quiet and methodical journalist who gets her results through hard work.

In *The Body Rock* (2001), Emma investigates an unexplained suicide and delves into the family affairs of hotel boss Todd Wilson, whose world is crashing down around him. As she pursues the truth she becomes embroiled in a mix of suspicion, lies, betrayal and murder.

*End of the Line (*2003) is set in the Dublin suburb of Lonsdale. The parish priest has been killed in a road accident, and when it becomes clear that it may have been orchestrated, Emma needs to know more. Soon she is involved in a tragic story of arson, sex and revenge.
www.ktmccaffrey.wordpress.com/

Eugene McEldowney

After growing up in the Ardoyne area of Belfast, Eugene McEldowney spent his journalistic career with the *Irish Times* in Dublin. After his retirement he wrote a short series of crime novels set in Belfast and Dublin about jaundiced, hard-drinking Superintendent Cecil Megarry — who although being a member of the Belfast police, turns up on holiday in Dublin for *The Sad Case of Harpo Higgins* (1996). Here he gets involved in a drugs case and is soon up to his eyes in violence and revenge.

In *Murder at Piper's Cut* (1997), a human head is found in the nets of a fishing vessel off the coast of Dublin. With a new female assistant, Megarry is called in to investigate.
www.fantasticfiction.co.uk/m/eugene-mceldowney

Pauline McLynn

Best known for her role as Mrs Doyle in the Channel 4 sitcom *Father Ted*, the actress Pauline McLynn is also a respected author, with a light comic touch. As crime novels her three Leo Street novels were lightweight, but they possessed enough readability to kick-start a writing career that continues today.

In *Something for the Weekend* (2000) Leo Street is a thirty-something in Dublin, working as a somewhat down-at-heel private investigator. In search of something exciting, she is delighted when a client invites her to County Kildare to keep an eye on his supposedly adulterous wife. However, her idea of pretending to be a high-quality amateur cook only leads her into trouble.
www.paulinemclynn.com

Graham Masterton

Though best-known as a prolific horror writer, Graham Masterton has written three novels about Garda police-woman Katie Maguire, who is based in Cork. She first appears in *White Bones* (2007), in which the dismembered bodies of eleven women are found on a remote farm. It is quickly established that they were buried many years ago. However, in the present day a serial killer is at work, with Katie in his sights, and it is soon clear that there are links between the two cases.

More recently, in *Red Light* (2014), a man is found shot dead in a grubby little flat in Cork. Katie knows exactly who he is — a Somali pimp involved in the sex trade. When a second pimp is murdered Katie has a dilemma. These are dreadful people, but vigilante murder cannot be justified... can it?

www.grahammasterton.co.uk

Stuart Neville

After three novels set in Belfast, Stuart Neville moved his setting to the Irish Republic. *Ratlines* (2013) is a story of moral complexity which is closely linked to Ireland's role in, and after, World War II. Three foreigners have been found murdered and all turn out to be Nazis, granted asylum in Ireland at the end of the war. Lieutenant Albert Ryan from the Directorate of Intelligence is ordered to investigate. However, having fought against the Nazis in the war, he eventually has to ask a vital question — whose side is he on?

See also: Northern Ireland

www.stuartneville.com

Andrew Nugent

Andrew Nugent is an author with an unusual back-ground, having been a trial lawyer, a headmaster and a missionary before becoming a Benedictine Monk. He has written three satisfying and witty police procedurals, all involving Inspector Denis Lennon and Sergeant Molly Power of the Irish police force.

The Four Courts Murder (2005) concerns the murder of a much-disliked High Court judge in Dublin. Though doubtful about a young man seen hanging about the courtroom, they suspect more than just a revenge attack. When a connection to art theft is made, Lennon and Power realise there is more to the case than meets the eye.

Soul Murder (2008) opens with a death — a house-master at a leading boy's school is murdered. Then a boy goes missing, and a former owner of the school building (a converted castle) is also found dead. Dark secrets abound, and Lennon and Power need all their experience and ingenuity to solve the case.

www.us.macmillan.com/author/andrewnugent

Niamh O'Connor

A high-flying investigative reporter for Ireland's *Sunday World* newspaper, Niamh O'Connor is also a novelist, with four books to her credit so far. Given her knowledge of the crime scene in Ireland, it is no surprise that these are authentic, gripping and thought-provoking.

The series centres around Dublin policewoman Jo Birmingham, a courageous, worldly-wise single mother divorced from her boss (Chief Supt Dan Mason), who struggles to balance her career with her family commitments.

In the first novel, *If I Never See You Again* (2010), she spots the vital clue in a series of appalling murders, and concludes that a serial killer is at work. Under internal force scrutiny as well as public pressure to find the killer, she embarks on a menacing investigation, in which she could easily be added to the list of victims.

In the fourth book, *Blink* (2013), Jo investigates the apparent suicide of a colleague's wife. Meanwhile the colleague, DI Gavin Sexton, is exploring a number of teenage suicides. When he meets a girl with the frightening "locked-in syndrome", he is horrified when she blinks out the single phrase, "I hired a hitman." But with his wife recently dead, can he concentrate on the case?

www.randomhouse.co.uk/authors/niamh-oconnor

Gerard O'Donovan

A journalist who has written for the *Daily Telegraph* and the *Sunday Times*, Gerard O'Donovan has also written two crime thrillers set in Dublin. Using his home city as backdrop has allowed him to capture its true feel and character.

Both novels (the start of a projected series) feature Inspector John Mulcahy and investigative journalist Siobhan Fallon, working to uncover the same murder mystery, but from differing perspectives.

The Priest (2010) Mulcahy, recently returned from a job in Spain, pitted against a vicious sex attacker with a religious obsession. When he is sidelined by his superiors, he joins forces with Fallon to uncover the truth. The ending is likely to shake even hardened crime readers.

In *Dublin Dead* (2011), Mulcahy is in the drugs squad, and links the killing of a Dublin gangster with a hoard of abandoned drugs. Meanwhile Fallon is trying to find a missing woman. When they realise the two cases are connected, they pool their resources and set out on a trail that ends in a bloody confrontation.

www.gerard-odonovan.com

Louise Phillips

A new name in the field of psychological crime fiction, Louise Phillips had award-winning short stories included in a number of Irish anthologies before her debut novel was published in 2012.

Red Ribbons (2012) is an exciting read, with a strong central character in criminal psychologist Kate Pearson, who is called in by the police after two schoolgirls are found murdered in the Dublin area. She uncovers a connection to Ellie Brady, imprisoned many years ago for the murder of her daughter, but in unravelling the case, she puts herself in terrible danger.

The author followed this debut with *The Doll's House* (2013), in which Clodagh Hamilton visits a hypnotherapist to try to understand the events surrounding her father's death. The sessions bring out another terrible tragedy from her childhood. Meanwhile Kate Pearson is working on an unrelated case — a body found in a Dublin canal. However, there turns out to be a connection to the Hamilton family, and now neither Kate nor Clodagh is safe.

The Doll's House won the Ireland AM Crime Novel of the Year in 2013.

www.louise-phillips.com

Michael Russell

A scriptwriter for the likes of *Midsomer Murders* and *A Touch of Frost*, Michael Russell was educated at Oxford and now lives in Ireland. He has so far written two excellent crime thrillers with 1930s Ireland at their heart. They are historical crime novels of considerable power and reach. Both novels feature Garda detective Stefan Gillespie.

In *City of Shadows* (2012), Gillespie arrests a German doctor for performing illegal abortions, and meets Hannah Rosen, a young woman searching for a friend who went to the clinic and never returned. When two bodies are found in the Dublin mountains, the trail leads to the German city of Danzig, and then back to Ireland where Gillespie must confront the all-powerful religious establishment — the Catholic Church.

In *City of Strangers* (2013), Gillespie is sent to New York in the summer of 1939 to arrest a suspected killer, currently working as part of a touring theatre show on Broadway. Then a chance meeting with an old friend lures him into the depths of the city, where danger lurks on every corner and the links to the struggle for Irish independence are strong. Suddenly the stakes for Stefan are very high indeed.

www.michaelrussellforgottencities.com

Peter Tremayne

The celebrated Celtic scholar and author Peter Beresford Ellis has used the pseudonym Peter Tremayne for a huge body of work written since 1977, including horror, fantasy, crime and several non-fiction works. Highly respected for his academic work on the Celtic world, he has set his crime series in Ireland in the seventh century AD, and in the nun Sister Fidelma he has created one of the great historical sleuths. She is an advocate of the Brehon laws prevalent at the time, which give her the right to investigate any crime in Ireland.

In *The Subtle Serpent* (1996), a headless body is discovered in a well at an obscure abbey in a remote part of south-west Ireland, and a crewless ship is found abandoned off the coast. Sister Fidelma is asked to help unravel the two mysteries, and finds that many people have something to hide.

A Prayer for the Damned (2006) sees Fidelma about to be married at Cashel, but unfortunately on the eve of the ceremony Abbot Ultan is found murdered, and the King of Connacht is charged with his murder. He appoints Fidelma to defend him, and it is soon apparent that the Abbot was not as devout a man as he might have been.

www.sisterfidelma.com

Ten Recommended Reads

1: *Holy Orders* by Benjamin Black (2013)
2: *The Guards* by Ken Bruen (2001)
3: *Slaughter's Hound* by Declan Burke (2012)
4: *In The Woods* by Tana French
5: *The Colour of Blood* by Declan Hughes (2007)
6: *The Rage* by Gene Kerrigan (2011)
7: *Ratlines* by Stuart Neville (2013)
8: *The Priest* by Gerard O'Donovan (2010)
9: *City of Shadows* by Michael Russell (2012)
10: *The Subtle Serpent* by Peter Tremayne (1996)

INDEX

379